THE
PEEP
DIARIES

THE
PEEP
DIARIES

HOW WE'RE LEARNING TO LOVE WATCHING OURSELVES AND OUR NEIGHBORS

HAL NIEDZVIECKI

City Lights Books · San Francisco

Cover photo by Adam Smith
Cover design by emdash

Library of Congress Cataloging-in-Publication Data

Niedzviecki, Hal, 1971–
The peep diaries : how we're learning to love watching ourselves and our neighbors / Hal Niedzviecki.
    p. cm.
Includes bibliographical references and index.
ISBN 978-0-87286-499-3
1. Sensationalism in journalism. 2. Gossip. I. Title.
PN5124.S45N54 2009
302.24—dc22

                          2009007522

Alternative Cataloging-in-Publication Data

Niedzviecki, Hal, 1971-
The peep diaries: how we're learning to love watching ourselves and our neighbors.
Includes material on bloggers and blogging, reality television, online social networks, surveillance, and privacy.

ISBN: 978-0-87286-499-3
1. Social interaction. 2. Technology—Cultural aspects. 3. Self-disclosure—Cultural aspects. 4. Blogs. 5. Reality television programs. 6. Electronic surveillance. 7. Online social networks. 8. Privacy. 9. Internet—Cultural aspects.

HM85N54
302

Visit our website at www.citylights.com

City Lights Books are published at the City Lights Bookstore
261 Columbus Avenue, San Francisco, CA 94133

Acknowledgments

I gratefully acknowledge the Canada Council for the Arts and the Toronto Arts Council for providing financial assistance toward the writing of this book.

I am grateful to the following people for their suggestions, advice, links to articles, and encouragement: Darren Wershler-Henry, Eamon O'Toole, Sally Blake, Andreas Ua'Siaghail, Jeannette Loakman, Stacey Lewis, Lindsay Gibb, and Andrew Blauner.

Adam Smith helped me set up BackAlleyCam and was otherwise on hand to take pictures of my exploits when required. Thanks, dude.

Rachel Greenbaum let me track her with the Snitch and, as usual, provided feedback, critique, and wise counsel.

Thanks also to everyone at City Lights Books, including my excellent editor, Elaine Katzenberger, for her support, enthusiasm, and acuity.

The following publications let me try out Peep ideas in their esteemed pages and otherwise supported the writing of this book: *Playboy*, the *Walrus*, the *New York Times Magazine*, *En Route*, and *Canadian Art*. Many thanks to those publications and their editors.

Finally, a big shout out to Paula, my sole Facebook party attendee. She dared to do what no one else would: break through the Peep.

Contents

Introducing Peep Culture

chapter one

Peeping Tom, a nick name for a curious prying fellow.
—Grose's *A Classical Dictionary of the Vulgar Tongue*, 1796

overshare (verb): to divulge excessive personal information, as in a blog or broadcast interview, prompting reactions ranging from alarmed discomfort to approval.
—Word of the Year 2008, *Webster's New World Dictionary*

In December of 2008, the editors of *Webster's New World Diction-ary and Thesaurus* chose the verb "overshare" as their word of the year. It's a new term—the aforementioned editors describe it as "emerging English." A weird word for a weird time, the awkward end to an awkward year, and, though it's unlikely to be remembered as such, a potent marker indicating a major cultural shift. In 2008 a dynamic new president of the United States was elected, Apple released the iPhone 3G, and global capitalism teetered, all turning points we won't soon forget. And yet that single ungainly word, "overshare," may prove to be more significant. For 2008 was the year we unequivocally and unceremoniously ushered in a new era: the Era of Peep Culture.

Peep culture is reality TV, YouTube, Twitter, Flickr, MySpace and Facebook. It's blogs, chat rooms, amateur porn sites, virally spread digital movies of a fat kid pretending to be a Jedi Knight, cell phone photos—posted online—of your drunk friend making out with her ex-boyfriend, and citizen surveillance. Peep is the backbone of Web 2.0 and the engine of corporate and government data mining. It's like the famous line about pornography: you know it when you see it. And you do see it. All the time, every day, everywhere.

Peep, like the sudden stunning rise of television in the 1950s, seems relatively innocent. Friends connecting. Overly enthusiastic teenagers pushing boundaries. People of all stripes and demographics gathering (virtually) to talk about their lives, likes, dislikes, and problems. But look at what happened with television: Such virtuous fare as *Rin Tin Tin*, *Gunsmoke*, *Father Knows Best*, and *You Bet Your Life* somehow led us to TV dinners, childhood obesity, and bowling alone. In less than a decade, television changed how we ate, socialized, and maybe even thought. Television changed society forever, but while it was happening it was hard to notice. We were too busy transfixed to what TV was showing (as opposed to doing). Elvis gyrated his pelvis, Sputnik pierced space, Cuba was blockaded, and we watched, somehow missing the big story.

It's the same today. While we monitor the overlapping "wars" on "terror," get close-up views of global warming, and access the intimate details of the lives of celebrities, how we socialize, shop, play, date, mate, and maybe even process information are all undergoing fundamental transformation. But there's nothing in particular to worry about or pay attention to. Kids will be kids, "overshare" is the word of the year, and if you want me, I'll be online, updating my status, posting my book reviews, and uploading videos of my root canal.

◻ ◻ ◻

The first indication that something new but not yet fully understood has taken root in our society is the sprouting of fresh vocabulary. That's where we were at the end of 2008: giving tentative names to the swirling miasma of strangely unsettling activities that can all be grouped together under the rubric of "Peep culture." A year to name names, 2008 is behind us now and it's time to ask: What do we really know about the world that these new words, innocent as babes in arms and portentous as armed teenagers, are trying to describe?

Take "overshare." It seems like the perfect (emerging) word. We immediately get it. Sharing is good, right? And so is networking, updating, uploading, tweeting, blogging, friending, messaging, and linking. But oversharing. That's like overdoing it. That's like having so much fun you end up face down in the gutter wearing nothing but your underwear. Sharing is fun, oversharing is even more fun—sometimes too much fun. Dig deeper and we find that a word like "overshare" raises more questions about Peep culture than it answers. Certainly it suggests the way Peep works: creeping in, promising good times, making it easy to say and do things you'd never thought possible, or, when you really stop to think about it, never considered advisable. But it doesn't even begin to tell us why we're suddenly so eager to share. Or who's on the other side, digesting those pictures of our loved ones, those details of our health problems, those lists of our top ten offbeat comedies. And, most importantly, how do we know when we've crossed the line from sharing to oversharing?

Let's move beyond labels. Let's ask ourselves: What are we really talking about here? For starters, there's what I'm calling Peep culture. Throughout this book, I use the term "Peep culture" (or just "Peep") to refer to what I see as a rapidly emerging phenomenon, a cultural movement steeped in and made possible by technological change, though it would be dangerous and foolhardy to dismiss it as a generational trend solely spurred by the arrival of a new array of techno gadgets. Peep is not just the tweens or the twentysomethings any more than it's the millennials, the boomers, the sandwichers, or the generations X, Y, Z. Young people dabble in Peep without knowing what the implications of their actions will ultimately be. Older generations ponder phenomena like reality TV and social networking, wonder where this seemingly unending narcissistic urge to self-revelation comes from, and then suddenly find themselves with Facebook pages of their own. Though there may be significant generational divides, we're all part of Peep culture. We're all learning to love watching ourselves and our neighbors. Peep's power is that it is widespread and elusive. It's a whispered, hypnotic idea: You need to know. You need to be known. In Peep we feel the cathartic release of confession, the allure and danger of gossip, and the timeless comfort of ritual. When we peer in on each other, we experience the thrill of performance, the purge of the talking cure, the erotic frisson of forbidden sex. Peep culture takes from all those things, but isn't any of them.

If you want to see what Peep looks and feels like, put down this book and turn on your television. (Don't do that: keep reading, watch TV later.) There are hundreds of television shows and at least three channels entirely dedicated to Peep culture. The shows you should watch include game shows (*Moment of Truth*), talent shows (*American Idol*; *America's Next Top Model*), cooking shows (*Hell's Kitchen*), sitcoms (*The Real World*), sci-fi shows (UFO Hunters, Ghost Hunters), detective shows (*Arrest and Trial, Dog the Bounty Hunter*), romance shows (*The Bachelor, A Shot at Love*), outdoor adventure shows (*Survivor, Crocodile Hunter*), home improvement shows (*Extreme Makeover: Home Edition*), travel shows (*The Amazing Race*), soap operas (*The Hills*), dramas (*The Real Housewives of Orange County*), self-help shows (*Intervention, Nanny 911*), sports shows (*Bound For Glory, American Gladiators*), business shows (*The Apprentice*), and comedies (*The Simple Life, The Surreal Life*). The channels you should watch are Fox Reality—"all reality all the time"; TruTV—formally Court TV (new tagline: "not reality, actuality"); and VH1—once MTV's nerdy light-rock-loving cousin but now the go-to channel for

B-list-celebrity reality TV (think of it as MTV's kind of crazy middle-aged aunt).

Now I don't want to give the impression that Peep culture is in any way confined to reality TV. In fact, I want to give the opposite impression: there are three specialty channels and hundreds of shows devoted to reality because Peep is so completely mainstream that it can, like golf, weather, and food, easily support dedicated twenty-four-hour streams of infotainment. I'm starting with reality TV because it's the one example of Peep we can all instantly recognize. The names and formats of the shows may come and go, but the concept—ordinary people watch ordinary people in settings from the domestic to the exotic—stays the same.

Reality TV is the most obvious incarnation of Peep culture, but the predominance of celebrity "news" runs a strong second. Celebrity gossip site PerezHilton.com alone gets 4.5 million hits a day. TMZ.com (founded by Harvey Levin—who made his name reporting on the O. J. Simpson trial—and now run in partnership with AOL) is widely credited for being the first to bring us such media events as the mug-shot photo and details of Mel Gibson's drunk-driving arrest and subsequent anti-Semitic rant; *Seinfeld* star Michael Richard's racist harangue at a comedy club; photographs of the interior of Anna Nicole Smith's "death fridge" stocked with methadone and SlimFast; and, last but not least, the complete audio of the raving answering-machine message that Alec Baldwin left for his eleven-year-old daughter, in which he calls her "a thoughtless little pig." (TMZ poll: Should the judge terminate Baldwin's visitation rights? Yes: 59 percent, no: 41 percent, total votes: 432,818.)

We're not just talking about the tabloid press here. Even the mainstream news media are crazy for this stuff, endlessly reporting on everything from the divorce of Paul McCartney to the possibly Nazi-themed bondage sex orgy of Max Mosley, the Formula One motor racing head, who, in summer 2008, won a judgment against the tabloid newspaper *News of the World* for parlaying a secretly recorded video into a front-page story and worldwide peeping. (According to his lawyer, Mosley's spanking was viewed 3.5 million times on the paper's Web site and on YouTube.)

All this, plus, of course, the seemingly unending travails of Britney Spears. "Now and for the foreseeable future," says an internal memo penned by Frank Baker, the Los Angeles assistant bureau chief of Associated Press, the venerable wire service, "virtually everything involving Britney is a big deal." The leaked memo, written three days after Spears was released from the hospital in the wake of a much-publicized breakdown, prompted one commentator to respond, "Not a good day for journalism as a discipline." More like not a good *decade* for a discipline that increasingly seems to function as an adjunct to the entertainment industry, which itself is becoming an adjunct to our hunger for a Peep culture that has spread to every conceivable medium and made true Andy Warhol's sardonic pronouncement on the perfect picture—"one that's in focus and of a famous person doing something unfamous."

Our daily lives are punctuated with urgent, expedited revelations regarding the problems of celebrities. Is it surprising, then, that our appetite for other people's issues, our need to be entertained by the "truth," spills off the pages of *People* and into our own lives? We don't need to wait for the next celebrity breakdown or pregnancy to have our fun. Online, in print, and of course on television, folks are openly and happily revealing and discussing their own particular problems, kinks, or lifestyle. This, again, is Peep culture: entertainment derived from peeping into the real lives of others, most of them ordinary, if by "ordinary" we mean not (yet) famous.

The new interactive possibilities of the Web have generated new ways to make our lives public, and more and more of us are trying out Peep. You can dismiss reality and talk TV and celebrity gossip as corporate distractions engineered to keep us happy and buying stuff while the world sizzles like Krispy Kreme batter in the deep fryer, but how do you explain the many millions who are emulating the tell-all culture of television through everything from blogs to online profiles to video uploads? A Pew Internet & American Life Project report estimated in 2006 that one in every ten adult Americans had a blog. And they weren't including the rapidly expanding cohort of people who use chat rooms and/or sites like YouTube, Blogtv.com, and Justin.tv to show and tell all. Not only are there are a lot of blogs, but there are a lot of readers of blogs. The same Pew study concluded that 39 percent of Internet users, or about 57 million American adults, read blogs. Three years later I think it's fair to say that at least 100 million Americans, a solid third of the country, read blogs.

Obviously blog creation and readership is a slippery number, but for our purposes all we really need to know is that these are big numbers, growing numbers, numbers that clearly suggest universal social acceptance: "Ordinary" people want to put their lives into the (mass) mediated environment. And other "ordinary" people want to read about those lives, which is why when you start a blog you never know who's going to read it. For every blog visited by ten, twenty or one hundred people, there are blogs like Jennette Fulda's *Half of Me*, about the Indianapolis woman's commitment to losing weight. Fulda's blog started like all blogs, with little or no readership, but now has almost 50,000 unique visitors a month who follow her attempts to go from 350 to 160 pounds.

And still the number of bloggers pales in comparison to the number of us who are regular users of social networks like MySpace, Facebook, Bebo, Reunion, MyYearbook, and LinkedIn. We're talking about over 200 million people with profiles, who every day post status updates, pictures of themselves and their friends, and more. In Canada there are ten million Facebook users, a staggering one-third of the country's population and second only to the thirty million U.S. users, which, though falling well short of Canada's Facebook obsession, is still a huge number: 10 percent of the entire U.S. population. (As of fall 2008 there were an estimated hundred million or so Facebookers worldwide.) Anyone who's ever lost a few hours clicking on the profile pictures of friends and friends' friends knows what Peep is all about. It's about feeling the hours slipping away as you drift wherever the current takes you. It's about wanting to know everything about everyone and, in turn, wanting to make sure that everyone knows everything about you. As with all things Peep, social networks are addictive and instinctual—why wouldn't you want to make "friends" with the click of button? In an age where parks are replaced by condos and fewer and fewer people know their neighbors, the urge to connect to like-minded people can be incredibly powerful. No wonder there are now social networks for recovering addicts; book lovers; divorcees; people with cats, dogs, and kindergartners; people living with chronic illness; and those who aspire to be on reality TV.

Social networking shares many characteristics with online dating—the posting of profiles, the eagerness to connect, the (often unspoken) promise that disembodied revelation might one day lead to actual physical interaction. So it's no surprise that dating sites continue to do a brisk business as both a way for people to meet and a way for people to peep each other. Popular dating site Plentyoffish.com attracts 600,000 people a day. Jdate.com, a site for Jewish singles, boasts 500,000 regular users, and Ashley-Madison.com, a site for married people on the prowl for discreet affairs, claims 125,000 daily visitors. You may not think of these sites as Peep culture but they are. Your dating profile is inevitably a source of entertainment for other users. I remember hanging out with a friend, recently divorced, who had joined several dating sites. We spent hours reading profiles, looking at pictures, contemplating the mixed messages behind the communiqués sent to him by possibly interested women. In the age of Peep, personals and dating sites are fair game as recreational Web surfing.

So how do you keep in touch with all your new friends, on-line sex partners, and fellow micro-beers-of-the-Pacific-North-west enthusiasts? You use Twitter, of course. Estimates for this mini-blogging service—that allows people to follow your short updates answering the question "what am I doing right now" via instant message or online—puts current users at around five mil-lion people (the Twitter creators don't make their numbers pub-lic). Here's a sample of the many million "tweets" sent every day: "bbq at amy + rd's. picking up wine first" (sent by "babiejenks" of Los Angeles, at 2:37 p.m., April 13, 2008). If Twitter's not your thing, you might consider using relative newcomer Sees-mic, which merges the brevity of Twitter with the functionality of YouTube to create a network devoted to what it calls "Video Conversation"—basically, people posting very short videos re-sponding to or initiating "conversations" with other users.

It's no wonder that another exploding Peep service is amal-gamating all of your various social networks, blogs, tweets, and other various connective applications into one easy-to-use stream that manages your online presence and those of the friends you follow. There are fifty or more such nascent services, with names like Ping, Lifestream, FriendFeed, Plaxbo, Digbsy, Profilactic (funny!), and the presumably ironic iStalker, which comes with a feature that lets you chart your life on a timeline. The value of Lifestream is ultimately that it's one-stop shopping for your pals to drop by and peep you. "Lifestream is a media and social aggre-gator," reads the accompanying promotional text, "that will keep you and your friends informed about what you're doing online at a glance and in realtime. With Lifestream you can put all your profiles and activity from your favorite web services on one page, making it easy for your friends to see your newest bookmarks, your favorite videos, your tweets, photos you've uploaded, your newest blog posts, and more."

As the need for Lifestream suggests, more than ever we're putting everything online, particularly photos and videos. On sites like Liveleak, RedClouds, VoyeurWeb, Dailymotion, Flickr, Shutterfly, Snapfish, Metacafe, Revver, and Brightcove, billions of images are uploaded and archived, millions more added monthly. Google, owner of YouTube, reports that roughly thirteen hours of content are uploaded to the video storing and sharing service every *minute*. Everything from sober family gatherings to drunken frat parties to kinky amateur sex parties are online all the time for all to see. We are creating public archives of the events of our lives like never before. Our friends and relatives appreciate our generous uploads. But who else is watching? We don't know, and we may not even care. This apparent lack of concern is a major aspect of Peep culture—we're not just, or even primarily, sharing with people we actually know. We're putting material out there for everyone to see. In doing this, we're showing ourselves to be naïve, optimistic, wildly enthusiastic, and more than a bit confused. The thing is, what we post online can and will be used against us. And what we innocently give away to the entire world has a hidden, potential value that most of us can't even imagine.

All these blog posts, images, videos, tweets, dating profiles, and friend updates can be easy to lose track of, which is why in the age of Peep culture we're not shy about searching the Internet for information about friends, coworkers, potential dates, and, really, anybody we want to find out about, including ourselves. Want to know how ingrained Peep culture has already become in our society? I've got one word for you: Google. Several studies have shown that using a search engine is the "solid No. 2" activity "among online tasks after sending and receiving e-mail messages." Sure, we use search engines to find out if a restaurant is recommended or what kind of soil grows the biggest turnips, but more and more we're using online searches to find out about each other. Yet another Pew Internet & American Life study determined that one in three Internet users had looked someone else's name up online and the searches were overwhelmingly for "personal reasons." More recently scholar Mark Andrejevic reported that in his own survey of Internet use "more than three-quarters of the respondents" said that they "had used the Internet to search for information about someone they knew." Half of those people reported that they did searches of that nature more than "several times a year or more." So who are they looking for? "More than two-thirds of those who said they'd searched for information online indicated they were looking up their friends, and almost two-thirds had looked up information about a current or former significant other." And why are they researching their friends online? "Several respondents indicated that googling friends online was a form of entertainment born of curiosity, it was just something to do when whiling away the time online."

It's getting harder and harder to keep a secret, so why not just go ahead and make your secrets public? A growing number of projects seem to exist exclusively to encourage confession and revelation as a form of entertainment. The "Cringe" and "Mortified" reading series in New York and Los Angeles, respectively, are ongoing events where you can regale a live audience with something embarrassing like a love letter or a diary entry written back when you were a hormone-addled teen. The widely popular series both have books out now, as well, featuring the most cringe-worthy and mortifying samples of hormonal penmanship. Then there are projects like PostSecret (anonymous secrets written on a postcard and sent to a Web site, also now a series of books and a traveling art show), Bar Mitzvah Disco (Web site and book featuring photos and stories about embarrassing seventies Jewish coming-of-age parties) and *Found*, a zine, Web site and book series dedicated to found notes such as "Mario, I fucking hate you, you said you had to work so whys your car here at her place?? You're a fucking liar, I hate you, I fucking hate you. Amber. P.S. Page me later."

You can't make this stuff up. That's why we're drawn to it. Again and again, Peep culture shows us how easy it is for reality to trump fiction. *SMITH Magazine* has started the online site Memoirville, which features various themed "memoirs" that are more like Twitters or blog posts than carefully considered reflections on life lived. The options include the "Six Word Memoir" in which you are charged with the task of telling your story in six words (there's a book of these titled after one of the submissions: *Not Quite What I Was Planning*). Or you can tell a story about a past relationship: "Everyone has an ex. Spill your guts, search your soul, and tell us all about it. You'll be glad you did." Then there's the invitation to recount "encounters with celebrities": "Tell us a personal story about an unexpected encounter with a celebrity as he or she entered your world . . . landing, like an alien, without warning."

The Sausalito, California-based journal *Memoir (and)*, proclaims that memoir is "*the* genre of the 21st century." It's a claim that's hard to dispute when, in the week I'm writing this, five of the top ten nonfiction hardcover books on the *New York Times* best-seller list are memoirs, including those of Tori Spelling, Julie Andrews, and Valerie Bertinelli, plus a father's account of his son's meth addiction, and, the number-one best seller, *Mistaken Identity*, a memoir by the families of two girls whose identities were confused after authorities dealing with a tragic car accident mixed up the victims. All this somehow inevitably leads to the publication in 2008 of not one but two books by white suburban couples in their early forties, both recounting the experience of making and keeping what I'm branding right here and now "the middle-class sex pact." In *365 Nights: A Memoir of Intimacy*, Charla gives Brad a year of sex for his birthday. In *Just Do It: How One Couple Turned Off the TV and Turned On Their Sex Lives for 101 Days*, hubby Douglas Brown tells us about the pact he and his wife made in 2006 to have sex every day for 101 days. Apparently, after the Browns completed their sex marathon, they went sexless for a month and now average what *People* magazine happily describes as "six to eight trysts monthly." Naturally one wonders:

which came first, these selfless acts of resurgent intimacy or the book deals and talk show bookings?

Does it matter? In the age of Peep, everyone wants to know everything (and everyone wants everyone else to know everything) about who they are, why they are, and how they are. After the memoir, one of the most notable mainstream cultural trends has been the rise of the documentary as a medium of entertainment/confession/personal revelation. Movies like Andrew Jarecki's *Capturing the Friedmans* (2003) have spawned a host of similar projects. These are documentaries that harvest home movies (on video or film) to tell the stories of seemingly normal people. The widespread use of video to capture the forgettable for all time creates immense banks of images to be picked over and turned into high drama, given the right (usually unfortunate) circumstances. Think of Werner Herzog's *Grizzly Man* (2005), a film that employs the personal video-camera footage of a wilderness recluse to tell the harrowing story of his mounting obsession with living in the wild among some of nature's most savage and unpredictable animals. Another must-watch example of the Peep culture documentary is Morgan Spurlock's *Super Size Me* (2004), a breakthrough, low-budget hit, in which a former extreme sports announcer chronicles what happens to his physical and mental health when he sets himself the task of eating only at McDonald's for a solid month. Movies like these made possible a project like Eric Steel's *The Bridge* (2006). In that doc, hidden cameras are used to catch actual suicides in the moments before and after they throw themselves off the Golden Gate Bridge. Though the film played to generally favorable reviews, it was hard not to notice the cat-and-mouse game the filmmakers played with the footage they had of the actual suicides—is that figure we're slowly zooming in on a happy-go-lucky German tourist or a despairing jumper? As one newspaper critic politely put it, "*The Bridge* raises age-old moral and aesthetic questions about the detachment from one's surroundings that gazing through the camera's lens tends to produce."

The same could be said of many of the current generation of Peep documentaries. The 2008 lineup for the Hot Docs film festival in Toronto, one of the world's premier festivals for documentary, was awash in the undertaking of personal journeys that, just coincidentally, happen to occur with the camera on. Randomly picking one day, I see that twenty-three films are playing. Eight of them, or just about one-third of the day's program, are part of what I consider to be Peep culture. For example, there's *Wild Blue Yonder*, in which Celia Maysles explores her acclaimed filmmaking father's absent presence in a "first-person search for answers in images, in the hope they might bring back the dead." Then there's *Second Skin*, which peeps into the lives of those devoted to Massively Multiplayer Online (MMO) gaming, including Second Life and World of Warcraft. In the film, "four friends bond and break up; a couple falls in love without meeting; a disabled man grows wings; a gaming addict enters rehab." Then there's *Searching for Sandeep*: "Poppy sends Sandeep a camera and we watch as their virtual long-distance crush blossoms into a very real physical relationship. But they face obstacles greater than the vast oceans that separate them. Sandeep is Sikh, lives at home with her conservative family and, at 31, is still in the closet about her sexuality." Finally, there's a documentary that tells the story of, as the title puts it, *The Art Star and the Sudanese Twins*. It's about New York artist Vanessa Beecroft's attempt to adopt Sudanese twins while making art that tackles the theme of Western neglect of Africa.

As Beecroft's creative choices, life choices, and "true story" merge, so too do the forms of documentary and art. Documentary is increasingly driven by the paradigms of Peep—real-life revelation for the purposes of entertainment and catharsis (entertaining catharsis)—and art is increasingly about turning individual life into a vehicle for self-revelation, narrative reinvention, and, inevitably, entertainment. I know of at least two projects centered around artists taking photographs of everything they've

eaten over the course of a month or a year. London-based Leba-
nese artist Mona Hatoum has exhibited photos and videos of the
interior of her body as a camera is inserted and passed through
various orifices. Berlin-based Canadian artist Michelle Teran
stages public screenings of CCTV camera feeds showing back al-
leys and baby's bedrooms. New Jersey art professor Hasan Elah
has put more than 20,000 time-stamped photos of himself online
after the FBI mistakenly put him on a terrorist watch list. Margot
Lovejoy's *Turns*, an online work displayed at the Whitney Mu-
seum of American Art, is composed of the contributions of viewers who write essays about important moments in their lives. The
essays can, in turn, be sifted through and sorted by viewers, who
are invited to add to the project. Finally and decisively, prize-
winning German artist Gregor Schneider has proposed putting
a dying person on display in a gallery. "The dying person would
determine everything in advance, he would be the absolute cen-
tre of attention," Schneider told the London *Times*. "Everything
will be done in consultation with the relatives, and the public will
watch the death in an appropriately private atmosphere." These
Peep artists, a small sample of what's out there, suggest not just
how much Peep is happening but how much remains yet to be
understood, explored, and known about this shift to Peep culture. Artists explore the gaps in culture, the cracks where meanings dissemble, and so it's no accident that they are increasingly
attuned to the multiple meanings and endless fragmentation that
Peep represents.

Art merges with documentary, documentary becomes more
like reality TV, and television becomes more like life. And life?
Life, it seems, seeks to become more and more like all of the above.
In Peep, life is lived on constant record because you never know
when you're going to want to be able to rewind something, see it
again, confront a family member, show it to the police, sell it to the
highest bidder, or post it on your blog. To assist us with this goal,
we are offered a powerful arsenal of Peep products and services.

Most of these products "empower" us to watch each other. In doing so, they undermine trust even among friends and family, and create further demand for services that, in previous eras, would have been both morally and technologically unimaginable.

First, the increasingly ubiquitous nanny cam, which comes embedded in a stuffed animal or a clock radio. You can check in online any time during the day, or review the footage after work, the kids tucked into bed, a cold drink by your side, your slippered feet propped up on the coffee table. Then there are special cell phones for kids that let you monitor who your child is calling and how long they talk. Plus you have the option of preventing undesirables from calling or being called, by blocking their numbers. Thanks to your monitoring, it's likely that your child will safely turn sixteen and apply for a driver's license. Now it's time to buy a GPS device that tracks where the family car goes, how fast it goes, and if there's erratic or dangerous driving. You can set this device to notify you if the car leaves a certain area or pulls onto a "forbidden" highway. Of course you'll want to know what your kids are up to: did they drink, do drugs, see that boy they're forbidden to get within 100 miles of? Why not pick up a portable lie detector device like the Handy Truster, a $99 portable "voice-stress analyzer." "Is she cheating on you?" the online advertising asks. "Is he really working late? What are your kids really doing?" And it goes without saying that you'll want to drop $50 on PC Pandora, a program that takes a screen capture of the computer it's surreptitiously installed on every fifteen seconds. Particularly handy for getting your hands on your kids' hidden passwords. Finally, your safety and security are not assured until you spend $65 on Advanced Spy, "a hi-tech tool that will help you to monitor and record all activities on your computer. Perfect for monitoring spouses, children, co-workers, or anyone else!"

Not all Peep products and services involve quasi-spying. A growing number of them, as with Twitter and Facebook, are more about consensual peeping. Loopt, offered by Sprint Nextel and available on Apple's iPhone, lets those in the mostly college crowd who use it see the locations of friends who also have the service and have agreed to share their whereabouts. They appear as dots on a map on your cell phone, with labels identifying your buddies' names so you can tell who's at the bar, who's getting their hair done, and who's staying home with a good book. (What book? Check their list on GoodReads or Facebook, or see if they've added anything to their Amazon.com reading wish list.) With Loopt safely ensconced on iPhone, around a million people are now using the service. And there's reason to suspect that more will sign up: almost 55 percent of all mobile phones sold today in the United States come equipped with the technology necessary to enable tracking services.

Obviously this explosion of new products is made possible by technological innovation, specifically those gizmos, gadgets, and programs that enable us to become increasingly integrated into wireless networks. Less obvious are the social forces that have led to our rapid adoption of Peep ideas and services. Peep emerges, at least in part, from our increasing and ongoing desire to adopt the mantle of celebrity and try out life lived in front of and for an audience. This desire has been slowly but inevitably merging with the notion that we are somehow safer when under surveillance, and that there's little or no downside to helping corporations and governments serve us better by allowing them to store and analyze our preferences and personal details. Meanwhile, the more we're encouraged to reveal ourselves, the more we're becoming used to being observed constantly and perpetually—whether by surveillance cameras on the street, our friends, our employers, or the banks, telephone companies, and ISPs that make our interconnected mass-mediated lives possible. And so we are increasingly tangled in the web of Peep. Are we the spiders or their prey?

One thing we know for sure: Peep culture is infectious. To come in contact with it is to be overcome with the urge to want

to see everything and, in turn, want other people to see *our* everything. In this way we restate the terms of privacy, community,
individuality, and even society. Even as we hide in gated communities and cancel out the world via the preprogrammed earbuds
of our cell phone/MP3 players, we show and tell all on our blog,
our various "my pages," in the photos and videos we upload, on
television, and anywhere where else we can think of. Peep culture
is human nature gone digital and electronic—which makes it
both all-inclusive and dangerously instantaneous. Despite all the
navel gazing, this is not primarily, or even necessarily, a culture of
reflection. It happens too fast, and it's too addictive, and we're all
part of it whether we like it or not, whether we think about it or
not. Peep culture's rapid propagation and allure are rooted in the
electronic grid that makes seemingly instantaneous pop culture
possible, but, like all major cultural shifts, it's more about radical
change to society than it is about what we're actually watching,
reading, or recording. Peep coalesces the sensibility of twenty-
first-century techno society into a never-ending spectacle of
bodies and souls bared in the name of entertainment, self-bet-
terment, and instantaneous recognition. Peep is a portal into a
collective consciousness no longer content to sit on the sidelines
and watch: We want to *do*.

But do we really know what we're doing? Once upon a time
we were taught to avert our eyes, not electronically enhance them.
We were taught that spying, peering, and peeking in on people,
is no way to behave. For centuries, the legend of Peeping Tom
has offered a cautionary tale to that effect. When Lady Godiva
rode naked through the town in a bid to convince her husband
to lower taxes on the peasants, all the townspeople were ordered
to avert their eyes and had the good sense to do so. All except the
tailor Tom, who was promptly struck dead, or struck blind, or
tarred, feathered, and excommunicated. Well, you get the idea.
Since then, poor Tom's been held up as the example, the go-to
nickname for curious prying fellows who like to watch.

The story of Peeping Tom coalesced into fable in the 1700s, though its origins are thought to be in Lady Godiva's Coventry around the turn of the first millennium. In other words, this is a thousand-year-old story, an enduring parable with an obvious, helpful moral: "Creeps who peep get what they deserve." But today we're apt to feel for poor Tom: He just wanted to get a little peek. What's so wrong about that? And obviously the good Lady Godiva, the medieval equivalent of the celebrity who arrives at the movie launch gala sans undergarments, wanted someone to see her. Why else tell us not to look? Anyway, she was lucky (or unlucky by the public relations standards of today) that Tom wasn't wielding a Handycam set to instant YouTube upload. Juxtapose the seemingly ancient definition of "Peeping Tom" with a new vocabulary of verbs like "overshare" and "Google," not to mention the exploding cyber hobby of amateur online nude posing (more on that later), and you get the ultimate culture clash.

Today we're all happily peeping away, seemingly free of social approbation. Governments, corporations, friends, and family all tell us (for different reasons) that it's okay to peer over the fence and see what's going on with the neighbors, particularly if what the neighbors are up to could in any way be construed as scandalous, scurrilous, seditious, or sexual— something entertaining enough to attract the millions of viewers up for grabs. Meanwhile, the neighbors are doing what they're doing precisely because they know that they are being watched. Just as we are willing voyeurs—no one forced us to look—they are willing performers. The voyeurs (us) and the people we're watching (us) are two groups acting together in cybernetic harmony, each one encouraging the other, neither stopping to think about what's happening and why.

When a thousand-year prohibition is readily cast aside, it's probably a good idea to wonder how that happened and what it means for the future of our society. What has transformed us into so many Peeping Toms? And will we, too, get our peeping comeuppance? The hidden forces pushing us toward Peep culture are also pushing us toward a new, unexplored, and in many cases unintended society. It's a culture of instant judgment, stolen innocence, and mass delusion, a culture that threatens to assign a price tag to every secret, scandal, and crime, every seemingly commonplace domestic moment. But it's also a culture of immense possibility, a culture of potentially widespread democracy and equality. Like Lady Godiva, we're innocently and optimistically baring our bodies and souls, not out of prurience but because we want to do good—we seek to connect, communicate, commiserate. But the difference between us and Lady G. is that we aren't ordering our fellow townspeople to stay inside and avert their eyes. We're begging them to look. Even better, take a picture. It's a difference replete with ramifications. Suddenly all things once sacred and private—from religious ceremonies to acts of copulation, to the last moments of life itself—are to be observed and consumed. This results in fundamental changes to our lives. Put a camera on something, introduce an audience, however small, and it's no longer what it once was. So what is it—and who are we now?

chapter two

Becoming a Peep (Product) Person

A pop person is like a vacuum that eats up everything. He's made up from what he's seen. Television has done it. You don't have to read anymore. Books will go out, television will stay. And that's why people are really becoming plastic, they are just fed things and are formed and the people who can give [the same] things back are considered very talented.
—Andy Warhol, *San Francisco Chronicle*, 1966

She calls herself Padme, though her real name is far less exotic. She lives in the Fraser Valley, not far from Vancouver, British Columbia. Her blog often features pictures of the snow-capped hills, lush foliage, and blue waterways that are so much a part of this Pacific Northwest rainforest.

Padme lives in a standard suburban community. Her husband works full time. She stays home and takes care of the kids. Her eldest turned seven not that long ago. When I say standard I mean that like most communities in the developed world Padme's is a quasi-community. Padme has friends and neighbors, though her sister, who she's closest to, lives far away. For most of us it's not a loose network of neighbors, companions, and relatives who are ultimately responsible for our health, safety, and well-being; those have become state responsibilities.

Padme is a little bit lonely. She doesn't have a lot of close friends. She describes her family as "looking like a typical traditional family." In 2005 she started a blog. The blog was a way to branch out, find new pals, and express herself. At first she was reluctant: "I thought who would read what I write? I'm not a very good writer." But she went ahead and started the blog anyway. She writes about her family life:

> I just found out that Chuck E Cheese where we are going to have Skywalker's birthday party had a pipe burst and they canceled his party on us. . . . The woman on the phone didn't seem to think it was a big deal but we have a ton of kids and people coming to the birthday later and now we have to try to find somewhere else. Also all the loot bags and cake and package was done through Chuck E Cheese. Now we have a lot of running around to do. Urg!!

She writes about her health:

> The surgery went well. I have to go back and see my doctor next week to talk about it further. They are doing some tests on the polyp I had removed from my uterus during the D&C that they did on me. I am not sure yet if I will need more surgery or not for my fibroids. The uncertainty of it all has me feeling cranky. I have no patience and I want to start feeling better soon.

And then there's this:

> The kids were back to school today and Master was back to work again after the holiday break. I was a bit worried I might be lonely today but I was glad to have the place back to myself again and I had also been given permission to use my Hitatchi [sic] and masturbate this morning. It's been weeks since I last had the chance for some private time with my favorite vibrator. I forgot how good it feels to start the day with masturbation. I had a really big orgasm and am feeling really relaxed today and getting back to normal with my routine again.

Yup, you read that right. Padme has a secret life. It's her secret life that has brought over 1.5 million people to *Journey to the Darkside* since it started. Padme's blog, with its Star Wars theme and evocations of the ominous allure of Darth Vader, garners 3,000–4,000 visitors a day. Not bad for a housewife writing about her kid's canceled birthday party. Padme also writes about her husband spanking her. She writes about giving him lengthy, elaborate fellatio sessions. She writes about her need to be dominated by the man she calls Master Anakin, the man she's been, as she tells me, "married to for 4 years, living with for 12 years, and best friends with for 18 years."

But the blog is more than just a way to make friends and express herself. Who is Padme? Depends on who you ask. If you live next door to her, she's a mom and a neighbor. If you are the random porn aficionado lurking on her blog, watching the videos she sometimes uploads of her round white ass being spanked crimson red, she's your wet dream come true: a middle-class, middle-aged woman so horny and willing she gives it away for free. If you are part of her geographically dispersed group of men and women in similar "total power exchange relationships" (as she puts it), Padme is a brave explorer of alternative sexuality, a fellow practitioner of a distinct lifestyle. ("He makes all the decisions," Padme tells me when I ask about the details of a "total power exchange" relationship.) She's the kind of woman who, in the same paragraph, can complain about her son's birthday party being abruptly canceled and note that it "doesn't look like I'm going to be getting my spanking today with dealing with all this birthday stuff."

Padme doesn't use her real name on the blog and doesn't show her face in the pictures and videos she uploads. So who is Padme? She's the (semi) anonymous citizen of Peep, denizen of a world in which the insatiable desire for the secret turns what is hidden into a precious commodity—so long as it is revealed.

"We're not just one specific topic," she tells me when I ask her about the popularity of her blog. "A lot of people seem to like that we're really open. We're not just spanking or sex. I think people are fascinated with us. There's definitely a lot of lurkers, a lot of return visitors. People are curious. They want to know what we're doing next."

Padme and Master have started an online store. They are making money from the blog. The economic potential of the site is growing with every visitor: "We've thought of doing clips for sale or getting into the video area more." Perhaps responding to the increasing popularity and potential economic gain, Padme updates daily, solidifying her unique place in the blogosphere by offering ever more intimate juxtapositions of family life and secret life. Meanwhile, the blog is featuring more videos and pictures of a salacious nature. Padme isn't an adult industry entertainer, she doesn't do porn for money. She does want to keep the numbers up and please the "lurkers." But it's a fine line. She doesn't want to alienate by going too hardcore. Details about a lot of the heavier "play" don't get posted to the Web site. "I did a post asking if you would like to see heavier photos, maybe if more people came out and said 'Hey I really want to see that.' At this point we share a lot of spanking photos, now we're starting to show the videos. I have opened up about heavy play, I just don't think it's necessary to put up all the photographs or whatever. I try to balance it out, it's all about balance."

The more successful the blog is, the more difficult it is to maintain proper balance, online and off. Some think she's over-stepping by mixing the kinky with real life. "I've been told by people that I should keep it separate, but I think it makes us real people. You're able to look and say, 'Hey that person is having a bad day.' We are real people, we do have a real life, there's more to us than just spanking or sex." Perhaps a greater concern for Padme is that in blending the domestic and the dominant, she is opening herself up to discovery. Padme worries that her non-lifestyle friends might stumble across the blog, or that her brother, also a Star Wars fan, might type some combination of words including "sex" and "Star Wars" into a search engine and come across *Dark-side*. But her biggest fear is that her kids might one day discover the blog. "I would hope that they don't ever come across the blog. I don't want them to know about the private details, just as I don't want to know about my mom and her private life."

But, I ask Padme, aren't you risking just that scenario by making your life public in a way that your mother would never have thought to do? Padme agrees that the surfeit of details in the blog would easily allow her to be identified even by people who only know her casually. Still, I can tell she doesn't really think that will ever happen. Even if you came across the blog, she muses, would you really go around telling people about it? After all, you'd have to explain how you found it and what you were doing there. The embarrassment defense is convincing to Padme. She'll keep things separate and no one will know, and everything will be fine. Only a few people in Padme's daily, "ordinary" life know about *Darkside*. Even her sister doesn't know. The bulk of Padme's unfiltered social existence happens online, in a state of partial anonymity.

It's the "community" that she has online that makes it worth the risk for Padme. The community supports her, and the community is the one place where she can confess her true feelings. "I don't drive, I don't work," Padme tells me. "I'm a stay-at-home mom and I'm alone all day. It's been a great way to connect to people." You can feel how much her community means to her by reading the posts she sends directly to the community of people (a small percentage of the 4,000 daily readers) who are her regular correspondents. She writes the following in a post updating her health situation:

> Thank you for all the comments and support during this last week. Southern Angel even did a LOLcat just for me this week and it cheered me up a lot. I got a lot of e-mails and e-cards. I'm sorry I haven't responded to them but I've been trying to recover

from the surgery and not feeling too good. . . . I want to be feeling better so I can start being more like a slave. Master's been taking care of me and helping out a lot but I hate not having my structure. The chores list and rules help me to stay centered. I miss feeling like a slave.

It's as if for Padme being a slave is only half of it. The other half is telling people about it. The same secret that isolates can also be a source of connection. But once you start spilling your guts, it's hard to know when, or if, you should stop. "It can definitely be addictive," Padme admits. "I've tried to cut back a bit. But you come home and you want to see who's left a comment. It can get out of control." So when is too much? When is it time to stop? "In our case you get to 1.6 million readers it's really hard to just walk away from that. It would be hard to stop at this point. We take breaks but to actually stop and not blog anymore, I can't even go a few days and I want to blog. We are very regular. I think people like that, they can count on a post being there."

❐ ❐ ❐

People are counting on Padme's posts, and Padme is counting on them to read her posts. What's happening in Padme's life is happening in lives all over the world. It's impossible to say how many people are using the details of their lives to gain attention and some semblance of community (however disparate), but I encounter their stories on a weekly if not daily basis. On holiday at my parent's house, I flipped through a copy of the staid *Washington Jewish Week* newspaper only to discover a feature on nine-year-old Elan Arnowitz, who, "after nearly two months of nonstop posting and updating to his site" about his battle against a degenerative disease that has left him bedridden, is now garnering thousands of hits and kudos from not just hoi polloi but "various celebrities and sports heroes as well."

Why are so many people, ages nine to ninety, seeking so much notice online? The easy answer is to say that they just want attention. And that's definitely true. But dig deeper and we find that most people aren't trying to become superstars; they're trying to meet a need that our society no longer seems able to fulfill. Those things that were once provided by community and regulated, in large part, by gossip and face-to-face interaction, are now the responsibility of corporations, governments, and bureaucrats. As a result, despite the seeming appearance of rampant individualism in our society, we are actually more observed, managed, categorized, and analyzed, and ultimately more conformist than ever. We fit in as pin-making drones, some of us suited for management, some for quality control, some for stuffing the pins in boxes as they roll off the assembly line. With community replaced by bureaucracy, there are fewer and fewer opportunities for us to feel like we are truly ourselves, recognized just for being. We live comfortably, maybe too comfortably, longing for something that we've lost: essential recognition of our humanness, intrinsic acknowledgment that we exist. Where in our regimented, highly organized society do we find that? Which store in the mall sells us back our essential self?

Peep culture is our twisted answer to the problem of the dehumanizing of humanity. When we present ourselves to be watched and commented on, we are, ironically enough, attempting to reclaim our individuality on our own terms. It's our attempt to show not how special and exceptional we are, but how ordinary and normal and deserving of everyday human interaction we are. Basically we're trying to show that we are human beings worthy of recognition just for being who we are. In that way, Peep is a reaction to, and a symptom of, our technocratic age of quasi-community, nonstop marketing, and global celebrity gossip.

With Peep, as Padme shows us, we fit in by turning ourselves inside out. We proclaim and reclaim individuality by offering up our daily lives to "the system." We don't fight against the system. Instead we embrace it. You want to know about me? Okay, I'll tell you everything. I won't leave a single thing out. As *Harper's Magazine* contributing editor Garret Keizer put it, commenting on the infamous Kinsey Report on sexuality, "That there are people who copulate with sheep neither surprises nor interests me; that there are people sheep-like enough to surrender that information on demand is a perversion I find altogether baffling." In other words, what's baffling is not the diversity of human sexuality, but how eager we are to be noticed—chronicled and counted and embraced by the system. From the Kinsey report to the BDSM family blog: Regiment your daily doings into daily reports. Quantify the exact number, length, and style of blowjobs you give Master and describe them in detail. Then do the same for the blog posts *about* the blowjobs. Then drop a bombshell about your son's canceled birthday. Reassert the peccadilloes and unquantifiable murkiness of human life, the need for a regular coterie of others to simply notice and reaffirm your existence, by embracing the techniques of alienation and reduction: exactitude, reportage, precision, anonymity, and, ultimately, ideally—commerce.

The grassroots revelation of your everyday life is the grand Peep culture experiment. Can sharing everything all the time bring us happiness, connection, even meaning? Many of us see this kind of sharing as some kind of weird perversion, but there's also a case for this cultural shift to be viewed as "progress." Glasgow-based professor Brian McNair, author of the book *Striptease Culture* and a keen observer of the British addiction to tabloids, reality TV, and closed-circuit television (CCTV) surveillance cameras, tells me that the rise of a widespread Peep culture could actually be a good thing: "It's not so much that we're all equal suddenly, but we're no longer quite so alien to each other—gay and straight, middle class and rich. Celebrity is a good example. The television show *Big Brother* turned people into celebrities, and now we have *Celebrity Big Brother* in which celebrities reveal themselves to be ordinary people. So there's a democratization going on there which is quite healthy."

An Australian research team from Swinburne University of Technology in Melbourne found that both blogging and social networking helped people feel more satisfied with their lives. First, James Baker and professor Susan Moore contacted people on MySpace and conducted a survey. They found that people who intended to blog were less satisfied with their social networks and lives overall versus people who did not intend to blog. "We found potential bloggers were less satisfied with their friendships and they felt less socially integrated, they didn't feel as much part of a community as the people who weren't interested in blogging," is how Moore put it. Then they went back two months later and did another questionnaire with the same people. They found that those who had started blogging reported feeling less isolated and more part of a community, as well as happier about their friendships both on and offline. Says Moore: "They were also more likely to use venting or expressing . . . emotions as a way of coping. It was as if they were saying 'I'm going to do this blogging and it's going to help me.'" Even those who didn't end up blogging felt somehow happier after being on MySpace for a few months. "Going onto MySpace had lifted the mood of all participants in some way," reports Moore.

Technology writer Clive Thompson talks about the way in which all the bits and pieces of information one can glean from following various blog posts, tweets, and status updates can come together "like thousands of dots making a pointillist painting." He writes: "Each little update—each individual bit of social information—is insignificant on its own, even supremely mundane. But taken together, over time, the little snippets coalesce into a surprisingly sophisticated portrait of your friends' and family members' lives."

At the same time, researchers such as social psychologist Jean Twenge have found a rather remarkable rise in the levels of narcissism and self-absorption in the young, college-age cohorts who have been the early adopters of these kinds of social networks. In her studies, chronicled in her book *Generation Me* and newer research papers, she gives psychological tests to college students and compares them to similar tests delivered to similar students in previous decades. She finds, to no one's surprise, that today's young people are more and more interested in themselves. Twenge isn't alone in reaching such conclusions: A study cited by Jake Halpern in his book *Fame Junkies* put the number of teens who thought they would one day be famous at 31 percent and the number who thought of themselves as "truly important" at 80 percent. (A similar study done in the 1950s shocked parents and educators by finding that—horrors!—12 percent of teens considered themselves pretty important.)

Another psychologist, John Suler of Rider University in Lawrenceville, New Jersey, has been researching what happens when the kind of ubiquitous narcissism that Twenge has chronicled (though her work is not without its critics) gets extended into the Web. In his sprawling interactive text *The Psychology of Cyberspace*, Suler explores, among other things, online disinhibition. "Some people are considerably more disinhibited in online life," he explains to me. "In real life they have needs they can't express, but online they have a vehicle and an environment where they can unleash, and they do it. It's pretty well known in psychology that if you have anonymity you are going to do things you wouldn't normally do. You can depersonalize the other person, that's another established principle, [and] when you depersonalize you can do things you wouldn't do. The combination is powerful. Online the special talent is to realize that there are other people on the other end of those wires."

So what happens, I ask Suler, if you can't seem to cultivate that "special talent" and you forget that behind every blog post or status update there's an actual flesh and blood human being? "When people go online they start off having the initial awareness that anyone in the world could read this. But then you start typing, and you aren't getting feedback in face-to-face situations, you don't have this feedback, you don't have this censoring process, you can lose that perspective. You start delving into tangents that maybe should not be said online." Finally, I ask Suler why it seems like so many people online seem to cling to what they call a community, though it's more like a bunch of people all doing similar things and encouraging people to do more of what they are already doing. "Cyberspace has become an incredibly powerful environment where anybody can have a voice and put out whatever they're thinking and feeling. But with so many people doing it the odds are you're going to have a limited audience, so I see people online dividing into all these subgroups and communities, mostly like-minded people gathering together to reinforce their own ideas."

From all these overlapping studies and theories we can conclude the following: There are two prevailing interconnected reasons why individuals do Peep. There's the seemingly virtuous search for connection and shared meaning, and the more vicious, pop-fueled desire for attention and recognition in which, as Twenge tells me, "Your identity is your product." Merged, we have the central tenet of Peep: that what I'm thinking and feeling and doing is as valuable and as important as what anyone else is thinking, feeling, or doing. We're all equally interesting, equally capable of providing advice, catharsis, distraction, companionship, and entertainment. We all have lives worthy of watching. We all have lives worthy of selling.

❏ ❏ ❏

For a year or so, Justin Kan's life was also his movie. Justin is the San Francisco mastermind behind Justin.tv. Justin calls what he does "lifecasting" and describes it as a kind of new entertainment paradigm, a complement and extension of the on-camera life we're already living. While Justin was still in the throes of lifecasting, I called him for an interview. I reached him at a coffee shop, a fact I knew before he told me so. Justin had a camera mounted on his head that broadcast twenty-four hours a day to the Internet. I could see on my computer screen everything he saw. So could anyone else who happened by his live broadcast. I turned up the volume on my computer speakers and also found out that I could hear everything Justin was saying and everything being said to him. I watched Justin leave the café and walk home. There he put me on speaker phone so his audience would be able to hear my side of the conversation. Immediately, that audience, all comfy and logged into an adjoining online chat room, started commenting on my questions and Justin's answers. Lifecasting creates an interactive, never-ending soap opera, featuring live people in real time. It's the nadir of Peep, and, according to Justin, it's the future.

"People fundamentally like having relationships and watching other people. Something like Justin.tv is a low-cost way of having a relationship either with me or other people on the show or the people online. It's almost like a coffee shop except it's easy—you don't have to go anywhere; it's TV plus Internet chat."

Call it surveillance with benefits. You spend so much time observing the life of someone else that you actually start feeling like you have a relationship with that person. Come to think of it, maybe you *do* have a relationship with your favorite lifecaster. Justin talked about his "longtime fans" who answered the questions "newbies" posed to him about "bathroom, sleep, sex." These fans also had strong opinions about the choices Justin was making. "I was at a cable industry trade show and someone said 'Justin doesn't know what he's doing, he's not a good networker, he doesn't get what trade shows are for.' Or 'he should have asked that girl out on a date.' I have a guy who watches a lot and he's like a father. He says, 'Justin, you don't eat rice.' He's called me 'boy' in the past; it's a little awkward—you don't really say that in real life.

Sometimes he says, 'You need a spanking.' I think: 'I'm a grown man but thanks a lot of for your opinion.'"

In the early days, Justin was getting a lot of opinions. So many that he had to disable the feature that let people text message him. He couldn't keep up with the stream of hundreds of messages pouring in everyday. Eventually he even had to stop logging in to Justin.tv and watching himself chat with the watchers watching him. But when Justin came back to the site months later, he was pleasantly surprised: "For a while I wasn't going on the chat room, and when I started going back I realized a lot of people knew what was going on in the site better than I did."

Justin, like Padme and other peepers, is obsessed with the numbers. While lifecasting, he was receiving a text message every fifteen minutes telling him how many people had logged in and were watching him. "Two hundred sixty-six," he said at one point in our conversation. "there are 266 people watching right now." The height of his popularity throughout our hour-long discussion was 269 people. Justin didn't seem bothered when his numbers dipped. As he told me, "Even if your blog is only read by five friends that's still five people paying attention to you." Again, like Padme and many others, Justin evokes not narcissism but community. He tells me that he's met tons of new people and made new friends both in person and online. "I was driving home from Sunnyvale, about 45 minutes south of San Francisco and I was, like, falling asleep on the road and people were freaking, they were trying to call me and I got so much feedback after: 'Justin we were so worried about you.'" As annoying as Justin's fans might be (one anonymous typer in the chat room on Justin's page describes watching Kan as "interactive voyeurism"), Justin seems to have a soft spot for them. "One person told me, 'You can't do this and expect people not to care about you.'"

But Justin didn't decide to turn his life into online spectacle so that more people would care about him. Community, friendship, and even potential celebrity are all welcome, if accidental, by-products. In stark contrast to Padme's haphazard approach to personal revelation, Justin went online with his life deliberately: "I'm not an actor. I was never really a fame seeker. I consider myself an entrepreneur; this is kinda the ultimate putting it on the line for the company." In many ways, Justin is the Peep purist. He transfers his person into mass-mediated product solely to build his business. "We're trying to build a show. We're getting a fan base and viewership for our Web site."

So it is that Justin goes offline some months after our interview. His site has launched and he's recruited a new generation of Justins to take over. (Most notably, conveniently named, precocious, blonde counterpart Justine, who comes across as the Reese Witherspoon of Peepdom and has since jumped ship to rival service Ustream.) They are the users, the ones who Justin has built his business around. Justin hopes they'll be watched. Why wouldn't they? "What's the difference between people watching this and people watching produced content? If you're watching six hours of TV a day, how is it any better or worse than watching online?" Justin's got a point. Either way you're putting your life on hold while watching other people go about theirs. But there is a difference. The difference, of course, is gatekeeping and accessibility. The several hundred people who were broadcasting on Justin.tv the last time I checked were doing so without any (immediate) financial reward, and without the benefit of directors, scriptwriters, cinematographers, and censors. Their broadcasts are ambiguous: What do they want? Why are they doing this? Mostly their "channels" are painfully boring. But, then again, you never know what's going to happen. In one case, a troubled nineteen-year-old from Florida, Abraham K. Biggs, actually committed suicide on Justin.tv, overdosing on pills while various strangers, associates, and members of his online "community" watched and left comments. The comments made while Biggs was dying suggest the kind of disconnect that can occur when real life (and death) becomes Peep entertainment for others:

"if you put full screen on you can tell its not a still pic but why isnt his top moving as he breathes"

"um guise . . . he looks like hes not breathing"

"desperate cry for attention . . . log off his stupid jtv site. . . . you're just making this retard act out worse than he would otherwise"

"You want to kill yourself OP? DO it, do the world a favor and stop wasting our time with your mindless self pity. For fks sake"

"should someone call the cops? no because no one cares. NEXT"

"someone call the cops. snitches get stitches brah"

"Called his fone and went straight to voice mail. Left message 'do it.'"

Finally the police arrive. Even as an officer covers up the webcam, the online "community" is still arguing the veracity of the scene, with some chatters eager to point out apparent inconsistencies in the "script."

Abraham Biggs died online more than a year after I talked with Justin. His death raised fresh questions in my mind about what happens when the banality of existence is merged with the inherent excitement of voyeurism. Are we ultimately going to measure our lives based on how "real" our deaths look on TV?

"We're trying to figure out how to do highlights," Justin told me back in happier times. "We want to let people bookmark interesting moments and share them with other people." But why do "we" want to encourage people to do that? And what does a world of prepackaged life highlights look like?

Hundreds on Justin.tv and tens of thousands on other sites are doing what we might think of as "partial lifecasting" online. They are regularly uploading clips discussing, and sometimes showing, moments (highlights) from their everyday lives. The prospect of tens of thousands of partial lifecasters using video and audio to broadcast their divorces, hook-ups, dislikes, successes, and thrills with many more on the way doesn't faze Justin. "What will that society look like? I don't think it will be that different from the society we have now. For twenty years we've been telling people, 'Maybe *you* can be a celebrity,' and now this is just an extension of that, maybe. But broadcasting yourself online is way of sharing what you're doing with other people; it doesn't necessarily have to be exposing your private life for entertainment."

It doesn't necessarily have to be, but it almost invariably is. What Justin doesn't seem to get and what Abraham Biggs starkly demonstrated is just how easy it is for your private life to become entertainment, regardless of your intentions. Justin is the entrepreneur, the untroubled tactician who takes a calculated risk— I'll exchange my private life for attention for a limited amount of time in order to launch my product. What is that product, if not a new kind of entertainment? Where once such exchanges were considered the stuff of science fiction, today they are commonplace enough to be a regular component of our popular culture. Quite simply, people wouldn't have been logged in to the final moments of Abraham Biggs if they weren't in some strange way being entertained.

Justin, Justine, and the late Abraham Biggs came along after the visionary artists, provocateurs, and engineers did their thing. When Ontario's Steve Mann did live point-of-view broadcasting to the Web from 1994 to 1996 while a PhD student at MIT, he was branded a cyborg freak. When Jennifer Ringley started JenniCam in 1996, offering live broadcasts of everything that happened in her dorm room (and later her apartment), she was attacked as everything from a porn star to, horrors, a performance artist. When a young Texan decided to mark the millennium by officially changing his name to DotComGuy and giving us webcam access to a life he vowed to live exclusively over the Internet for the entire year 2000 (including courting women via online chat and furnishing the initially empty suburban house he moved into for the stunt), he was widely viewed as a corporate stooge and, well, a bit of a loser. (Public perception didn't improve when he changed his name back to Mitch Maddox in 2004.)

All these people, and others, like video artist Willoughby Sharp, whose 1974 work of performance art consisted of his living in a four-by-eight box for 300 hours while broadcasting to an exterior audience, made possible Emmalene Pruden. Emmalene is a twenty-one-year-old YouTube enthusiast. She's married, and the mother of a two-year-old. She lives in Hamilton, Ontario, hometown of original cyborg Steve Mann. Hamilton is an industrial city between Buffalo and Toronto, with a population of roughly three-quarters of a million people. There's nothing about it that would make it seem like a hotbed of Peep culture. Then again, Hamilton is the kind of place where you might easily decide that it's up to you to make your own fun. Emmalene's been posting videos on YouTube about her life and times since 2006. To date, she's posted 179 videos, including a three-part series showing her moving out of her in-laws' house and into her first-ever apartment, accompanied by her daughter and husband.

Emmalene, with her braces and baby face and propensity for appearing in pink sweat suits alongside her collection of stuffed animals, could easily pass for thirteen. She's bubbly and excited in front of the camera. She often opens her videos with a hearty, "Hello, YouTube!" Like Padme of the *Darkside* blog, she tells me that she started her video blog out of loneliness. After her child, Alice, was born, they had to move out of her mom's house and into her husband Mike's parents' house in a completely different part of town. Emmalene found herself cut off from her friends: "I was sitting at home. I didn't know anyone. Mike was still at school, Alice was still a baby. So I just started watching people talk on YouTube." Emmalene found herself drawn to the various oddballs revealing themselves online. She began thinking that YouTube might be the kind of place where her outgoing personality could find an outlet. Despite being an extrovert, Emmalene tells me that she has problems making friends. Deep down, she's shy. YouTube was a good solution to both address her shyness and the fun, attention-seeking side of her personality. "I like to entertain, I like to make people happy so I figure if my video blogs make people happy that's good. I started it as a way to be out there talking to people because I've never been good with it. It hasn't been a replacement but it's been a good Band-aid. There's times when you can't stand to be alone so you just go online and there's a message for you. It's a bit of sunshine on a cloudy day." (Echoes of JenniCam: When NPR's Ira Glass asked Jennifer Ringley why she decided to continue with the webcam experiment in her new apartment after she graduated from college, she replied, "I felt lonely without the camera.")

Emmalene has come along way since her first upload. "My first video blog I was actually reading from a script. I just sat there really nervous in the chair and I was all shoulders up. I was performing in front of a crowd and I didn't know if they would like it."

Turns out they did like it. Emmalene added tags so that her video would appear on YouTube search engines. Pretty soon she found herself with an audience. "At the start I got about a hundred views and then it kind of slowed down. Most of my videos are in the hundreds now, but sometimes in the thousands. That's kind of scary, when you think: 'Who's watching?'"

It's a good question, and I put it to Emmalene: Who is watching? "I get messaged all the time and people tell me I have a way of talking on the camera. It actually kinda makes me feel good if I somehow manage to connect to someone. Sometimes it's creepy . . . but it's actually quite exciting when you think about how many people know me, how far away they are. A lot of people say 'I know you, I've gotten to know you through your video blogs.' But I think, 'these people don't really know me.'"

They know Emmalene, which is exciting. But they don't *really* know Emmalene, which is reassuring. So which is it?

The viewers might not know Emmalene, but they do know

an awful lot about her. They know she's in college for carpentry, they've taken the tour of her in-laws' house, they've met her daughter; they've heard Emmalene on getting braces, they've seen her a little bit drunk with her friend, they've watched her struggle with a part-time job, finding child care, and saving for a place; and they've watched her move into that place, complete with a tour of her new apartment stacked with half-open boxes. Anyone who drops by and watches Emmalene's videos will certainly know much more about her life than they would if they met her at a party and talked with her for ten minutes. But that level of intimacy with strangers doesn't bother Emmalene. In fact, she seems to sense that it is these quotidian revelations that make her enticing to her viewers. They are, in a way, all she has to offer: the intimate details of her life. And so she feels inexplicably duty-bound to respond to her viewers. I ask her how that works: "Okay, well," she tells me, "so-and-so has asked me this, so I should answer them because we're building a community." Someone, for example, asked Emmalene if she was still attending school. So she took her camera to college and gave everyone a tour of her classrooms. Doing stuff like that is part of what Emmalene calls "the community part of YouTube," a community of random video bloggers and watchers scattered all over the world. "They are people like myself and some members on a forum I belong to. For us it's an important part of the day, we religiously upload."

The community is all-inclusive and so includes any number of creepy lurkers and actively aggressive pranksters. Emmalene has had to deal with nasty comments about her looks, her ideas, and her singing (she likes to play guitar and sing on her video blog, and even tried out for *Canadian Idol*, an event much ballyhooed in her videos though she didn't make it to the show). She had one serial crank banned from YouTube after he made a project out of harassing her: "I ended up getting his account suspended. He was leaving tons of comments, calling Alice a 'fetal parasite,' calling me names; I don't think people should say 'You're a bitch' . . . I would delete his comment and he would come back a million times more, with harsher comments. That's where the sense of community comes in . . . my viewers came in and defended me."

There are problems outside of the virtual community too: her husband, Mike, doesn't like her video blogging and is visibly uncomfortable when she turns the camera on him. "He doesn't get it," Emmalene says. She seems perplexed by this: "It's weird because I've found fellow YouTubers, customers I meet at work, and we have our own language." If it wasn't for Mike, Emmalene says she would probably "have a camera on me at all times to include my lifestyle with everyone." But Mike is private. He didn't like it when Emmalene blogged the day of their wedding, for instance. Random strangers could see his bride in her wedding dress before he ever did. "He thinks I include too much of our lives. He's a very private person. We are total polar opposites. I go out at night and he stays at home. We've reached a compromise where I'll go a few weeks at a time without making a video so when I do upload it's not as if it's happening right now. So they don't get the update as if they were family. It used to be [that if] something happened I'd make a video, and he'd say, 'You're including them way too much.'"

Despite the compromise, the tensions between Mike and Emmalene over her video blog persist. But Emmalene isn't giving up on video blogging. It's become too important to her. "YouTube," she tells me, "has become a lifestyle as opposed to just a boredom time filler."

Emmalene, one of Justin's many prodigies and contemporaries, is taking advantage of the new Peep services and turning a part of her life into a kind of show. She does so as a hobby, as a way to announce the fact of her existence, as a way to connect to others. As is often the case, some are made uncomfortable. What Emmalene and others are doing with their partial lifecasts feels too blatant, too much a violation of—something; we aren't sure what. We just know it makes us uneasy. At least one reason it makes us uncomfortable is because Peep culture demands a reassessment of what the contemporary individual is. Are we people, products, performers, pretenders, or just plain pathetic? When people do Peep to themselves, they invoke, ironically but without irony, the end of the human. We're talking here about the ghostly, frightening image of the cyborg citizen, the heavily armored record-all, tell-all machine; a walking, talking television station protected against incursion from all comers—be they criminals, police, panhandlers, or paparazzi—by the instant upload camera. It's JenniCam meets Padme meets YouTube meets RoboCop meets Emmalene. It's many things, but it isn't pretty, and it isn't anything like what we like to think of as human. Because turning your secrets into entertainment for an anonymous mass feels intrinsically wrong, and because this process inevitably relies in large part on relatively new technological applications that seem ever more perversely fused with what we think of as biology, Peep culture adopters seem to be veering away from humanity, even as everything they are seeking—attention, community, interaction—is pretty much at the core of what humanity is all about. As a result, neither traditionalists longing for the old days nor futurists evoking the wonders of techno-capitalism can truly embrace the new Peep culture lifestyle. Even those actually doing Peep seem unwilling to fully admit their cyborg status. There's a profound discomfort about the whole process of trying to fit the square peg of humanity into the round hole of product. It's like trying to shove a videotape into a DVD player. It doesn't work. Bits and pieces of us get left behind, our lives edited and reinvented, slashed and burned as our inner director seeks to ensure that the final film runs a theater-friendly hour and forty-five minutes.

Call it the cyborg effect. It's the discomfort we feel when people meld with technology and become their own ongoing project and product. This discomfort expresses itself in disparate ways that join like pieces in a puzzle and give us a pretty good sense of where Peep and everyday life conflict: Mike, Emmalene's husband, doesn't want to be on camera and doesn't particularly want Emmalene to be on camera either. At least one anonymous viewer flagged one of Emmalene's videos, a seemingly innocent upload showing toddler Alice in the bath naked from the waist up; the faceless viewers were seeking, perhaps, to protect the guile-less-seeming duo of Alice and Emmalene from the pedophiles who apparently lurk in every corner of the Internet. "YouTube took that video down," Emmalene says regretfully. She doesn't agree with the decision: "There could be a pedophile watching when we're walking down the street." Another viewer flagged a harmless video of Emmalene wearing a crop top: that video was then slapped with an "adult" content warning.

There's a difference between the mediated, ever-present loop and the intangible, unrecorded moment. We have a habit of projecting our own needs, desires, and insecurities onto the video image. Walking down the street isn't a kind of provoca-tion, isn't a demand that others acknowledge that you exist as a kind of mediated product and are worthy of their attention and viewing for the simple reason that you exist. Video turns people into characters. And characters are reproductions that exist to be watched on terms no longer their own. Characters are products, not people. So it is that young, perky Emmalene seems to attract more than her share of anonymous lurkers posting messages of anger, perversion, and lust. People who would never dare go up to Emmalene on the street feel free to accost her on a regular basis via virtual reality. With her image, her character, they feel free to do what they like: use, abuse, project their self-doubts and basest desires. They are the disinhibited lurkers, the silent voy-eurs empowered to a kind of solipsistic interactivity with their imaginations via Peep.

Of course, in some ways Emmalene provokes them. In the

crop-top video, she exposes and discusses the state of her post-partum belly; in another she shows her panties; it's hardly *Girls Gone Wild*, but whether she's aware of it or not, she is on camera, mediated. She is a young, female, televised product. No matter what her intentions, she will be viewed as a sexual object. Jennifer Ringley of JenniCam spent a lot of time explaining that her site wasn't pornography, but there's no doubt that the fact that you might see her undressing, masturbating, or going to the bathroom fueled interest in her experiment and helped her attract thousands of paying customers. Emmalene promises nothing nearly as explicit. And yet the videos still feel candid in an almost physical way. It's the way they're set in her bedroom. The way she appears in her pajamas. The way the camera points at her, at her body. And Emmalene herself seems to relish interactions with her online "community" no matter how base their point of view:

> OneillZmed: Can you do another video in a belly shirt? Are you wearing underwear in this video, you are hot!
>
> Emmalene: yes I am wearing underwear, no I don't really own belly tops.
>
> OneillZmed: What kind of underwear were you wearing? Can you do another video in the belly shirt from the video, you have a sweet bellybutton!
>
> Emmalene: I don't really disclose what type I wear over the internet . . . but feel free to use your imagination! I don't like doing belly videos because the comments I get tend to creep me out, to be perfectly honest.
>
> OneillZmed: I did not mean to freak you out, I would just like you to do another video in the belly shirt you are wearing in the video. Can I guess what kind you are wearing . . . G-string or thong?
>
> Emmalene: ha ha I won't be doing a video wearing just that shirt . . .

OneillZmed: No I meant another video with you wearing that same shirt. Also, were you wearing a G-string or thong?

Emmalene: apparently someone has flagged my video . . . I never thought ironing was overtly sexual . . . but ok . . . and I never thought a belly was very sexual either. . .

Snuf13: Yours is. . . ;)~

kurbsyde: Damn girl, Mike's one lucky guy, hahahaha. Take care and again, thanks for the shout-out >:D< to you and yours.

So, what to make of this? Emmalene is, like so many others, a little lonely, a little isolated, a little misunderstood, and feeling very much in need of a community that, by and large, supports her desire to be seen and known. But that same "community" reduces her, uses her, turns her into a product to be consumed as they please. (As social media researcher Danah Boyd told a reporter: "They can observe you, but it's not the same as knowing you.") Meanwhile, old-style social constraints, whether they take the shape of a disapproving husband or still-prevailing conservative ideologies about sexuality, reign in Emmalene, keep her from going completely Peep. Emmalene doesn't tell (or show) all. But she tells (and shows) enough. She has subscribers. Followers. Watchers. In her own way, maybe even somewhere in the back of her own mind, she's a bit of a celebrity.

◻ ◻ ◻

British social theorist Nikolas Rose echoes Jean Twenge when he talks about the modern individual as an "entrepreneur of him or herself" who is "to conduct his or her life, and that of his or her family, as a kind of enterprise, seeking to enhance and capitalize on existence itself through calculated acts and investments." The modern individual, then, seeks to have more and more relationships with others that are essentially "parasocial," the term social scientists use to describe the kind of one-sided relationships we have with celebrities. (We know everything about them; they don't know we exist.) Danah Boyd has argued that the constant flow of detailed information about people we don't know is creating a whole new class of people in our lives—people we follow closely online and come to know intimately though we have no actual relationship with them and they don't necessarily know we're watching them.

A good example of this kind of twenty-first-century individual is Julia Allison, the New York socialite turned online celebrity. Allison isn't a household name, but she is well-known within tech-geek-gossip circles. Well-known enough to earn her a cover spot on *Wired* magazine. In the ensuing article, she tells *Wired* that her fame is no accident: it's something she set out to achieve through careful cultivation of a certain kind of persona. "I treat it like a fire," she explains. "You have to add logs, or it'll be like one of those YouTube videos that flame out." But Allison, in a posting on her blog that is much more interesting and frank than anything she tells *Wired*, is also aware of the drawbacks of such an obsessive cultivation of attention: "The irony, of course, is that Publicity is a full-time job," she writes. "I did over two dozen print interviews and 350 television segments in the last year—and probably over 500 in the last two years. I taught my brain to think in soundbites, in PR nothing-speak, to project authority on subjects I have no real knowledge about. It's a game . . . but I'm a bit tired of playing it. Now I need to unlearn much of that."

Can we unlearn it? Everyone I've spoken with about blogging has said in one way or another that it's addictive. I've felt the pull myself. As I go about my day, I suddenly wonder: Did I blog yet? Would what I'm doing right now be a good thing to blog about? Or I might wonder: What's Padme up to? What's Emmalene doing? The next thing I know, I'm spending an hour or two finding out. It's an addiction, a hunger that can never be sated. There's always more to be revealed or discovered. There's always the looming possibility that the next post will go viral. There's always someone out there willing to read, comment, and at least seem to care.

We're addicted to the rush we get when people we don't know pay attention to us. It doesn't matter if they're trashing us or heaping praise on us. Julia Allison finds herself the cover story of a major magazine. The reaction from the general public is less than flattering. As a result, Allison announces her intention to back off, even as that announcement brings further attention to her life and perpetuates a cycle of Peep that seems far too pervasive and all-encompassing to simply unlearn or walk away from. As with Emmalene's experience on YouTube, the comments might be hateful or lewd, but that doesn't mean they are any less thrilling to receive. People care about me. They care enough about me to hate me or turn me into their fantasy. I'm in the big time now. Reality TV here I come. Next stop: celebrity!

◻ ◻ ◻

Stardom didn't invent itself. A cohort of glamorous, rich, inaccessible talents who are worshiped worldwide and completely dominate our mass media didn't just spring up like orchids, shockingly vibrant blooms, rare and deserving of our attention. Stardom, like Julia Allison's celebrity, is constructed and created. The concept of the "star" emerged from the rise of an industrial, urbanized society in which we live "alone in the crowd." Stardom came along at a time when the way human beings live was being altered on every level. As film came to the fore in the late nineteenth and early twentieth centuries, human beings were moving from the country to the city, from the old world to the new, from the edicts of kings and queens to the scientific tautologies of bureaucracy and democracy. Everything was changing and it was getting harder and harder to know what to put one's faith in. Community was becoming pseudo-community. The tribe was disintegrating. Religion was under attack. What would emerge to offer people wisdom, solace, distraction, amusement, awe?

Enter the nickelodeon. For five cents you could see a movie. Cheap, accessible, easy to understand, film quickly took on the trappings of ritual and transcendence. Film allowed for rare moments of shared cohesion in a world of near total fragmentation. "The motion picture offered no linguistic barriers," wrote early film historian Terry Ramsaye. "A story on the screen was a picture alike to Pole, Slovak, Russian, Magyar or Italian. And it was cheap, the price of a glass of beer." Motion pictures like *The Life of an American Fireman* (1902) and *The Great Train Robbery* (1903), both directed by Pennsylvania film innovator Edwin S. Porter, are straightforward and exciting. A fireman is asleep in his office. He is dreaming. The dream, shown in an inset, depicts a mother putting her baby to bed. The fireman wakes up with a shock. He must save the mother and child! He does, of course, save the mother and child. *The Great Train Robbery* is even more straightforward—it's Indiana Jones, John Wayne, and Clint Eastwood, all in one. It's the archetypal American western told in twelve minutes of nonstop, thrilling action and technical innovation. *The Great Train Robbery* would tour for five solid years, and be the main attraction at the first nickelodeon that opened, in Pittsburgh, Pennsylvania, in 1905, a phenomenon that was quickly imitated in cities across the United States and then the world. It would start a craze for the movies that continues to this day. Theater critic Walter Eaton seemed both peeved and admiring when he wrote in 1909 that "in New York City alone, on a Sunday, 500,000 people go to the moving picture shows. . . . You cannot dismiss canned drama with a shrug of contempt. Here is an industry to be controlled, an influence to be reckoned with."

Motion pictures were becoming an industry, but their product was stories acted by people, not pencils or applesauce. As the industry moved from documentary to drama (drama made up 17 percent of the offerings in 1907 and 66 percent in 1908) the power brokers in this fledgling big business quickly realized that they needed to make sure to stay on the good side of potential censors. Phrases like "here is an industry to be controlled" sounded alarm bells in their ears.

To quell concerns, the industry turned to the "players." Hey, everyone, come meet our stable of squeaky-clean, noble, kind-hearted members of the common folk (particularly in contrast to the venal bohemians and moral-ingrate intellectuals found prancing around on the stage). This kind of promotion served to underscore the idea that the moving-picture industry was a moral industry populated by upstanding craftspeople who just wanted to tell a good story. A new marketing strategy was discovered: not only can you promote the motion picture, you can promote the fascinating, upstanding actors in the picture. The actors became personalities as worthy of discussion as the characters they played. Before 1909, the public was pretty much ignorant of the names of the actors in the films. But by 1912, the bulk of the "players" had been "discovered." Attendance swelled, and the star was born.

This isn't something people clamored for. It's something that, to this day, is relentlessly manufactured. In February 1910 a contributor to an early film commentary magazine, the *Nickelodeon*, noted, with perhaps some degree of embellishment, that "picture theater patrons are demanding of exhibitors a better acquaintance with those they see up on the screen . . . the development of the art has produced actors in the silent drama second to none on the legitimate stage, and they richly deserve the public recognition which is even now awaiting them." By 1911 film trade publications were commenting on the Edison Company innovation of listing the members of the cast on a title card at the beginning of the film. Edison would take this to the next level two years later, beginning each film by showing the image of the actor along with his or her name and the name of the character being played. These and other innovations had the desired affect. A 1914 issue of the popular movie periodical *Photoplay* featured an article titled "Loree Starr—Photoplay Idol." It had a very distinct subtitle: "A Fascinating Serial Story Presenting a New Type of Hero." This marks an escalation in tone: The actors aren't just common craftspeople of moral character. They're one step above that—they're heroes. Here's another quote from a movie magazine of pre–World War I Hollywood: "And even in these days of the all-seeing camera-eye there are scores of heroic deeds, of patently self-sacrificing acts, performed by the film folk which never reach pictures or print." The article ends by asking: "Is your REEL hero ever a REAL hero?" Already a fascination with the secrets behind the cellular facade. Already the exaggeration and adulation, the deliberate strategy of marketing individuals as the new gods, REEL heroes and REAL heroes.

Today the idea of integrating your person seamlessly into your product and becoming your own media property is as hypnotic and elusive as anything on the big screen. Today, more than ever, we want to be the stars, and we're told that, yes, we can and should and probably will be stars. After all, anybody can be a celebrity in the age of reality TV, blogging, and social networks, can't they? In fact, the corporate-owned mass-media outlets are only too happy to facilitate this fantasy with an endless series of specious examples of this kind of "success." They are not only enhancing and deepening the myth of the star that so much of their (Peep) programming depends on, they're also inculcating us with another myth: that the rise of the "everyday" celebrity in some way represents a rebellion in which we get to rush past the corporate gatekeepers, smash in the door where all the stars live, and loot the liquor cabinet.

Many have been suckered into the idea that the ubiquitous celebrity marks a successful overthrow of the old elitist methodology of superstars and their admiring millions of swooning fans. This load of bunk has crystallized into a prevailing sentiment: that the age of the star—the movie star, the rock star, even the porn star—is over. Today the far more egalitarian and grassroots "celebrity" rules. The star, distant and inaccessible, was ultimately an elitist insult to the masses. Enter the new and improved celebrity. A celebrity doesn't need, and usually lacks, any discernable skill or talent. A celebrity is someone whose everyday life is entertainment. A celebrity is someone whose allure is ever-present presence (made possible by ongoing access to the conduits of mass media). Celebrity is more Peep than pop because a celebrity doesn't actually have any particular skill, and is known, first and foremost, for being himself or herself. Paris Hilton is a celebrity. Julia Allison is a celebrity. Marilyn Monroe was a star.

Is the celebrity really a radical overthrow of the ideology of stardom? The rhetoric that tells us that we now live in a time when anyone, anywhere, can suddenly become a celebrity seems as much a fantasy as the star discovered in a diner while bringing pancakes to the table of the famous director. The conventional wisdom is that first we had stars, and then we had celebrities, and now we have ubiquitous "amateur" celebrities—an inverse progression that either reflects the broad-based dumbing down of a society saturated in quick-fix media or the egalitarian, rebellious nature of the new Web 2.0 entertainment universe. But in truth, rather then one replacing the other, all three categories can and do exist at the same time. There are still plenty of stars who have risen to prominence through hard work, skill, and that extra-special something that makes people want to like them and be like them. Some of these stars, though not all of them, are also celebrities. They are stars who have learned to incorporate not just their exceptional talents and enviable charisma, but also the quotidian details of their daily lives into the project of their brand. Meanwhile, many, if not all, celebrities—people like Paris Hilton and Tila Tequila who rise to prominence through sheer calculated ubiquity—continue to seek the legitimacy of stardom. Consider a comment made by Tila Tequila in an interview with the *New York Times* at the height of her success with the *Springer*-meets-*The Bachelor* show *A Shot at Love*: "The press and the media have glorified the celebrity thing and brainwashed people to live in that world," Ms. Tequila said. "People try to stand out for nothing and they end up getting quote-unquote famous. I'm not into that at all. If you're just into fame for fame, I'm like, 'Okay, but what are you good at? What can you actually do?'"

Before her seedy mating show, Tequila's claim to fame was based largely on a *Playboy* spread and the fact that she had 1,771,920 MySpace friends. And yet even she, at the pinnacle of Peep culture, seeks to lay claim to a discernable, tangible talent, to something other than the ability to tell all and show all, all the time. Celebrity does not replace stardom, it simply creates more tiers, more ways to categorize and calculate, more ways to legitimize our watching.

The Peep celebrity isn't becoming so prevalent in our culture because we're finally freeing ourselves from the shackles of an entertainment industry that for too long controlled who and what we watched. Would that it could be so, but sorry, no. In fact, the opposite is happening: the Peep celebrity is indicative of just how entranced we are by the media machine's ability to create the star-celebrity; we are drawn to the person-product who seems to fit so effortlessly into a society organized around the principle that people can and should be reduced to hits, ratings, views, box office gross. In such a system we are encouraged to believe that our participation could lead to us being recognized and lavishly rewarded just for going about our lives. Meanwhile, we are led to believe that our participation is in some way "against the system"—we happily perceive ourselves as rebels even as we actively seek to join the system in ever-more cyborg-like symbiosis.

◻ ◻ ◻

"Sometimes knowing that we're not alone with our weird habits or our uncomfortable feelings makes us less ashamed," writes Lisa Sargese on her blog. Sargese started blogging as a way to tell the truth about her life as a morbidly obese, single woman determined to return to mobility and health via stomach-shrinking surgery. "There's stuff out there about this kind of surgery," she tells me when I reach her by phone at her home in Clifton, New Jersey. "But it's very tame and not gutsy enough for my taste. I wanted to tell the truth. On a blog nobody gets to tell me what to say. I can tell it all."

And she does. Lisa has blogged daily since 2006. She doesn't shy away from any subject, whether it's her post-surgery re-emerging libido or her pre-surgery experiments with self mutilation:

> Friday, December 15, 2006: The Burning Flap
> My abs hang down to my knees. Feeling like this makes me want to curl up in an ass-ball and hide from the world. I have some nerve trying to make it in the world in this deformed state. Or is it just the enemy talking? My abs are hanging like loose drapery. I've heard it called "the pannus." Sounds like a droopy bread basket. Maybe that's exactly what it is. It pulls on my upper carriage. The skin folds burn. I feel ugly.

> Tuesday, December 12, 2006: Hearing Other People's
> Experiences = HOPE
> My story doesn't matter. At least, I didn't think my story mattered until folks started to thank me for sharing it. My fear, my low self-esteem, my aversion to exposure and confrontation made me want to hide . . . for years. And I did hide. I hid behind a mountain of fat. I'm still fat, at least by society's standards. No one takes into consideration that I can walk from my classroom to my car without sitting 3 or 4 times. No one looks at my big ass and applauds me for getting off it. No one is sympathizing with my impending reconstructive surgery to cut off all the inevitable loose skin. No one does, unless I tell my story.

> Monday, April 16, 2007: Blog Therapy
> I see a shrink, not a therapist. When I say "shrink" I mean psychiatrist. She prescribes my magical, and I do mean magical,

cocktail of meds that keep me somewhat sane. . . . I WAS in therapy . . . on and off for 20 years to be exact. Some of my therapists were cruel and unhelpful. Most of them were compassionate and helped me heal. They listened, encouraged, gave a little advice and I did the hard work of changing. It's a fair cop. Someday (soon) when I have tons of money and good health insurance I'll get back into therapy. For now, Blogging is my therapy. A friend of mine suggested I call my book "How Blogging Saved My Life: Putting My Heart, Guts and Mind on the Line Online." Kinda wordy but catchy, right?

Monday, June 2, 2008: Renewed!
What goes up must come down and vice versa. My dark mood has lifted, though I say that hesitantly so as not to jinx it. I'm feeling hopeful. I went to my bariatric surgeon's office today for a check-in. I lost over 20 pounds over the past 10 months. Maybe it doesn't sound like an OH WOW amount of weight but considering it's weight I WILL NEVER GAIN BACK it is an Oh Wow amount. Considering how strong I've become and how well I've been eating and the progress I've made overcoming my eating disorder my 20 pounds lost is an OH WOW amount. Plus, the year isn't over.

Early on, Sargese railed against the silence that met her posts. "LEAVE ME A COMMENT," she begged in all caps on December 13, 2006. "Let me know you're out there! :-)" Lisa isn't begging for comments anymore. Today the comments arrive with enough frequency so as to have convinced Sargese that her future isn't in academia (when I spoke to her she paid the rent by lecturing part time at Montclair State University) but in pursuing a career as a celebrity therapist. "What is this DRIVE I have to be some bad-ass, rock star celebrity?" she writes on her blog. "I don't know why I want more, I just do."

And so she's gone from simply wanting to communicate and reach out to others, to believing that she may well be the next Oprah. Despite having just recently earned a master's degree in

counseling, despite having just made a comeback from a debili-
tating physical condition which reduced her mobility to nil and,
at its awful nadir, landed her in the hospital for two months,
Sargese is ready to take on the world. She tells me that her goal
isn't simply to lose weight and regain her health. Her ultimate
aim is to look "hot" and achieve stardom as a self-help guru. All
this from a woman, who, when she began blogging in 2006, was
embarrassed to leave her house.

I ask her if maybe she isn't deluding herself a bit. After all,
there's a big difference between being encouraged by a small
group of ardent readers and believing that you're destined for
fame. Lisa, unruffled by the question, points out to me that tem-
pering fantasy with reality won't help her much. "The people who
are successful in life are not the most talented," she says. "You see
a lot of hacks that make it, so even if I'm deluding myself, well, if
it perpetuates the delusion that people can be rich, famous, and
successful that might just give them the inspiration to continue
doing it, and just by their persistence they will succeed, so it will
have been worth it."

Note how Sargese slips into the third person. It's as if she's
already "made it" and is now practiced at encouraging her faceless fan base to dream big like she once did. Turning your life into
an entertainment product gives you the power to invent a new
person—the person you think you should be, as opposed to the
person you actually are.

Lisa herself says to me, "I've created a persona." She talks
about being who she wants to be on the blog, so that it can happen in real life: "Even if it was just my friends or just me reading
it, I've still created this character: I am the girl who exercises, I am
the girl who's going to win at this by seeing it there in a concrete
way in the writing and doing of it everyday." Today, Lisa is talking
about becoming a "motivational speaker" and "needing a product to promote." Her product is her blog, that is, herself: "That's
the product I'm promoting, people write to me and say 'I do your

exercises every day." People who are pre-gastric bypass, they can't get out of bed, who's going to help them, encourage them? It's exciting, it's something I wanted but didn't know if I could achieve. Every time I give a talk I get a few more regular readers. After I give a talk the blog hits will get 200 a day, then it simmers down to 50 or so. It's no longer just about me."

Again the numbers. Again the idea that there is a community that needs you, a community in which you can be a star just by being yourself. The reality is that Lisa is a part-time lecturer at a New Jersey college. She wants to find a full-time job. She wants to become a self-help guru. She wants a book deal. She needs health insurance and a steady source of income. She thinks her blog will help her, but maybe the opposite is the case: do employers want to hire someone so open about their mental and physical problems? Does a publisher not look at this and say, "Hey, this story has already been told for free online?" The real Lisa and the projected future Lisa are at odds, and the blog is where they meet in a daily struggle to accommodate fantasy to reality.

❑ ❑ ❑

Many who do Peep culture forget that there is still a social order out there, still a quasi-community that makes normative judgments based on a previous, tribal way of constructing communal existence. You step into the fantasy world and, the more the fantasy becomes reality, the less you are able to judge how others might see you. You are fusing with mass media and (often unconsciously) turning yourself into product. But society is uneasy with such blatant transmutation. As a result, there's always the chance that people will perceive unfiltered openness as a kind of desperation. Not every shape shift into Peep product leads to a book deal or a reality TV stint. There's always the chance that people will see you as damaged goods and decide they don't want to have anything to do with what you're selling.

Consider the story of Beauty, a petite, middle-aged mom who lives comfortably in a small, working-class, Canadian city and works from home part-time as a tutor.

Before meeting her second husband, Beauty had always thought of porn as something for losers and perverts. But, as she told me, her new husband introduced her to a variety of amateur porn upload sites at which point she realized that "billions of people look at porn." Pretty soon hubby suggested that they take pictures of Beauty nude. "I was so enamored of him and I trusted him so I was completely open to it. Sure enough we found a little deserted beach on vacation and took some pictures. They were pretty good so we decided to put them on Voyeurweb." They put the pictures up on the Web site—"tasteful nudes" Beauty told me—and they called the woman depicted in them "Beauty."

The reaction from the five million or so people from around the world who drop by Voyeurweb on a daily basis was exciting: "We won newcomer of the month and 300 bucks. We thought, 'Wow this is really fun.'" Naturally, that wasn't going to be the end of things. "It soon became a habit for us—I should say a hobby. It was a hobby. It was just a great fun hobby, taking pictures, sorting through them and putting them on Voyeurweb. For whatever reason we very quickly became popular contributors. I don't know what it was. It's not that I was the most beautiful woman on the site but for whatever reason our pictures resonated with the viewers; every time we would put a contribution in we were voted #1 and we were stunned because there are millions of contributors."

Beauty and her husband became more and more devoted to their hobby. They sought out exotic locales. They booked vacations based on the terrain's ability to provide picturesque solitary spots for ever more elaborate photo shoots. They also started to let loose in terms of showing Beauty's face. "Of course the women who would win the most money would show their face. We started half showing my face and then in the end we were fully showing my face." Fully revealed, Beauty was winning even more of the popularity contests. The money rolled in—ten to fifteen thousand in prize dollars over a year and a half. "Voyeurweb was our little world where I was pretty famous. Checking the computer every day to see the rankings and comments . . . I think we probably got caught up in it. We would use our Voyeurweb money to take vacations and take more pictures, so it was great. We planned a vacation when we were really in the thick of it, we went and the first day there my husband had too much tequila and was in the water taking pictures and the camera got ruined. We had planned this whole vacation to take pictures and here we were without a camera. It was a bust. It was kind of a reality check for us at how addicted we had become to it, and we came home from that really disappointed because we didn't get any pictures and had spent a fortune on that vacation. We thought, 'Is this our wake up call that maybe we're too involved?' But we didn't believe it. We bought a new camera went right back to the same place."

Then the real wake-up call came. While the couple was on that second vacation, someone back home connected the suburban mom and tutor to the online model. "They were on the site. Somebody recognized me, told someone, who told someone else, who came to me." A woman came to Beauty, "a straitlaced Christian woman," who condemned her and withdrew her child from tutoring. Beauty and her husband were frantic. "I just went into complete panic mode." They didn't know how far this could go. Could the husband be fired from his job? Would the kids be ostracized and mocked at school? Would they have to move? Immediately they asked the site administrators to take down all their pictures. Beauty said that for the next six months her heart leapt into her throat every time the phone rang. She and her husband held their breath and hoped that the storm would blow over.

Weeks and months passed and no one else came forward. The rumor had died out. What was left was a feeling of absence— Beauty missed posing nude and posting the pictures. "Wow, we can't do this anymore. It's such a big part of our life. It was very—I hate to say devastating—that's not the right word. But it certainly was a downer." Absence turned into anger and frustration and disbelief and even a bit of self-disgust. "We got pretty addicted to it. We took huge risks." Then again, Beauty mused, "We made a lot of money from it. It's been an unbelievable part of my life. If you told me ten years ago I'd be doing this I'd [have said], 'You're out of your mind.'" Despite the shaming sense of addiction, Beauty couldn't stop thinking about what she was missing out on. So why don't you just go ahead and go public with it? I asked her. If it's that important to you, why not just go ahead and do it? "It's about my family and my community. It's because of my children. And my parents would just die. That's the reason I don't do it. I don't resent that because they are more important than anything. Sure, I wish I could, but I don't know if there will ever be a time when that's an acceptable thing to do."

Months passed, and Beauty, despite the dangers of exposure, couldn't shake the need to be online. So they started up again, this time more cautiously, posting without showing Beauty's face, on Voyeurweb's more explicit sister site RedClouds. RedClouds is safer. It has a smaller base of viewers because people have to pay to access the site. Their first entry won them $2000. People on the site were excited. One commentator succinctly captured the buzz on the site, writing simply: "Beauty is back!"

◻ ◻ ◻

The first blogger to openly lose her job due to oversharing was Heather Armstrong, fired in 2002. In one of several now infamous posts penned for her blog Dooce.com, she wrote:

> I hate that the Enabling Producer enables nothing but my
> never-ending agony, that she never knows what she wants and so
> gives directions as vague as, "Mock up something that, you know,

says something," without even telling me what I'm supposed to say something about. And after I mock up something that, you know, really says something, something about nothing because I have no idea what I'm supposed to be saying something about, she freaks out and says, "That's not saying something. I hired you to say something."

You can see why the higher-ups at her company might have been a wee bit ticked. Since Armstrong, a steady stream of people have been, as Web slang now puts it, "dooced," including Catherine Sanderson, a British secretary in Paris who was fired in 2006 after writing about the accounting firm she worked for. Sanderson blogged anonymously, though she did post her picture. In her blog she mocked her employers for wearing "braces and sock suspenders," and joked about deliberately revealing her cleavage during a video conference. Eventually someone found her blog and connected her to her office. After that, it was only a matter of time. Sanderson actually filed a complaint with a French workplace tribunal, but really, what did she expect?

Years after Heather Armstrong, you'd think people would start to know better. But the stories keep coming: An adjunct journalism professor is fired from teaching a course at Boston University after posting his thoughts about his first day of teaching. He'd written : "Of my six students one (the smartest, wouldn't you know it?) is incredibly hot. . . . It was all I could do to remember the other five students." A journalism professor, no less! Then there's the lecturer at Southern Methodist University who starts the blog *Phantom Professor* in which she mocks rich female students, whom she calls Ashleys. She also trashes a new full-time hire she calls Professor Wideass, implying that it was the color of her skin, not her scholarly work, that got her the job. When the anonymous blog is finally tied to the writing instructor, she is asked not to return after the spring semester.

People don't just get fired for doing Peep, they also manage to get themselves sued. The best example of this is Jessica Cutler (another one of Peep culture's early mavens). Cutler's anonymous blog *Washingtonienne* was about a Capitol Hill employee (then twenty-six and working as a mail sorter for Senator Mike DeWine, an Ohio Republican) who bragged about sleeping with six different men, some for money. *Washingtonienne* listed her partners by initials and occupations, from the married "Chief of Staff at one of the gov agencies, appointed by Bush," to her current boyfriend, a fellow Senate staff member who she identifies by his real initials and depicts as being into submissive women and handcuffs. Anyway, this went on until she was outed by another blog—double Peep!—the popular Washington gossip blog *Wonkette*. *Wonkette* interviewed her, revealed her identity, and made it pretty easy to figure out who her boyfriend was. While Cutler reveled in her sudden fame, posed for *Playboy*, and grabbed herself a quarter-million-dollar book deal, her boyfriend became a laughingstock and found his career in tatters. But Cutler had no regrets: "Some people with blogs are never going to get famous," she told *Playboy* in the short interview accompanying her photo spread. "And they've been doing it for, like, over a year. I feel bad for them." She may feel bad for them, but she doesn't seem to feel bad for her ex-boyfriend Robert. He decided to sue for $20 million. Cutler, by now living in New York City, promptly declared bankruptcy, asserting in court documents that she was unable to pay her bills, legal fees, and student loans. Broke, unlikely to get another book deal after her first novel got predictably lackluster notices, still Cutler relentlessly markets her persona. I drop by her Web site and the first thing I notice is a "donate" button. Cutler writes underneath it: "I need money for slutty clothes and drugs!" (A year later, Cutler was still at it, peddling "exclusive blog posts" concerning her nuptials to Manhattan lawyer Charles Rubio to blog site the *Daily Beast*.)

Cutler's story is well-known and documented, but the lawsuits are still coming. Laurie, a Manhattan mother, was sued by her soon-to-be-ex-husband after she started podcasting on DivorcingDaze.com during her divorce in 2006. According to Laurie, as many as 10,000 people downloaded each episode of her podcast. They were treated to such information as how she found out that her husband was having an affair (by looking at the e-mail on his BlackBerry), and how her husband had told their daughter that he wasn't cheating (because, as far as he was concerned, the marriage was already over). Even though she didn't divulge her husband's last name or her own in the broadcasts, hubby found the content, as court statements put it, "obnoxious, derogatory or offensive" and in violation of the terms of the divorce settlement, which stated that his wife not "harass" or "malign" him. A New York State Supreme Court justice disagreed. The court wrote that while Laurie's statements were probably "ill-advised and did not promote co-parenting," they were covered by the First Amendment.

In a similar case, a court in Vermont ordered William Krasnansky to take down a barely altered, supposedly fictional account of his own divorce, in which he described his ex-wife in an unflattering light and blamed her for forcing him to sell their home at "a ruinous loss." Mr. Krasnansky's ex-wife called the online story "defamatory" and a judge agreed. But a few weeks later, after an eruption of criticism regarding free-speech rights, the court changed its mind and Krasnansky was allowed to continue publishing. One more entry on this list: Tricia Walsh Smith made a YouTube video announcing that her husband, theater executive Phillip Smith, hoarded Viagra, pornography, and condoms, even though they never had sex. The couple was in the process of divorcing at the time. Smith's lawyer protested, but didn't sue, perhaps heeding the results of the previous cases.

To call all this material "revenge blogging" isn't necessarily accurate. In fact, many of the people who find themselves accused of crossing the line into defamation, libel, and oversharing are people who have already been bloggers or podcasters for a while. When things go sour, so does the tone in their online communications. As a reporter notes: "For some ex-spouses, revenge is not the point. Writing about divorce can be good for readership." This theory is affirmed by one Penelope Trunk, the author of the *Brazen Careerist* blog, who has spent quite a bit of time writing about the demise of her fifteen-year marriage. "The bloggers who are doing the best are those who are injecting their personal lives," she notes. So obviously if your personal life is scandalous, tragic, or otherwise notable, you're going to "do" even better.

In a study led by Fernanda Viegas out of MIT, nearly 500 bloggers were interviewed. More than a third of the respondents said they had "gotten in trouble" for material posted on their blog. Another third said that they knew other bloggers who had gotten into trouble with family and friends. Bloggers who admitted to frequently writing about "highly personal materials" got into the most trouble, most frequently. As one mournful fellow explained, "I lost a prospective girlfriend, who found that I'd blogged a brief amount about our date." Nearly two-thirds of the bloggers Viegas interviewed said that they rarely asked permission before using other people's real names, though they apparently "became more sensitive to the importance of using pseudonyms after their friends and family objected." The kind of trouble you can get into while turning yourself into a pop-Peep product is varied and endless. While I was working on this book, the good people of City Lights Bookstore (which sits below the offices of my publisher, City Lights Books) alerted me to a blog called *Whale Ship* by a young woman attending Berkeley, who in one of her posts bragged about shoplifting books from the store. The blog doesn't include her name, but she has posted a picture of herself, which City Lights Bookstore staff have seen. (They hope that she'll return.) The blog, which reeks of a carefully cultivated, hyper-aware, bad-girl persona, was probably only read or even noticed by her friends until a simple Google alert for City Lights

Bookstore brought up her name. (Tip to future rebels intent on showcasing low-level criminality: Mentioning on your blog the names of stores, dates, and details about items stolen isn't the smartest thing to do.) Anyway, this scourge of the San Francisco literati is hardly alone in putting up information about herself that may have unintended consequences. A study done by Dr. Dimitri Christakis of the Seattle Children's Research Institute and Dr. Megan Moreno of the University of Wisconsin analyzed 500 randomly chosen MySpace profiles of eighteen-year-olds. They found that "54 per cent of the publicly available accounts they checked contained information about high-risk behaviors: 41 percent mentioned substance abuse, 24 percent sexual behavior and 14 percent violence."

In the Peep culture era, the era of the persona-product that constantly reaffirms the new ideal of celebrity while undermining our crumbling sense of community, it's harder and harder to know where to draw the line. The legal squabbles over free speech and defamation are less interesting as law cases and more interesting as evidence of just how divisive Peep can be. Over and over the desire of individuals to use intimate details of their lives as the building blocks of online persona-product collapses into the reality of what we consider allowable in our society. Culturally we're half in the past, half in the future, and wholly uncomfortable with these new self-proclaimed cyborg tell-alls. So when former *Gawker* blogger Emily Gould blogged about her soon-to-be-ex-boyfriend and set off a tit-for-tat article and blog frenzy, reactions ranged from repulsed to perplexed to fascinated— often all at once. For those of you lucky enough not to have heard this story, Gould blogged about her boyfriend (also a *Gawker* editor) when they were dating and after. This prompted boyfriend to write an article in *New York Magazine* about her writing about him in her blog. Gould then retaliated with a piece in the *New York Times Magazine* about him writing about her writing about him. The article centered around Gould announcing (like

Julia Allison) that she had finally learned her lesson: From here on in she would be "doing something unexpected: keeping the personal details of my current life to myself." Of course, as with the case of counterparts like Allison and Cutler, even this has to be taken with a grain of salt since, obviously, by writing the article she was again revealing the personal details of her life, and promoting her blog (which is still going). Plus, as countless other blogs have pointed out (themselves only too happy to jump on the bandwagon and peep Gould while she peeps herself), Gould continues to blog on *Gawker* and elsewhere. Meanwhile, *Gawker*, her past and occasionally present employer, can't get enough of the story. As *New York Observer* "Media Mob" columnist Matt Haber noted, "*Gawker*'s first post officially linked to Ms. Gould's *Times Magazine* story received 9,133 views and 170 comments. A follow-up post clocked in at 8,814 views with 149 comments, while a post announcing comments had closed on NYTimes.com received only 4,150 views and 83 comments. Sadly, another, about the article's photos, topped out at only 2,556 views and 55 comments. Finally, it seemed, for *Gawker*, the horse had been kicked to death."

All of which is to suggest a more complicated, less flattering truth about lessons learned in the age of Peep: what Gould and many other Peep cyborgs are learning isn't that they need to stop using their real life to create their product, but that they need to be smarter about managing how and when they reveal their personal details—when to back off, when to go on the offensive, when to feign being offended. As such, for now and the foreseeable future, Peep will continue to engender horror and confusion even while it fixes our gaze in fascination. Good citizens from Manitoba to Michigan will wonder: What's wrong with these people? Why can't they stop?

◻ ◻ ◻

I can't stop.

We might easily make the mistake of thinking that Lisa Sargese, and a cast of Peep characters that includes Padme, Justin, and Emmalene, are feckless extroverts with too much time on their hands. But I've tried to do what they do. And guess what? It's hard work blogging twice daily, sending twenty Twitters a day, constantly generating video. It takes time, focus, and commitment. We're not talking heroic effort or anything, but we're definitely talking a considerable amount of energy devoted to creating an external, mediated, parallel, Peep-friendly self.

I started blogging on January 16, 2008. I called my blog *The Peep Diaries: One Man's Journey Into Self-Exposure, Surveillance and the Future of Voyeurism.* I started blogging for two reasons. First, I wanted to see what it would be like to be a blogger, to write about my everyday life to an audience of total strangers the way Lisa does. To that end, I would blog about my personal life and day-to-day existence. The second goal was to create a forum for ideas and developments in Peep culture. This would be an ongoing blog of interest to anyone who cares about media, celebrity, privacy, surveillance, and, well, pretty much all aspects of contemporary society. Naturally, of course, as with most blogs by the authors of books, I also hoped that in the long term, the blog would lead people to my book, and the book would lead people to the blog, which would then lead them my other books, and so on and so forth. (Hey, a guy's gotta make a living, right?)

My first blog post was typed on a train to Kingston, Ontario. I was on my way to do research for this book. Here's some of what I wrote:

> So a bit of a peep into my morning: The train left at 7 am. I woke up at 6:10, five minutes or so before my cab was supposed to show up. Actually I didn't wake up, W woke me up. Who knows when I would have gotten up if left to my own devices. I was counting on the kid to wake us both up at 6 am exactly, like she

does every morning. Today, the little bugger decided to sleep in. So, much to W's annoyance I ended up waking them both up as I fumbled for something to wear and stumbled into the bathroom to brush my teeth.

Anyway, I grabbed my carefully packed bag, kissed everyone goodbye and jumped into the waiting cab. Five minutes later I realized I had forgotten my laptop, so we turned around. I ran back into the house past W and kid, and bounded up the stairs. W, who is the kind of person who has to get everywhere at least an hour early, shook her head in horror as I waved yet another frantic goodbye.

At this time in the morning it takes less than 10 minute to get from my house to the train station so I got there with fifteen minutes to spare—time to hit the bank machine and grab a coffee before the train pulled out. Stepping onto the train a few minutes before it left the station reminded me how annoying flying is and how great train travel is. High speed rail, please!

I haven't told you why I'm going to Kingston yet: On Monday, while compiling peep related links for this blog I dropped in on a site I'd been meaning to visit but hadn't gotten around to yet. It was the website of the Surveillance Project, founded by sociologist David Lyon and located at Queen's University in Kingston. I noticed that they had a talk scheduled on Thursday. A criminology prof from University of Montreal was coming to talk about public perception of CCTV surveillance cameras. Perfect material for an article I'm writing for *The Walrus* magazine and for the peep culture book I'm researching. So I called them up and asked if I could come visit the Surveillance Project and talk to David Lyon and the University of Montreal prof. They set me up with 3 interviews—Lyon, the prof and a grad student doing research on Facebook. That plus the talk seemed to make it more than worthwhile to spend a day in Kingston. I'll be arriving in about ten minutes, so we'll soon see if I'm right. (By the way, 2 more audible cell phone conversations took place on the train while I wrote this: one woman trying to coordinate a meeting and one woman just chatting about her life.)

It's way too long. There's no single compelling idea or key-word for search engines to glom onto. There's nothing that would make others want to link to this or quote this in their own blogs. Furthermore, it reveals very little about how I feel. I know now that a successful Peep blog post—like a successful Peep blog—is going to be about how your blog persona feels at a specific mo-ment. I could have, and should have, broken the blog into three separate posts—one about the Peep possibilities of overhearing people talking on their cell phones in public places, one about my trip to the Surveillance Project, and one about the fact that this was my first-ever blog post. In all cases, this material should have been about my feelings. Successful personal blogs like Lisa's and Padme's are not about events, they're about emotion—Grrr, I hate people who talk on cell phones in public places! Arrgggh, I forgot my laptop! Ah, so nice to travel by train. A short, solid rant on each subject would have stood me well. Instead I composed a fluid, well-balanced summary: decent exposition, but terrible Peep culture.

Unfortunately I'm a bit of a slow learner. The first post set the tone for the next few months of blogging. I reluctantly churned out too-long posts about a new holiday in Ontario called Family Day, watching reality TV, and the Eliot Spitzer call-girl scandal. I avoided personal revelation and didn't really say all that much interesting about Peep, either. Moreover I was finding that these blog posts were taking forever. Who has the time? I started post-ing once a week or so, as opposed to the planned daily update. The result—a few months went by with nary a comment and when I finally got around to finding out what my stats were, they were pretty sad: sixty-seven visitors, spending an average of two minutes and eight seconds on the site.

I was seriously contemplating giving myself a good online spanking. That, at least, would get me some much-needed at-tention. I've never kept a diary or a journal. I've yet to utter the phrase, "I'm hurting inside, can we talk about it?" I tell my wife, my daughter, and my mom that I love them, but that's about it when it comes to revealing my inner feelings. Now all of a sudden I'm supposed to be gushing about my hidden self every single moment of the day? What readers I did have seemed disappointed and underwhelmed. My one regular commentator only bothered interjecting to tell me that I was revealing nothing. After yet another lackluster post, this single nemesis-commentator wrote:

> Who is this Hal (calling for the real Hal Niedzviecki . . .has anyone seen him)? And what the f%#k are these Peep Diaries anyway? An excuse to publish a book? Each time I have returned, I have sincerely hoped to find something different than the usual scratch-the-surface voyeurism (which seems to be all there is to be found here), and professional backslapping. Big, big yawn. Hal, if you can't deliver the "peep" goods yourself, why not invite others to post on your blog who do: who are not afraid to risk everything to reveal an entirely new realm of social experience which is emerging and evolving right before our eyes?

Ouch. That hurt. And it was all true. My reader was getting more and more frustrated and, to tell you the truth, so was I. In July of 2008 I made a pledge: "So here's the new plan: for the rest of July starting today I swear to blog twice a day. Yes, that's right! At least one Hal life update a day plus some other report relevant to Peep culture. It will be a merciless onslaught of Hal's everyday existence. Wait for it!" I figured if nothing else, the sheer need to add to the blog would force me to start blogging about my life.

I didn't keep the pledge. It was too much work. Again I ask, who has the time? But I tried my best to update at least three times a week, and focus on my life and my feelings.

The results of my reinforced vigor, call it my own Peep troop surge, were immediately noticeable. I blogged about fighting with my brother, I blogged about tracking my wife via GPS Snitch (more on that later), I blogged about the challenges of fatherhood. I tried to be honest, focused, and less reserved. I tried to say something about how I felt. Slowly, more people seemed to be dropping by. I started reaching thirty to fifty a day. My only online antagonist wrote in to encourage me: "I like the changes. You are really beginning to close the gap between the private and the public Hal Niedzviecki. More photos. More videos. You're really on to something here, Hal." I was still nowhere near Padme's 4,000 readers, but, hey, I hadn't been at it for four years straight, nor was I blogging about blowjobs and spankings.

In fact, regardless of my vaunted need for honesty, I couldn't bring myself to blog about anything having to do with my sex life whatsoever. Maybe if my blog was anonymous like Padme's I might have been able to get more explicit. But, well, I kinda doubt it. I was also extremely reluctant to blog about my professional life. Every time I considered a post on that subject, I pulled back. I just couldn't bring myself to put the stories of editors sometimes rejecting my work out there in a public forum read by everyone and anyone. It's part of the whole stiff upper lip thing. I want people to see me as a success—who doesn't? But, of course, one's life isn't just a string of impressive victories. I should have been blogging about my failures and, most importantly, how I felt about them. Instead, I concentrated on maintaining a convincing aura of success.

I did blog about the domestic sphere. I was, weirdly, pretty comfortable posting about my difficulties thinking up something to cook for dinner, or letting my readers in on an argument I'd just had with my wife. My wife works in the mental health field and told me from the beginning that she would not like to be identified by name or shown in pictures and videos. I called her W, and, when I blogged about the travails of raising a preschooler, I called the kid E. Strange that I found it easier to write about E and W, than to write about H, myself. It was as if the personal details of my public life were more private to me than the private details of my private life. Maybe that's one of the reasons that the personal blog comes relatively easy to us. Everybody argues with their spouse, struggles to raise their kid, can't think of anything to make for dinner. It's personal, but it's also, well, kind of generic. Blogging about your work, about your dealings with the world of publishing, for instance, well, that's messing with not just how you make a living, but also your own fragile ego. That would involve me telling people stuff I really don't care for them to know.

Still, even the relatively pedestrian material about raising the kid or fighting with my wife and brother were far more popular than items about the nature of Peep culture or the latest celebrity scandal. It seems contradictory: Wouldn't people rather read about Max Mosely or Britney Spears than me? But they didn't want to read my words about those other people. They wanted to read Hal on Hal. Posts about my life got more readers and comments and were even occasionally referenced by my real friends in my real life. After a post about arguing with my brother, several people in real life asked me how things now stood with my older sibling. They weren't people I would normally discuss a family squabble with. But they'd read the material online and obviously felt no compunction whatsoever about bringing up the subject. When friends and acquaintances asked me about the whole brother squabble, I downplayed it, saying, "It was really nothing, we fight like that practically every third day." Nevertheless, for whatever reason that particular post kept coming up. A reporter doing a short piece on my Peep culture ideas mentioned it in his article. On a trip to Montreal, my loudmouthed uncle asked me about it. Then, over at my brother's house, my brother's ten-year-old kid showed me the newspaper article the reporter wrote and asked me, "Why does it say you're fighting with my dad?" The fight with my brother was nothing, a minor dustup. But online, it became dramatic and exciting—certainly more exciting than the real thing. In order to make blog life match real life, I felt like calling my brother up, insulting him, and then promptly hanging up the phone and rushing to the blog. Update: Bigger, Better Fight with My Brother!

Blogging is all-encompassing. Even a feckless blogger like me goes through the day constantly thinking about blogging. It's not just always feeling the perpetual need for a steady stream of inconsequential thoughts and information. It's the big picture. The whole concept of having a blog, of wanting to have a blog. It's an all-encompassing admission: I want other people to know about me. To blog the way Padme does, the way Lisa does, you have to be willing to submerge your self into your self. I'm a bad blogger because I think too much of my "real life" self. Lisa, Padme, Justin, and Emmalene are fantastic Peep bloggers because they perceived themselves as having nothing to lose and everything to gain. As such, they were each far more willing to merge their real-life person with their online persona. They did the work, laid bare their personas, and now they're looking for payoff. Meanwhile, skeptical, emotionally reserved H, who thinks he's too good to blog, who thinks he has something to lose by baring all, doesn't deserve a payday. Held back by his existing persona, he fails to attract the kind of disparate but dedicated online community that the great peepers of cyberspace seem able to trap like ants in honey.

But every once in a while I felt it. That sense of a community of strangers rooting for me (as if I was a celebrity). That sense of having a bunch of people out there who actually cared about what I had to say and, moreover, cared enough to consider my problems and feelings, and to advise me on them. After I posted one of my most open and vulnerable posts—about my frustration around my inability to reveal my innermost feelings—other bloggers rallied to my defense: "I hear you," went one response. "I'm a professional blogger and know I'd get more traffic if I blogged about my feelings, my kids, my husband, my troubles, etc., but I just can't open up (or don't want to) the way, say, *Dooce* does. But, I feel like privacy has its place in the blogosphere and we've got to draw a line somewhere. For the record: I really enjoy your non-feeling, no-sex, anti-personal-marketing posts."

That's it. That's the addiction. There's someone out there who loves me. Or likes me. Or sympathizes with me. Or understands me. Or enjoys me. The person I'm trying to be. It's not much, is it? But what if I could get more of that? What if every day someone left a comment like that, encouraging me, praising me, even rebuking me in a gentle, helpful, caring way?

◻ ◻ ◻

Six months after I first talked to Emmalene, I noticed that her YouTube video postings were slowing down to a crawl. Her only recent video was a short, cryptic monologue about being in a bad place and needing to get her life together. I wondered if Emmalene was having a different experience than people like Beauty, Lisa Sargese, and Padme who, if anything, had intensified their online efforts since I first talked with them. Was Emmalene's seemingly waning interest a portent for the others, or an anomaly?

I called up Emmalene and we agreed to meet in Limeridge Mall in Hamilton, Ontario. I met her and her daughter in front of Old Navy and we headed over to the food court to eat Taco Bell and talk. Emmalene, it turned out, hadn't necessarily lost her enthusiasm for YouTube and self-exposure. But life had started making her more cautious. In addition to the "fetal parasite" incident and her husband's ongoing disapproval, real-life responsibilities were taking precedence. It had proven too difficult to juggle college with the demands of regular video blogging, so Emmalene had decided to put that on hold. Instead she was working retail on the strip near the mall. A lot of her time was being spent in the store. But she was reluctant to blog about work, fearing a customer or her manager might take offense.

After lunch, we moved to the benches around the mall fountain. Emmalene's two-year-old threw pennies in the water and danced around. "I basically grew up on YouTube," Emmalene told me. But things have changed: When she isn't working, she's with Alice. When she does have time to video blog, there just doesn't seem to be that much she feels she can safely say.

Emmalene, one of the youngest of the bloggers I talked with, seems to have the most well-developed sense of the consequences and possibilities of her hobby. As much as she wants to explore her creativity and even her sexuality (to the extent that she obviously enjoys the attention she receives), as much as she is attracted to the possibilities of online community and the potential to develop audience and even celebrity, she also realizes that her online life is in many ways in contrast with her real life. The online community may be exciting and supportive, but faced with the challenges of taking care of a two-year-old, settling on a career, and paying rent, there's just too much at stake to keep growing up in public online.

At the mall, our conversation was tapering off. Emmalene pulled out her camera and suggested that we make a video. I agreed. "Hello, YouTube!" Emmalene said cheerily, pointing the camera at her face. Then it was my turn. I introduced myself. After that, we rambled on, neither of us sure what the point of the video was. "Well, okay," Emmalene eventually said. The camera wavered between me, her, Alice dancing by the fountain, and passersby heading for the food court. Finally, mercifully, Emmalene blew a kiss into the lens and we faded to black.

chapter three

Faking the Real: Everyday Secrets and the Rise of Peep TV

We're scouring every aspect of American life for stars. We're expanding the concept of "star."
—Richard Stolley, editor of *People* magazine, 1977

Meet John Egly of Poolesville, Maryland. He's going to take us all the way back to the year 2004 when reality TV was still relatively young and pop culture's move to Peep still seemed temporarily exotic, like Richard Hatch grilling a rat.

So, 2004. San Francisco issues marriage licenses to same-sex couples as an act of civil disobedience. Billy Crystal hosts the Seventy-sixth Academy Awards and *The Lord of the Rings: The Return of the King* wins eleven Oscars. The infamous Abu Ghraib prisoner abuse photos are released to widespread revulsion. Ronald Reagan dies and George Bush Jr. is reelected. With the TV industry still riding high from the blockbuster success of 2000's *Survivor*, Fox Television premieres the show *Trading Spouses* to decent ratings and the general amusement of all.

Enter John Egly. He doesn't know it yet, but 2004 will be the year when the real estate appraiser and his family exchange a week of their lives for a $50,000 paycheck and the chance to be on national television. John Egly isn't the first person to agree to such a trade. Nor will the outcome of his decision be particularly earthshaking. But that's exactly what makes his participation notable. Who is John Egly? He's a middle-income, middle-American father and husband. He's the everyman of Peep. He's 2004's nobody of the year, the already forgotten reality TV star who symbolizes the moment when, just about in the middle of first decade of the millennium, Peep culture went suddenly mainstream. John Egly is the guy who's going to show us how normal and everyday watching the neighbors (on TV) has become.

When Fox called our Peep "everyman," John Egly was surprised. He'd never seen *Trading Spouses*, a new show at the time, or imagined himself on television. In fact, it was his then fifteen-year-old daughter who had sent in the requisite application without telling anyone else in the family. "I picked up the phone," says Egly, "and they said 'This is *Trading Spouses* calling.' And I said 'Thank you very much but we're not really into that.'"

But guess what? The Eglys *were* into it. And so was Fox. A fun-loving, liberal, Jewish couple living their version of the American dream, complete with four kids and seven horses, the Eglys seemed eccentric enough to be interesting, and normal enough to appeal to the mainstream. "They explained that my daughter had e-mailed them. She told them that we lived out in the country with seven horses and that we're Jewish and that's what's unique. I wasn't really sure because I'd never been in this situation, but I was excited and wondering what the next step would be."

The next step was for Fox to send out a representative and check the family out. Egly tells me that the initial interview lasted four to five hours. The family was asked about school, work, what they did for fun. "They didn't really at that time emphasize the Jewish part, it was more or less about being out in the country."

After an initial interview at their home, the Eglys were

invited to fly to Hollywood for a tryout. As John Egly tells me: "It was like *American Idol*, you know? 'You're going to Hollywood.'" For five days, the Eglys were guests of Fox, quartered in a luxury hotel. In return they were poked, prodded, psychologically evaluated, filmed from every angle. They were asked about their politics, their religion, their family dynamic. "They paid for the whole family to fly out and they put us up in a five-star hotel for five days. We went to two or three interviews per day plus a mental and physical examination. We were evaluated by psychologists and psychiatrists; they wanted to make sure we weren't crazy. And there were interviews with producers; if you've ever seen a movie star interviewed, this is what they did to us, they put us in a room alone with an interviewer. I've never been a star, and it really felt great. They asked us if we were proud to be Jewish. We didn't feel uncomfortable; they did it in a way that was very relaxed, kept us excited about this whole thing, maybe we were going to be on TV. They gave us $1,000 just to spend. They went all-out."

A mere three days after returning home, they got the call: they were *in*. "A week later," says John Egly, "they were out here filming."

The speed of the transition from initial phone call to total takeover of the Egly family's life left little time to reflect, let alone worry. "We had a contract that we had to sign, it was two hundred pages, covering everything. They could sue us up to seven million dollars, they actually specified seven million dollars. They own you; we couldn't say anything about the show without their permission up to two years afterwards. They put two interior cameras on the ceiling, one in the living room and one in the kitchen. Even if the camera men aren't walking around, you're always on film. They explained to us that we were going to be on camera sixteen hours a day for the week." In return, the contract specified that the Egly family would receive $50,000, no strings attached, despite the fact that *Trading Spouses* always ends with the two families telling each other how they have to spend the money. As John Egly says, "that's a hoax, that's just part of the show."

With total control established, it was time for the filming to start. "In terms of filming it was a real reality show. They never said 'move to your left a little bit, give us a big smile,' they didn't do that at all. The whole thing was very exciting. When I came back from working and got on the property I had a person that attended to me; they called them handlers, they get you coffee. If I wanted a Starbucks coffee she would hop in her car. You've got a camera there, people waiting hand over foot on you, you're making fifty thousand dollars week. It's a dream come true."

John Egly's new "spouse" was Ann Marie Doverspike, a middle-aged, born-again Christian, stay-at-home mom, living in a Southern California suburb. At first, it seemed like the producers were going to try to play up the suburban-versus-country angle. "They basically said 'do what you do everyday and try to include her in what you're doing.' She was out there mucking the stalls; she had never even seen a horse up close before. Anne Marie helped me do the stalls. We actually got her onto the horse; we had a lot of footage, a lot of funny stuff going on, with the horse, and she stepped on poop, but in the end they never even showed anything with the barn."

When they weren't mucking around in the barn, they were going on field trips. "Ann Marie's second love was Bush. She thought he was the best thing in the world; she wanted to go to Washington DC to see the White House. Finally we hopped in the Suburban and drove to DC. Three or four camera crews went with us. It looked like the CIA, it was three black Suburbans, and we drove up to the Lincoln Memorial and they parked right in front of the Lincoln Memorial, and you can't even walk there hardly. It was unreal. I really felt like a movie star then: everybody was looking at us—'Who are these people? Why are they filming?' It was just unreal. I was waving to the crowd—we had a crowd—people who were like, 'I don't know who he is, but what the hell.' There were loads of people watching us. When in your life would that ever happen to you?"

The trip to DC didn't get much play in the final product. Nor did scenes of Ann Marie having a great time learning about horses. Instead the show focused on perceived religious and cultural differences. Over in California the other half of the trade was getting all the attention: "They made my wife out to be a real Jewish bitch," explains Egly. "They had a Bible meeting one morning, and invited her to come on over, and it started at ten o'clock. They made sure she was late, she got there around twelve o'clock, you saw the meeting started at ten. . . . They were trying to make it look like she [didn't] give a shit. Still everybody was super friendly when she got there. She said, 'I'm Jewish and we believe in the Old Testament,' and everybody said, 'Have a seat and if you want to leave, you can up and go, we understand.' These people were nice. So what they did [was to show] her come in late and have her say 'I'm Jewish,' and then they had her looking bored, she was there for two hours, but in the twenty seconds they showed they had her squirming around, putting make-up on, and then they showed her just getting up and walking out. And they filmed her going down the hallway and they have a voice-over from another interview saying, 'Boy, I'm glad I got out of there, I couldn't stand being there.' She was talking about who-knows-what from another interview. I resented that, I didn't like that."

Even the scenes in which Egly was a direct participant ended up being out of his control. "The way they edited things was unreal. Anne Marie was crying and I went out there and said "What's wrong?' And she said, 'Well, I just miss my kids.' But what they did is they showed her crying and in the background they had her saying stuff about changing us, making us better. They showed her crying and used a voice-over saying, 'I tried and I guess it just isn't going to work out.' But she was crying because she was missing her kids, she couldn't care less about converting us to Christianity."

"So," I say to John Egly, "I guess you regretted doing the show in the end?" But Egly doesn't regret it all. His biggest disappointment, as it turns out, is that there was ultimately only a single half-hour episode based on the Egly/Doverspike trade, as opposed to the customary two episodes. Egly tells me that if he ever has a chance to do it again, he'd let loose more. He regrets censoring himself. Looking back, he wished he hadn't been so reserved. "I guess there just wasn't enough conflict. All these shows now, they usually get kind of a nut on there, screaming and crying and yelling, that's what sells the show. Our show was too calm and normal. Anne Marie and I just didn't do that."

The show presented a gross distortion of his family, but Egly tells me that, sure, he'd do it again in a second. "The whole seven days was very exciting, it was fun. Everybody actually had a good experience. The bad experience was the way they did everything at the end, turning it into a Jewish-Christian thing, and they made my wife look kind of bad, but people who know us know we're not like that. So we were lucky nothing turned out too bad." It's almost as if there were two different experiences: the fun reality of being a star for a week, and the less fun reality of the show which turned them into characters and caricatures, but which ultimately could be ignored, despite the fact that the show was the whole reason everybody was there in the first place.

Immediately after John Egly's week on camera, Fox sent a mental health professional to the house to help him and his family deal with the conclusion of the weeklong shoot. "In the end they had a psychiatrist come to the house and talk to us," Egly tells me. "She actually said, 'You may become depressed next week.' And she was right, the intensity of filming and the excitement and then all of a sudden it's gone. It was depressing."

What depressed John Egly was the sudden void: for a week you're surrounded by cameras and helpers; you feel like a star; then it's gone. "It's very addictive," he tells me. What exactly was addictive about making the show? "It's your fifteen minutes of fame," he says. "Just to be on TV. Everybody is looking for that. Even if they don't say they are, they are. When it presents itself, and it's there, you go ahead and do whatever you have to do. We would have done it even if they just gave us five thousand dollars."

What we're talking about here is the kind of heightened, camera-is-on attention you can only get from an entertainment universe that no longer excludes a real estate appraiser from Poolesville, Maryland. John Egly and family gave up their privacy and all control over how they would be depicted. They are a loving family. They have friends, jobs, spirituality, economic stability. And yet something still made them feel in need of "it." Something still made them want to sell a week of their lives. They not only traded their time and privacy, but they sold the right to control any possible story fabricated from that week. That was the deal they made, the only deal they could have made if they wanted to see themselves—the Eglys—brought to the attention of the world.

Would the rest of us make that trade? Under the guise of reality TV, Peep culture has spread from network to network, channel to channel, home to home. It dominates not just television but the American imagination. So the answer to the above question seems obvious: "Hell, yeah!" In fact, the real question is not, "Will you make the trade?" The real question is "how much?" How much of yourself will you give away and what will you be left with? This is a central question in Peep culture, one that each of us struggles with everyday, whether we know it or not.

Reality television is the first, the best-established, and arguably the only truly profitable Peep industry, an industry in which entertainment professionals are charged with turning random, "average" lives into for-profit Peep culture. Peep culture didn't start with reality TV, but reality TV is undoubtedly the first prolonged exposure that the vast majority of us have ever had to the idea that people's "regular" lives might be used as entertainment fodder in place of actors, singers, and dancers ("stars"). Reality

TV, with its infinite variety, unexpected consequences, and wild-West spirit of innovation and daring, is a portal into a particular kind of Peep culture that has set the tone for everything else that's now happening and is likely to happen. If we want to understand why so many of us do Peep culture, we have to understand why so many of us "do" reality TV. We have to figure out what makes reality TV, and good old John Egly, tick.

◻ ◻ ◻

"Uh, I have a question." A girl in the middle of the pack of a hundred or so Vancouver teens waves her hand in the air. "Yes," I say encouragingly. "Uh," the ninth grader wants to know. "Is *The Hills* real?"

The teens were bussed in to hear me give a talk based on a book I wrote for young adults about making your own "indie" pop culture. So while the question wasn't exactly on topic, I was willing to take a stab at an answer. Is the popular reality show about young, rich, good-looking white people in their early twenties "working" in Beverly Hills real? Standing up there in front of those kids, I could have said a lot of things. I could have dismissed reality TV with a wave of my hand—no, it's fake, it's crap, go read a book. But telling young people that their favorite show is garbage isn't going to change anything. Plus it's not true: reality TV isn't always garbage, isn't always meaningless junk. But is it real? I could have tried to explain how the word "real" is being met with more and more skepticism in an age of virtual environments, online love affairs, and movies based on memoirs based on "true" stories. "What's real?" I could have shot back. But they know what's real. Real is what really happens. And they want to know if *The Hills* really happens. "Well," I vacillate. "Sorta. Kinda. I mean, what happens really happens. Only not exactly in the way it's shown. And the stuff that happened might not have happened if there hadn't been a TV show. So, sure, *The Hills* is real. It's as real as if you were hired to play a girl who had your same name and did the same things you did, only you weren't really her, you were just pretending to be her for the cameras. Does that make sense?" The young lady and her compatriots don't look convinced. I don't blame them. It's a trickier question than it seems.

"In my opinion," writes Patricia Plinsker, another *Trading Spouses* participant I got in touch with, who declined an interview but e-mailed me a short statement, "'Reality' television only creates the appearance of a breach in privacy. The final product that is assembled from heavy, multi-faceted, deterministic editing is nearly unrecognizable from the unedited footage. The final construct is, therefore, fictional. One's privacy is only breached to the degree that an actor, playing a part in a piece of fiction, experiences a breach in privacy."

"Is it reality?" says Kaysar Ridha, a star on *Big Brother 6*, who I met at a reality TV convention in Nashville (more on that soon). "Well, it really happened. But it's misleading. These are all created circumstances. Someone's behind the scenes with the weather machine, creating the storm clouds, creating the sunrise."

"So it's fake then," I can hear the ninth grader in my audience mutter, disappointed. Well, yes. But also, as I already tried to point out, no. Not exactly. Let's try a different approach. Law professor Clay Calvert took a stab at the question in his book *Voyeur Nation*, published in 2000. In it he uses the term "mediated voyeurism" to describe reality TV and other related genres. He defines mediated voyeurism as "the consumption of revealing images and information about others' apparently real and unguarded lives, often yet not always for purposes of entertainment but frequently at the expense of privacy and discourse, through the means of the mass media and Internet." All manifestations of Peep culture are mediated. When we peep into someone else's life via reality TV (or blogs or Facebook or YouTube) we're not watching them directly, we're not looming over them as if they lived in a miniature world, utterly oblivious to all the giants

84 | Hal Niedzviecki

staring at them; we're experiencing their lives through the media, through mediation. Which is to say that someone—directors, editors, or the same person who's posting what they want read or watched online—is mediating our access. They are deciding what we should see and how we should see what we see. As the defenders of reality TV often point out, just putting real life in all its "unguarded" glory on television would be boring. What reality TV does, then, is give us real-life highlights—a montage shaped into an exciting story.

"Yeah, okay," your inner ninth-grader blurts, "but is it real?" Well, Clay Calvert is obviously no fan of reality TV, so he imbeds a critique into his definition, noting that the entertainment value of this voyeuristic programming "frequently" comes "at the expense of privacy and discourse." Calvert is suggesting that when reality is mediated and turned into story, truth gets fudged, points of view are altered, and the opportunity for "discourse" that might be generated from a group of people seeing something that really occurred is lost. This is obvious from the *Trading Spouses* episode featuring John Egly. The differences and similarities of a liberal Jewish family and an ultra-conservative, born-again-Christian family are explored but only in as controversial and emotional a way as possible. Points of connection are ignored. The scene at the barn is dropped. Emotional dramatics trump discourse. In that sense we can determine how much of any particular episode of a particular reality TV show is "real" by asking: How much of any given show would be left if you removed the scenes that are sensational, emotional, and over-the-top? Strip away the drama, stunts, and mood music, and you probably get something real. But strip all that away and what's left? Would that be entertainment?

❏ ❏ ❏

It's the job of people like David Lyle, the Los Angeles–based president of the Fox Reality cable channel, to entertain us, not show us reality or the truth. Lyle's been in the reality business as long as anyone. Among other things, he's worked on *American Idol* and he was the producer of the controversial and widely watched series *The Swan*, in which "ugly duckling" women were given costly makeovers, including everything from face-lifts to body modifications, dental procedures, and short stints with psychologists. Naturally enough, Lyle makes no apologies and no promises.

"Think of scripted programming," he begins. "You have to go through a lot of buildup and character exposition before you reach the emotional highs and lows. On Fox Reality we run and rerun a lot of reality TV and one of the reasons it's easy to watch a second time is that you come in there and you know something's going to happen—there's going to be an emotional moment, you're going to laugh, gasp, cry."

What about the argument that in the pursuit of the "emotional moment" anything relating to actual reality is lost? "In very rare circumstances you might take a suspicious look from two days later and lay it in to allow the viewers to understand why someone did what they did. But that's only to help with the narrative. The moment when someone goes off on someone or hops into a hot tub actually happens. If someone spits at someone else it's not the editor that made them look fairly gross."

Lyle goes on to tell me about a show called *My Bare Lady* which takes four women porn stars and sends them to London for acting lessons that will lead to a special one-night-only performance in a famous London theater. "So they had to learn something from *Romeo and Juliet*, and one of the dear porn stars, god bless her, said 'It's wonderful to do Shakespeare, she really knows how to write for women.' You couldn't have scripted that, you couldn't have written that. And later one of the stars who did go to London fell truly in love with the actor playing Romeo and you couldn't have scripted that in your wildest dreams, [that] a girl who made 200 porn films is going to lose her heart over a fey English actor. So the reality just constantly surprises you."

But what if the entire thing is a setup? Who knows if a particular person playing herself might not just decide (or be encouraged to) find a love interest because she knows it will get her more attention, more on-screen time, and possibly more opportunities in the future?

"That misses the point," says Michael Hirschorn, executive vice president of original programming at VH1, and the man in charge of developing programs like *Flavor of Love* (and its spin-offs) for the cable channel. "It's about real people put in semi-artificial or produced situations. What's the mixture that creates the most dynamic and interesting environment? We're trying to do really interesting social experiments through the premise of reality TV."

In other words, reality emerges from how people act in these fake situations. If they decide to do things specifically because they want more screen time, well, then, that's their decision and that becomes their reality. For Hirschorn (who left VH1 and formed his own reality TV–focused production company soon after I spoke with him), a good example of this is the popular show *The White Rapper*, which he says "taps into a lot of issues about what is authentic. Can white people rap or not? By placing them in the South Bronx and making the judge and jury the people of the South Bronx, it's taking cultural questions and playing them out in real time." So forget the idea that only when the truth is shown—the facts and just the facts, ma'am—are we able to engage in a fruitful debate about what happened and what's going to happen next. Assume, instead, that everybody is pretending, scheming, trying to get the most out of their opportunity, the most out of the situation. Then take a bunch of white teenagers, ideally rich and from the suburbs, and have them rap in front of a hostile audience of inner-city kids (ideally black and poor). To worry about how much of it is acted, manipulated, or mediated through editing, is irrelevant. Reality TV teaches us that what happens on TV creates a kind of reality that, because of its permanence and potency, is in many ways more pervasive, more *real*, than actuality. So this is the most important lesson that reality TV has for Peep culture: truth is less important than the appearance of truth. Which doesn't mean that to succeed in the brave new world of Peep you have to be a liar. It means that you have to accept that lying isn't lying, it's creating a new you: lying creates its own reality. The lie, broadcast on TV or uploaded and made available online, can, in the right circumstances, become more real than your "reality."

For VH1's Hirschorn, the power of reality TV to reshape the real comes from its air of authenticity. "You almost believe something more if you can't quite hear correctly and the picture is off," he says. "It's an aesthetic." The grainy home video, the hidden-camera footage, the whispered dialogue so quiet it has to come with subtitles, the shifty, greenish, night shots—all standard techniques in the reality TV repertoire, become a kind of stand-in for actual reality. They are a signal that "reality" is taking place. The set-up is fake, but the obvious fakery is what makes it somehow seem more real. Reality TV trumps truth by paying close attention to the aesthetic, the feeling, of being behind the scenes. In Peep culture, something that feels revealed and behind the scenes is always powerful and compelling, even if it never really happened.

Reality TV, like Peep culture, is here to stay. Right now, as I type this sentence, Fox Reality is airing the following lineup: *Arrest and Trial, Real Stories of the Highway Patrol, LAPD: Life on the Beat, Extreme Dating, Blind Date, Battle of the Bods, Maximum Exposure, Meet My Folks, Pushing the Limit,* and *Now See This*. The description of *Maximum Exposure* on the Fox Reality Web site is particularly instructive here: "Some home video clips aren't meant to collect dust on storage shelves . . . so they appear on *Maximum Exposure*! The show takes videos and gives them the slow-motion analysis and fast-paced action sequences for your enjoyment! Anything and everything is given maximum exposure!" In other words, it's your private home videos reconceived as entertainment through dramatic editing and stylistic flourishes. That's the premise of Fox Reality and, in many ways, that's the ethos of Peep culture: it's your life restated; it's your life, if not necessarily better, then at least far more entertaining, exciting, and exposed. And that, essentially, is why reality TV is going to dominate American television for many years to come. Don't believe me? Here's a list of just some of the casting calls I recently received in my inbox courtesy of the Web site RealityWanted.com:

The Bad Girls Club Season 3 Now Casting

Family Court With Judge Penny Now Casting

Did A Family Member Ruin Your Life? Now Casting

FUSE TV Casting Bands for Reality Show!

Don't Forget the Lyrics Open Casting Call

Now Casting College Basketball Players

Casting Divorced Couples

ABC's "Opportunity Knocks" Now Casting Families

Casting Softball Players

Casting Prom Queens and Kings

NBC'S The Biggest Loser! Now Casting

FUSE TV is Now Casting for contestants for a new game show that will test how far you would go to see your favorite artist!

Family Court Casting Sibling and Mother/Daughter Conflict

Cook Yourself Thin! Now Casting

MTV's True Life I'm Addicted to Meds Now Casting

What Not to Wear Now Casting

Cook With Rocco Now Casting

CELEBRITY MAKEOVER Show CASTING PLAIN JANES $200/day

◻ ◻ ◻

The capacity to reveal something more "real" than everyday life is why the moving picture, just a curiosity a little over a century ago, is now such a powerful force in society. The (Peep) history of the moving picture began in 1895 when Louis Lumiere created a five-kilogram camera known as the cinematographe. This film camera, hand-cranked so it didn't require electricity, was also a projector and a printing machine. It was a precision item that offered many of the conveniences of its future incarnation, the digital video camcorder. Its small size allowed the operator of the cinematographe to roam anywhere, record footage, develop it, and project it, all in the same day.

In 1895 this magical apparatus was revealed to the world. Lumiere demonstrated the invention with a short film, *Workers Leaving the Lumiere Factory*. He followed this up with another film, *Arrival of a Train*. In this film, a train approaches, moving "from long-shot to close-up." The camera, "placed on the platform near the edge of the track," captured the hurtling metal conveyance's approach with such accuracy that spectators ducked, dodged, and screamed.

Do you notice anything in particular about these early films, shown, as film historian Erik Barnouw writes, "on every continent except Antarctica"? People were fascinated by them because they were "real." When Lumiere operatives went around the world armed with the precious cinematographe, they did so with instructions to make films of actual events. In Russia they filmed the coronation of Nicholas II, in Australia they captured the Melbourne Cup. In Proctor's Pleasure Palace in New York, in March 1897, the program included:

The Baby's First Lesson in Walking

The Electrical Carriage Race from Paris to Bordeaux

Fifty-ninth Street, Opposite Central Park

A Scene near South Kensington, London

The Fish Market at Marseilles, France

A Sack Race Between Employees of Lumiere & Sons' Factory, Lyon.

People flocked to these screenings, hoping to see themselves, or people like themselves, on screen. Film was not yet five years old, and already the masses wanted a piece of it, wanted to use it to subvert the normal expectations of life and death, of temporary presence and eternal absence. "Now that we can photograph our loved ones," mused a Paris journalist in 1896 after seeing a cinematographe show, "not only in stillness, but as they move, as they act, as they make familiar gestures, as they speak—death ceases to be absolute."

In the next couple of decades a wild period of global competition ensued, featuring a vast array of makeshift cinemas, showing everything from the battles of the Boer War to faked footage purporting to capture the 1906 San Francisco earthquake as it happened. "The technical possibilities of the camera were so unexpected," writes Eric Rhode in his history of early cinema, "that they seem to have inhibited the imagination. Everybody had turned out trains entering stations, babies at table, men at cards. The notion of film direction, of mise-en-scène, of using the actual to some other purpose than that of doggedly recording appearance in a single shot, was undiscovered; and so was the distinction between reportage and fiction." But a major change was underway. By 1907 "fiction films were increasing in number and beginning to dominate audience interest." Around the world documentary very quickly took a backseat to fictionalized entertainment. And yet, in a surprising twist, the rise of the fiction film was not the end of an early flirtation with Peep culture—it was its true beginning. Made-up tales turned out to be extremely compelling, even more compelling than real events. And fiction was particularly compelling when made to *look like the everyday*.

In a surprisingly short amount of time, fiction films became obsessed with realism, with rendering the fake in as exacting a way as possible.

As early as 1919, American director Cecil B. DeMille was paying intricate attention to costume and detail to create a heretofore unmatched sense of verisimilitude and sensuality. Describing the beginning of the infamous *Male and Female* (1919), British film critic Alexander Walker writes: "The still invisible Swanson has the way prepared for her by maids . . . busily displaying outsize bottles of bath-crystals, king-size powder puffs, etc. Now Gloria rises . . . she lets the bed-wrap slide off her shoulders while the maids raise a towel to exclude the intervening gap of bare flesh." No detail is unconsidered, no garment or accessory is placed by accident. Ridiculous and over the top, and yet the scene must be real—must, in fact, be realer than real. Legendary filmmaker King Vidor meticulously re-created moments that the audience could never experience for themselves, moments that reverberated into the kind of psychological "truth" that critics would later warn devalues actual, in-person experience. Vidor directed, for instance, *The Big Parade* (1925), an epic about American soldiers in France during the first World War. Its final battle scene is a fever of "night panoramas of luminescent smoke, spiraling flares and a syncopation of shell-bursts that phantasmally conveys the din in the fields of death." A year later came the first version of the epic *Ben Hur*, with tens of thousands of extras and millions of dollars spent re-creating ancient Rome. Upon its release, the film set box office records. "The more [intense] and flawless his [the film producer's] techniques," warn Max Horkheimer and Theodor W. Adorno in their dour 1944 dissection of the power of mass culture, "the easier it is today for the illusion to prevail that the outside world is the straightforward continuation of that presented on the screen."

It is amidst this remarkable innovation and energy devoted to verisimilitude that documentary made a comeback or, perhaps more accurately, came into being as the hybrid genre we know to-day. The first nonfiction feature-length film to reach a wide audience and establish the conventions of what we now understand to be documentary is Robert Flaherty's *Nanook of the North*. When it was released in 1922 there was not yet a word for what it was. The noun "documentary," meaning documentary film, wouldn't appear until four years later, to mark the occasion of Flaherty's second feature, *Moana* (1926). The word was used by Flaherty's fellow documentary innovator and moral antagonist John Grierson (among other things, founder of the National Film Board of Canada), who described the documentary as the "creative use of actuality."

The "creative use of actuality" perfectly applies to *Nanook of the North* and future incarnations of the nonfiction film. Nanook was the product of a long obsession the American Flaherty had with filming the people then known as the Eskimo. Flaherty, first exposed to the Inuit people when he was sent north to prospect the land in advance of a planned railroad to Hudson Bay, wished to capture on film a chronicle of the daily life of these northern hunter-gatherers, in part because that traditional life was already disappearing. So the problem is obvious: how do you faithfully show the authentic life of a people whose authentic lives began to become "inauthentic" some several hundred years earlier, when the Europeans first took root in their midst? The answer is Flaherty's genius: take the conventions of the feature fiction film and apply them to reality. In other words, re-create actuality. When Nanook harpoons a seal and pulls it out of a hole in the sea ice it is obviously already dead. Nanook and his family pretend to be tucked in for the night asleep in an igloo that is, in actuality, half of an oversized igloo built so that Flaherty has enough room to film in and enough daylight to film by. Flaherty banishes rifles and Western clothing from the eye of the camera, then sends Nanook and others on a dangerous walrus hunt undertaken solely for the purposes of filming the endeavor. The result is a film rife with all the moral ambiguity of contemporary reality TV and Peep culture, and audiences went crazy for it when it opened on Broadway. *Nanook* became an instant hit. Viewers weren't bothered at all that some of the movie was "faked." They particularly loved Nanook's family life, Nanook and his wife mugging for the camera, and Nanook teaching his kids to hunt. Flaherty turned these real people into sympathetic, entertaining characters, and in doing so he used the conventions of fiction film to attach us to the drama of surviving in the Arctic wilderness. We root for Nanook and his family, are drawn into their lives, in part because we know they are real and in part because they are presented as fiction. The critic who reviewed this first documentary for the *New York Times* wrote that the film was "far more interesting, far more compelling purely as entertainment, than any except the rare exceptions among photo-plays." Audiences agreed and the film made millions around the world, firmly establishing the documentary as a new genre.

Granted, some critics weren't as complimentary, dismissing the film as a fake, fixating in particular on the scene in which Nanook triumphantly pulls out that dead seal. "But they missed the point," writes Eric Rhode, echoing Michael Hirschorn's take on reality TV as having more of a feeling of truth than a commitment to exactitude. "Flaherty was not trying to compile an anthropologist's case history . . . he was trying to show how filming was something else than the record of fact. How it needed to include the fantasies and poetry which suffuse experience and give it meaning. He was trying to project a beauty which was more than scenic; a beauty to be found in the generosity and courage which certain men reveal under stress; and this beauty had to be reconstructed."

Only now, with the full flowering of Peep, are we seeing what a concept like the "creative use of actuality" can mean. Only now, one hundred years later, are we coming to grips with the notion that things happening specifically for the benefit of the camera are not necessarily fake, can be more compelling, more real, more "suffused with experience," than anything that happens off camera or goes otherwise undocumented. A hundred years later, in the age of Peep culture, in the age of reality TV, we are forced to confront head-on the collapsing distinctions between true and false, and the way that those collapsing distinctions can result in a mediated "reality" that is "far more interesting, far more compelling purely as entertainment" then anything we could ever make up.

Flaherty went on to film several other *Nanook*-type epics, but despite receiving ongoing critical plaudits he never repeated the global success of his first documentary. And Nanook? Well, two years after the film—his film—premiered on Broadway, he starved to death in the Arctic on a hunting trip.

◻ ◻ ◻

John Egly and his peers are the next generation of Nanooks. Their willing participation is changing the face of entertainment and even culture as we know it, just as Nanook's collaboration with Robert Flaherty created an entire new entertainment genre, the documentary. But why are they—why are we—such willing participants? Did Nanook sense an opportunity for immortality as he mugged for the camera and pretended to bite into a gramophone record in puzzlement? Who was using whom?

"If you can pay them they'll do it," Los Angeles–based casting director Tamra Barcinas tells me. Barcinas has been in the business going on ten years, and though she doesn't want to specify the particular shows she's cast, they include big-name dating shows, docudramas, renovation shows, family-dynamic shows, game shows, and even the Peep documentary *American Teen* (2008). I ask Barcinas how hard it is, a hundred years or so after *Nanook*, to get people to hunt polar bears with their bare hands for the camera. "If something's potentially embarrassing, money makes that fear go away. When you offer a large amount of money, people don't see the consequences as much as they see that paycheck."

Barcinas isn't saying that money is why people go on reality TV. She's saying that money is an enticement, it's what puts them over the edge and sends them hurtling off the precipice into the vortex. John Egly told us that he didn't do it for the money. Then again, he did mention the money several times as part of the whole experience, the whole "dream come true." It was almost as if the money couched the transaction as a legitimate, bona fide dream deal. Sign on the dotted line, put in your week, get your fifty thousand. The money legitimizes the aura of celebrity that reality television implicitly promises. Fifty grand a week—that's celebrity money! Celebrity and money go together, but on their own they don't determine participation. "The allure of celebrity doesn't happen so much with family shows or anything dealing with mature adults," says Barcinas. "That's more maybe twenty-seven and under, and that's more the crowd that does the MTV dating shows, anything where there is a competition like singing, dancing, comedy, some sort of way where they can show off what they believe is a talent."

Okay, fame and money obviously help, but they aren't it. So what seals the deal? How does Barcinas pitch participation to people like our everyman, John Egly?

Barcinas talks to me about selling the reality TV "opportunity." As she says: "It's an experience, it's a life experience that they really can't get anywhere else; this isn't something you can go get at Disneyland."

This rings true to me. Remember that John Egly, too, talked about the opportunity. As he said about the trip to Washington, or the week of having his own personal handler, when else are you going to experience any of that? When else is Nanook going to have a bunch of guys following him around with cameras while he builds fake igloos and spears dead seals? Being paid attention to is addictive. It's at the core of what reality TV offers.

Opportunity is attention, attention is being noticed and remembered, and being noticed and remembered is a kind of immortality, the only kind of immortality we've so far figured out how to bestow. Reality TV, like ubiquitous surveillance and so many other manifestations of Peep, is compelling on several different levels. It offers both the instant satisfaction of money and fame, and the underlying promise that cinema has offered since its inception—the promise of life after death.

In a *Washington Post* report on the twentieth anniversary of the iconic reality show *Cops*, John Langley, producer and creator of the storied franchise, reports that more and more perps are eager to sign the releases that permit their images to be shown on *Cops*. "Twenty years ago, it was harder to get releases," he says. "Now, it's way over 90 percent of people who sign. We live in a celebrity culture and people are almost always willing to be on TV—even if it's committing a crime."

"They're not doing it for the money," Fox Reality's David Lyle assures me. "They're doing it because they want to." Lyle goes on to make an interesting point that connects the reality TV performers with their watchers. "For years," he says, "we were all convinced that the motivation was always to make money. And yet the biggest interactive form of television in the history of the medium is [*American*] *Idol*, and people interact, vote by phone, in numbers higher than any national election—in every country more people voted for *Idol* than for the leader of the country, and they do it not to win a bean, they do it altruistically, there's no self interest."

❏ ❏ ❏

Why do more people vote for *American Idol* than for the U.S. president? Obviously people have become steadily more disaffected with politics over the last century or so. But that doesn't necessarily explain why reality TV has so many dedicated fans, why so many millions watch, cast votes, shed tears, and even go so far as to try out for the shows. What's in it for the fans who not that long ago seemed perfectly happy to bawl their eyes out at the site of a giant ape falling off a skyscraper without necessarily wanting to be the ape, the woman in the palm of the ape, or the guy in charge of directing the ape?

To find out what fans of reality TV think about the genre's appeal, I headed to the second annual Reality TV Convention at the Radisson Opryland Hotel in Nashville, Tennessee. Picture a handful of reality TV personalities signing autographs and hobnobbing with their fans—the small cluster of diehards who still remember *Survivor Vanuatu* and *Big Brother 3*. When I say "small cluster" I mean far less than the thousand *Apprentice* addicts the organizer promised. And when I say "handful," I mean roughly half of the "stars" advertised on the conference Web site.

Still, these are the serious fans who came from across the United States to meet their favorite reality TV personalities. Denise Runevitch works in market research in Cleveland. When I caught up with her at the conference she'd just met her hero, *Big Brother* "star" Kaysar Ridha. Barely pausing to take a breath, Runevitch told me about how she used to stay up all night watching Ridha on live feeds. As Denise explained, for a monthly fee you could watch the *Big Brother* housemates, live, online, as they went about their confined days, scheming, loving, and cheating. "You get to see them as they really are," she told me. "What they show you on TV isn't what really happened." This was a recurring theme at the convention—fans all agreed that the "reality" we're treated to is anything but. At the same time, they've become accustomed to finding other ways to get deeper into the "real" experience. They pay for extras like live feeds, relentlessly discuss the happenings on Internet conversation boards, and track down the tiniest tidbits of gossip. What bothers them isn't so much the fakery or manipulation but when the manipulation is done badly, such as when, as Runevitch told me, there is an obvious and blatant difference between what she saw on the live feeds and what appeared on the show.

So long as appearances are maintained, a show can feel (if not necessarily be) true. And what feels most true is the notion that the participants are regular people, just like us, and therefore any one of us could be the next one plucked from normalcy to appear on the big world of the little screen. That, more than anything, is what keeps the fans watching. A psychological study done in 2001 concluded that "the attitude that best separated the regular viewers of Reality Television from everyone else is the desire for status." Apparently, regular fans of these shows are much more likely to agree with statements such as "Prestige is important to me" and "I am impressed with designer clothes" than are other people. The authors of the study go on to note that reality TV "allows Americans to fantasize about gaining status through automatic fame. Ordinary people can watch the shows, see people like themselves and imagine that they too could become celebrities by being on television. It does not matter as much that the contestants often are shown in an unfavorable light; the fact that millions of Americans are paying attention means that the contestants are important." Another important lesson that we take away from reality TV and into the broader world of Peep culture: when we watch, no matter what we watch, we always seem to see ourselves. We may say and even act otherwise, but somewhere deep down inside us, we are seeking our own redemption through the immortality of being noticed all the time by everyone.

❏ ❏ ❏

"There are moments," casting producer Tamra Barcinas tells me, "where it's like 'I can't believe you would say that out loud, how embarrassing.' But they'll have a screening party back home with their friends and family, and they're so thrilled that they actually got to be on TV. That was their moment."

The thrill doesn't last very long. Those who have been on reality TV report reactions ranging from angry to sheepish, from embarrassed to grateful, if bemused. Many are still trying to milk the last remnants of their reality TV experience—for cash, but also to make the "opportunity" linger. In Nashville I spoke with some of the cast of *The Real Gilligan's Island*, a low-budget, gimmicky, *Survivor*-type show that ran for two seasons on the TBS network. The show cast "ordinary" people (with a few models thrown in) who looked like the original *Gilligan's Island* characters, and then had them compete against each other. Mark Groesbeck, nickname Gooner, is a thirty-one-year-old fry cook from Weedsport, New York. He told me that he saw a casting-call ad on TV and immediately thought of himself in the Gilligan role. (I'm jealous—*I* would have made a great Gilligan.) Lanky, almost seven feet tall, and a born clown, Groesbeck told me that "my mama, god rest her soul, always said I was put here to entertain people. People come up to me and say, 'you made me laugh my ass off.' So I just did it. Why not? I like to be the center of attention." Despite his happy-go-lucky attitude, Gooner is still upset about the circumstances surrounding his departure from the show, as well as the fact that the network was third-tier and couldn't attract the kind of audience he was hoping for. He speculated, for instance, that his unwillingness to be seen on camera putting the moves on Mary Ann might have been one of the reasons he didn't advance to the finals in the show. "They wanted me to hit on her. They wanted Gilligan and Mary Ann to hook up. I said, 'Do you want to pay for my divorce?' " So why is he here, three years later, at a conference he paid his own way to travel to? Gooner shrugged. Why not? The experience continues.

Randi Silvers played Mary Ann on the other season of *The Real Gilligan's Island*. She's at the Nashville conference too, along with a couple of Skippers and a Ginger. She wasn't crazy about how she ended up being portrayed in the show either. "It's a distorted reality. I was made out to be the bitch because I'm opinionated. I was working in a bar for a long time. If I don't like you, I'm going to say so. The producers can hear everything, they have microphones everywhere. They create drama by listening in, telling you what other people said."

Those who played the game found out it was fixed. They were pigeonholed and manipulated. No matter what they did, they couldn't change the path that the directors and producers had laid out for them. And when the show was over? In many ways, the former characters are still playing themselves. At the conference the women wore a lot of makeup, stuffed themselves into short skirts and tight dresses. They sold signed pictures of themselves for ten dollars. Guys like "Chicken" George of *Big Brother* talked really loud and told anyone who would listen about their extraordinary good luck having been chosen for the show. In a way, that's true: Thousands tried out and they were the ones to be picked. But now the ride is over and it's clear that despite the fact that few of them made money or achieved even fleeting fame, no one is completely prepared to go back to their regular life.

"You don't know the extent of it," Kaysar Ridha told me, still sounding bewildered by the whole experience of being a fan favorite of *Big Brother* 6 and 7 (All-Star edition). "I got voted in, there were five million votes cast. I was getting e-mails from France, Iran, Iraq, New Zealand. I became known all over the place. My world, my reality, got flipped upside down." I asked Ridha why he came to this convention and what he saw in his future. "I came at the last minute," he said. "It's more of a learning experience for me because eventually I want to continue making a social impact, go into television and movies, retain that platform to do other things." He paused and looked around. "It's not very glamorous, is it?"

The kind of people Tamra Barcinas and David Lyle are looking for—extroverts who demonstrate a high opinion of themselves—are also the kind of people who are, by their very nature, vulnerable to the inevitable disappointments that arise from being just another widget on the assembly line of mass culture. You expect a lot from yourself. You think it's just the beginning. You think reality TV is your big break. Next up, more fame, more acclaim, more opportunities to really show what you can do.

"It is difficult for reality stars to know how to parlay that stardom into a career," notes David Lyle. "More often than not, they didn't have a lot happening before their reality show and now they're trying to see if they can get the second or third show. Again, the personality types you're looking for are larger then life, they live big and they do enjoy being the center of attention, so it's difficult to go back to working at a gym in Kansas. To some extent the show has to let them down gently. There's some psychological care put into them to bring them down to normality. However all the care in the world can't overcome that delight in being semi-famous. It's always been so in any form of showbiz."

So that's it? You send them to the shrink for an hour and they're on their way? Well, most shows don't even bother with the shrink part.

"That's not the norm—sending psychologists—and that's a more responsible approach," notes Barcinas. "Most shows do the show and leave the participants to go about their day. I would encourage more shows and more production companies to actually follow up with their participants." I ask Barcinas what she thinks she might find if she followed up with the people who have been on shows she's worked on. "Some of the consequences that I've seen happen were actually very surprising to me," she reports. "For instance with the renovation shows and makeover shows that are larger than just one room, the people have not been able to maintain the homes that have been built for them or some of the fantastic appliances that we've put in. They haven't been able to pay the electricity bills. The truth of the matter is these people couldn't pay the taxes on them, they couldn't afford to maintain all the changes we put in almost overnight."

But, I press Barcinas, the consequences can be even worse

than just a foreclosed home, can't they? "It depends on the popularity of the show, it depends on how large it actually is. Absolutely they're not prepared for the meteoric rise and consequently the
meteoric fall of that attention. There's a power surge and when it
goes away, sometimes that is devastating. The thing is that those
people are often in some sort of crisis—do they need help with
their children? I've worked on those kind of shows, and, yes, they
need help with their children. But with all of these shows there's
a template, there's a formula: In the end it will be solved in a nice
little package and you'll feel better when you turn off the TV." We
can turn off the TV. The producers can pull the plug and wrap
another episode. But those people whose lives were turned into
product don't have that luxury. In many cases, their problems
remain, only worse now that they've been advertised to an audience of millions. In other cases, the feeling of stardom makes
returning to normal life a depressing disappointment.

"The bottom line," says Barcinas, "is that reality television
is an industry where we have a product and that product happens to be episodes of people's lives, emotions, and experiences.
And that product needs to be turned over and made, just like
any other industry, as if it were shoes or peanut butter. We have
orders that we need to fill."

◻ ◻ ◻

Reality TV's legacy is not just bringing a new kind of cheaply
made, family-friendly entertainment to our living rooms. For
those who have actually been on reality TV, there's another legacy
entirely. That's the legacy of the first-ever Peep-culture industry
plowing through lives and homes like a tornado, leaving a wake
of broken promises, shattered dreams, lawsuits, and even deaths.

There was trouble right from the beginning. Consider the
first bona fide fly-on-the-wall docudrama-type reality TV program in North America, the PBS creation *An American Family*,

which aired in 1970. The show chronicled, on film, the real-life problems of the Louds, a family from Santa Barbara, California. Starring William and Pat Loud, along with their five children, the series featured son Lance coming out of the closet and his parent's apparent refusal to acknowledge that he was gay. As the show proceeded, it captured the sad breakup of the Loud family, including the moment Pat tells her husband William that she wants a divorce. A camera crew lived with the Louds for seven months, long enough to film the material they needed for the twelve-hour series, long enough to witness a family breakdown that William Loud would later allege was at the very least helped along by the show's focus on the negative aspects of his family's life.

It is in the spirit of wrecked families and damaged lives that reality TV developed. The tone continued to be set with the rise of talk TV. In 1995 a never-aired episode of the trashy talk show *Jenny Jones* was filmed. It set up a guy by the name of Jonathan Schmitz, by telling him that someone had a big crush on him which would be revealed live on air. Turned out that someone was Scott Amedure, a gay man. Schmitz, not gay, seemed to take it well on the show. The next day, though, a depressed Schmitz, with a history of mental difficulties, shot and killed Amedure. In 1999, with reality TV on the verge of exploding onto American television, the *Jenny Jones* show was found to be civilly liable for the whole tragic set of circumstances, and was ordered to pay $25 million to Amedure's family.

One disturbing case was settled and another began. With producers riding along with the West Virginia state police for an episode of *Real Stories of the Highway Patrol*, which ran for six seasons from 1993 to 1999, police got into a high-speed pursuit that ended with an innocent young woman killed in a car accident. She was in the wrong place at the wrong time, but a subsequent investigation revealed that the makers of the show were egging on the state trooper behind the wheel by yelling, "Go get him, stay on his tail, Kevin!" Ultimately the state police settled for $775,000 and Fox, which ended up owning the footage of the accident, also settled for an undisclosed sum.

A death, then a spate of near misses: In the 1999 season of *Real World*, a young woman drove off in a van after drinking heavily and after being "warned" by MTV employees not to drive. She got behind the wheel anyway, and, with the cameras rolling, the MTV crew pursued her and finally demanded that she get out of her vehicle. As Clay Calvert, author of *Voyeur Nation*, acidly notes: "The trials and tribulations of a 21-year-old woman with an alcohol problem (seen in one episode falling down drunk in a disco and throwing up half naked in the shower) may account for hefty ratings in 1999." No wonder coproducer Jon Murray told the *Wall Street Journal* at the time: "We're documentarians who want to document young people's lives. If we as older, perhaps wiser adults, step into every situation and try to solve it for them, were not going to wind up with a program that deals with the problems." Murray added that the cast members "know very much what they are getting into."

As it turns out, Murray's attitude has continued to prevail. Consider a *New York Times* report on the popular A&E TV show *Intervention*, which has been on the air since 2005. "On a recent episode of *Intervention*, A&E's documentary series about addiction, no one was stopping Pam, an alcoholic, from driving." In the episode in question, Pam staggers to the front door and stops at the refrigerator for a last swig of vodka. You can hear a producer then say: "You have had a lot to drink. Do you want one of us to drive?" Pam's not interested: "No, I can drive. I can drive," she mumbles. Pam gets into her car and drives away with the camera crew following her as she tries, writes the *New York Times* reporter, "to keep her turquoise Pontiac Sunfire between the lines." A&E's *Intervention* is one of that network's top shows; up to two million viewers per episode watch various crack, heroin, pill, and booze addicts mess up their livers and lives, then finally get help.

"This is their life with me or without me," says Sam Mettler, *Intervention*'s creator and executive producer. And that may be so. But one wonders what effect the camera has on their lives, as well as the ability of people so clearly messed up to make rational choices about life-changing issues like having their addiction become a permanent part of the corporate entertainment landscape. The show, of course, is well aware of the moral border zone it occupies. To avoid lawsuits it does things like "[requiring] potential subjects to undergo psychological evaluations and keeping a family member of the addict on call 24 hours a day during filming." The makers of *Intervention* are also kind enough to promise that if anyone puts herself or himself in immediate danger, they will stop filming and intervene. That's comforting to know and may have saved the lives of some of the people who have appeared on their show, such as a crack addict named Tim who crawled into a drainage pipe and threatened suicide, and the wealthy, divorced alcoholic Laney, who swallowed a bunch of pills off-camera, then admitted what she had done to the producers.

Technically, the cast and crew filming *Intervention* didn't have to do anything to help. There's no law compelling you to stop someone from doing something very stupid or potentially dangerous, even if they are doing it on camera or doing it expressly because they're on camera. I'm not saying there should be one, I'm just saying that the moral ambiguity is extremely hard to avoid. Even the generally inoffensive VH1 managed to get themselves in murky moral water when former child actor Danny Bonaduce (*The Partridge Family*), in an episode of *Breaking Bonaduce*, got behind the wheel after he had been drinking, and bragged how a car crash would make great television. Legally, producers don't have to do anything to stop a Bonaduce or anyone else. And, well, like Danny said, a car crash makes for great TV.

Still, it's bad PR to let someone kill himself while your production crew looks on happily. Generally reality TV stops just short of snuff. But once the cameras are packed up and the producers have moved on, things happen, and it becomes even harder to assign moral or legal responsibility. An early Swedish version of *Survivor*, called *Expedition Robinson*, that aired in 1997, led to one contestant, a thirty-four-year-old Bosnian refugee by the name of Sinisa Savija, throwing himself in front of a train four weeks before the show aired. No one knows why he did it, but it seems reasonable to assume that the mentally unstable fellow might have been troubled by the fact that he was the first person voted off the island. Scandal ensued, a producer was fired, and the show was briefly banned. That death is widely credited for the now standard use of psychological testing on prospective reality TV participants.

Despite adding the preshow mental screening to the repertoire, Savija's death wouldn't be the last time someone involved with a reality show would commit suicide after not making the cut. In 2004 the sister of a woman who killed herself after an appearance on ABC's *Extreme Makeover* sued the network. The contestant, trying to win free plastic surgery, mocked her own appearance on national television. She didn't win the surgery, and committed suicide soon after. ABC settled the case for an undisclosed amount in 2006. In 2005, Philadelphia boxer Najai "Nitro" Turpin, twenty-three, one of the sixteen contestants appearing on NBC's *The Contender*, a boxing reality-competition show, killed himself in a parked car before the show aired. There were many issues in Turpin's life, including a possible relationship breakup and the stress of supporting a younger brother, sister, niece, and nephew, all of whom he'd been responsible for since his mother had died when he was eighteen. Who knows how the prospect of being shown on television failing to make the final rounds had registered with this troubled young man?

Over in the UK, where many of the American reality TV formats get premiered before being brought across the ocean, the consequences are less dramatic but still evident. Consider the story of Jan Melia, whose appearance on Channel 4's *Wife Swap* program was so embarrassing that she moved her husband and three teenage kids from her native Nottingham to Belfast. "They appeared to decide we were poor and common, and that my home was filthy," she told a reporter. "All the filming was manipulated to that end, to make it look as if I neglected my children and Ollie was a feckless ne'er-do-well who never did any work. It simply wasn't true." Told that it was going to be just harmless fun, the family became pariahs after the show aired, with people pointing at them on the street, and at least one of the children physically assaulted by a gang.

Meanwhile, Kerry Hillhouse found a picture of herself on the Sunday morning cover of a tabloid newspaper after the Ayr resident appeared on an episode of *Supernanny*. The headline of the paper read: "Is this the worst mother in the world?" The twenty-nine-year-old reported that she couldn't even go to the supermarket without people shouting, "There's that woman off the telly who can't control her kids!" Additionally, her relationship with her husband had "broken down," in part because of how they were depicted on the show. "All I wanted was some help, and I ended up being vilified."

Maybe people should know better and maybe it's their own fault. As David Lyle pointed out, you can manipulate all you want, but the moment when someone freaks out really does happen. When you turn your life into entertainment, you have to know that people are going to try and push your buttons, and that some people are going to judge you negatively, and that you might have to deal with the failure of not winning the grand prize. But then, what about the kids? Did John Egly's kids all get the opportunity to think deeply about whether or not they should be on TV? Do the kids who regularly appear on *Supernanny* or *Nanny 911* get a say in whether or not they want to be immortalized forever as out-of-control animals? *Kid Nation* attracted 9.1 million viewers for the premiere episode of a series based on a bunch of kids sent to New Mexico to live on their own for forty days and forty nights.

The audience was huge, in large part due to the media reports about parents suing CBS, an attorney general's investigation, and the American Federation of Television and Radio Artists looking into the twenty-two-page liability waiver the parents were given to sign. In that now notorious document, parents gave up their right to sue if, among other things, their child died, was seriously injured, or contracted a sexually transmitted disease. Talk about moral ambiguity—the kids were each given a $5,000 payment, described as a stipend, so that the producers could claim that they weren't employees and thus that no child labor laws were being broken. It then came out that the show was shot in New Mexico to avoid the more strenuous labor laws around the use of kids on film and television productions in other states, like California. Let's also not forget that the parents signed away their children's rights to privacy, agreeing that during the course of filming participants could only expect to be off camera when they went to the bathroom. Can an eight-year-old really make a decision like that? Then there was *Brat Camp*, the show on which troubled teens were sent by their parents to a wilderness adventure camp where they could only leave if they learned how to get along with the group and meet challenges. But after the show, the brats were back in trouble, suggesting that televised therapy maybe wasn't the best route to mental and social stability. Among other incidents: Isaiah Alarcon was charged with spray-painting racial slurs in front of a home and Jada Chabot faced multiple police charges after she and her boyfriend slammed a speedboat into a family. The sheriff in Isaiah's town had this to say: "These kids had some real serious issues that needed to be dealt with in a long-term process, not a multi-week TV program for entertainment."

No discussion, however brief, of kids in reality TV would be complete without mentioning VH1's *I Know My Kid's a Star*. The host/judge is none other than Danny Bonaduce, a man whose own life was all but ruined by his stint as a child star. Who better, I guess, to introduce kids to the misery that is show biz? On the show, prepubescent kids have to perform song-and-dance routines while their parents look on threateningly. Critics and viewers have suggested that the show borders on child abuse, and they have a point. I've never seen such callous use of children to create adult entertainment. The show is really about the parents, you see, about how far they'll go to ensure that their children perform up to standard for Danny. They rage, rant, ridicule, and then order their kids to get out there and smile. (On an early episode, one of the kids actually threw up.) *Daily News* TV critic David Hinckley gave the show half a star and wrote, "What is true is that when the contestants and parents line up, none of the kids seems to look very happy. . . . For a show about cute kids who can sing or dance, *I Know My Kid's a Star* has surprisingly little joy or fun. Mostly it's sad, which is not the same as 'bad.'"

The moral ambiguity of using kids on these shows merges nicely with the overall question of whether or not we want a society in which people are subjected to physical and psychological torture on television for our amusement. Consider the program *Solitary*, produced for David Lyle's Fox Reality, in which the contestants battle it out to see who can survive longer and longer periods of isolation and mental torture. Twenty-three-year-old photographer Phu Pham, a contestant on the show, told the magazine *Mother Jones* about hallucinating gray rabbits and being scared out of his mind after two days of isolation in a small box with just a few hours sleep, almost no food, and a soundtrack consisting of the amplified wails of crying babies. After hours of this kind of torture, one of the contestants, known as Number 4 to the audience, a tough thirty-year-old woman originally from Romania muttered, "This is a psychotic-experiment show, not a reality show." Pham eventually won the show and the $50,000 grand prize. But he reported being haunted by the voice of "Val," the disembodied computer woman (a take-off of my namesake Hal) who communicates with the contestants. Pham dreams of Val, even eight months after it's all over. Still, he says it was worth it. "It's very hard to explain. You're trying to ham it up and let yourself have fun, entertain them, making the best of a pretty horrible situation. It's like when you're on death row. How sad can you be on death row? You've got to at least have as much fun as you can when you know you're coming to an end."

The sad fact is that Pham wasn't even the first and probably didn't even go through the most. Japanese show *Susunu! Denpa Sho-nen* featured a fellow who agreed to be interred in a locked studio apartment for eighteen months for no prize money at all. Writes a commentator for *Salon*:

> For a segment called Sweepstakes Boy, a struggling young actor code-named Nasubi agreed to be locked naked in an empty apartment until he could win $10,000 in prizes from magazine contests—surviving only on the prizes he won. His reward, he was told, would be fame. After 18 months of puttering around the apartment, slowly losing his mind and eating a large shipment of free dog food, Nasubi, his hair and beard grown out into a scraggly mess, was escorted victorious from his apartment and into a bare anteroom—whose walls collapsed around him, leaving him naked and blinking in the middle of a roaring studio audience. He'd been on TV the whole time!

It's these kinds of shows, coupled with what we see on more mainstream fare, that led scholars Sam Brenton and Reuben Cohen to argue, "Reality TV's production techniques have aspects in common with torture." The scholars cited Article 5 of the Universal Declaration of Human Rights that states that "no one shall be subjected to torture or to cruel, inhuman or degrading treatment or punishment." Well, the academics wonder, is a show depicting panic-stricken model Catalina Guirado ordered to get into what she thinks are crocodile-infested waters (actually remote-control dummies) torture? What about shows like *Fear Factor* and *Survivor* and even *The Real Gilligan's Island*, that regularly subject their contestants to confinement, starvation, and degrading activities? On *Endurance UK,* "players bobbed for false teeth in buckets of pig eyeballs and ate quiches full of maggots." On the Spanish game show *El Gran Juego de la Oca,* players were required to "escape from flaming coffins and bomb-rigged cages." And don't forget the British, American, and Australian versions of what's known in the United States as *Fat March* and in the UK as *Too Fat to Walk.* On those shows, obese contestants are sent on forced marches, purportedly to lose weight. If they fail to make the walk in the assigned time, their fellow contestants suffer. Are these shows torture? Well for a lot of people they're torture to watch, but ask the contestants and the creators and they'll tell you that no one forced anyone. What transpires isn't torture. It's "opportunity."

◻ ◻ ◻

Since its inception, pop culture and television have been accused of hateful, mindless voyeurism—the lunatic expressions of our group mind projected back at us with mesmerizing intensity. And so, Peep culture: an audience of disconnected strangers huddled in their darkened abodes, uneasily awaiting a "moment of truth." And yet, for all that may be wrong with reality TV, I have problem with the idea of the Voyeur Nation, a country of greedy, fixated perverts. Voyeurs are hidden snoops watching the unsuspecting. But we aren't voyeurs. The people we watch are willing participants (with the exception of the kids). Nobody goes on reality TV or talk television to be reticent about their emotions. We want them to spill their guts, and presumably they want to spill their guts. That's not voyeurism. That's Peep culture, a culture in which a desire to be watched and to watch others being watched pervades almost everything we do.

Like most people, I'm drawn to Peep culture. I love the excesses and outbursts that characterize reality TV. I watch the stuff and, again like most people, I'm very curious to know how I would fare on one of the shows. At the Nashville Reality TV Conference, there was a production company casting for a show to be aired on the Discovery Channel. I decided to try my luck. I'm funny, a little awkward, okay-looking in a yes-that's-my-paunch kind if way. Why not Hal for reality TV? The show had something to do with surviving on your own in the wilderness. Hey, I camp. I paddle a canoe. I live in the city, but idealize nature. It's perfect for me. I filled out the form. They asked a lot of questions. They wanted to know where I lived. Hmm. Toronto probably isn't the right answer. Americans want to see Americans. Plus, if they think I'm Canadian they'll probably think I have an unfair advantage 'cause we can't feel the cold and we learn how to hunt moose with our bare hands in primary school. I put down my parents' address in Maryland. Next up: profession. Again, a problem. If they think I'm a writer or a journalist they probably won't want me. They'll figure I have ulterior motives. But if I make something up, they might sense my fakery. I skipped it. Next: wilderness experience. Do they want someone who can kayak rapids or someone addicted to Diet Coke, Price Club, and minivans? Should I portray myself as an urban nebbish, a weak bookworm who can't leave home without his David Sedaris books on tape and his eighteen prescription medications? I go for the middle ground and tell the truth: a city dweller, yes, a book-loving intellectual, true, but also a camper of modest abilities, with backwoods canoeing experience, though I've never hunted or stayed out in the woods longer than a week or so.

Finally I handed in my form. The young woman at the desk looked it over. "If you don't mind me saying," I said, "you look a bit young to make casting decisions." Turned out she was just the intern. If I met certain criteria she'd send me on into the next room where they'd ask me questions in front of a video camera. My heart leapt. The girl read down my application. Had she just said "video camera"? I was one room away from national TV. "You left employment blank," she noted. "I'm, uh—" I'm a terrible liar is what I am. "I'm—I wasn't sure what to put," I said. "Do you have a job?" she asked helpfully. "Not—" I say, "not exactly." "So you're unemployed?" Unemployed. I didn't like the sound of that. The people on reality TV are warehouse managers, army recruiters, or aerobics instructors. Sometimes you get stay-at-home moms and college students, but the jobless? They don't qualify. "I work," I said quickly. "I'm a writer." She frowned. A writer? I write short stories. And novels. Fiction. You know, made up stuff? Okay, she said brightly. She dropped my form on top of a bunch of other forms. I'll pass this on to my boss, she told me reassuringly. "But what about—" I gestured at the door behind her. "That's not necessary at this point."

Back home, the sting of disappointment lingered. I could still see my form thrown in there with all the other forms more likely to be recycled than filed. So I signed up on Reality-Wanted.com. The Web site sent me daily news about casting calls and let me apply for auditions. Every day I dutifully scanned the calls, but there didn't seem to be too many shows that were looking for a middle-class, mid-thirties, white, married, *Canadian*, Jewish writer with a three-year-old kid. I don't need to go to rehab (at least not yet), I'm not fat enough for any of the fat shows (at least not yet), and I'm not divorced (at least not yet, my wife might add). I don't dance, sing, or even have a hidden talent lame enough for *America's Got Talent*. I find a few possibilities, but there's always a catch: A casting call for a show to be called *A New You* is looking for "the accountant who wants to be a rock star" and "the housewife who wants to be a race-car driver." That could work for me: How about the writer who wants to be a reality TV star? Ah, but they're only taking applicants from Florida. ABC's *Wife Swap* is seeking "families with stay-at-home-dads." Cool. I could be a stay-at-home dad. I stay at home and I'm a dad, right? But the fine print says my kid needs to be six or older. My daughter, ticket to the big time, turns out to be holding me back.

Maybe I'd have better luck closer to home. I ask a few people I know in the television business in Toronto (yes, there's a television business in Toronto). Turns out there's a surprising number of Canadian reality TV shows, mostly knock-offs and copies of U.S. or overseas shows, created to fulfill government-mandated Canadian content requirements as cheaply as possible. (Thank you, Ottawa!) Someone tells me that they know a production company casting for a show about married men and their mothers-in-law. Perfect! Saying that my mother-in-law and I have had a few run-ins is like saying I'm a little bit known for talking too much. They'll love us! We hate each other! But then I find out the wife/daughter has to participate too. I broach the subject with my wife. "Are you crazy?" she says. I'll take that as a no.

I was beginning to suspect that I wasn't a good candidate for reality TV. I called up Tamra Barcinas again, casting director extraordinaire, and asked her what she thought. She said that I'm too married, too normal, too well-off, not well-off enough, too known, not known enough. She asked me if I'm willing to emote, to really tell all on television. "If someone is not going to be open enough with their emotions, then it's boring," she told me. "You're not seeing tears, you're not seeing fear, you're seeing hesitation."

Okay, I get it. I'm basically in the middle, a vast category of people who make "boring" television. Tamra offered to set me up with a few auditions just for kicks. But I shouldn't get my hopes up, she assured me.

I decided to decline her invitation. It's all just a big lie anyway, I told myself. Despite the predominance of reality TV on the small screen, the number of so-called "regular" people who actually end up on television is still tiny, an infinitesimal fraction of the population of North America. A handful get paraded around in front of the cameras and we millions are still at home, in the dark, doing what we've always done since the inception of television: passively watching. The idea that we can all try out and have our chance, that idea that we'll all get our fifteen minutes of tele-vised fame, is as much a pipe dream now as it was twenty or fifty years ago. It's the lie of fame restated for the lazy and complacent. Now you no longer have to work hard and devote every fiber of your being to attain your dream of stardom. Now you can just roll out of bed, pick up the phone and say, "Hey, I'm a fry cook at a restaurant. I'm skinny and tall and funny, I look just like Gilligan and so obviously I'm the perfect candidate for *The Real Gilligan's Island*. So how about it? Can I go on your show? Please? Can I?"

◻ ◻ ◻

At the Nashville conference, I had met a documentary crew who, as it turned out, were also from Toronto. They were sniff-ing around the idea of doing a documentary about reality TV for Canadian television. A few weeks later, I met up with them again and I told them about my sense that reality TV was just part of a larger trend—the overall shift to Peep culture. They were inter-ested in this idea and thought there was potential for a documen-tary on the subject. So we hatched a plan to make a documentary in which I explore the rise of Peep by doing everything possible to be watched by others. It wasn't quite reality TV, but what the hell—it was my chance to get on TV and I was definitely going to take it.

A few months later, the producers came to my place to film footage for a promotional trailer. The idea was to get some shots of me going about my normal life before we started fly-ing (pending funding, of course) all over the place, in search of wild and crazy Peep experiences. Apparently, as the producers patiently explained to me, first my normalcy had to be demon-strated—people would only care about my quest for Peep if I was perceived as a normal, everyday schlub. To show my normalcy, I was told to take out the garbage. I actually ended up taking out the garbage about ten times. Then we headed into my backyard where I was fighting a battle with a bunch of ants that I was trying to keep from coming inside the house. I had spread lines of cinnamon in front of the backdoor because I read online that ants won't cross the cinnamon (sadly, not entirely true). The filmmakers wanted to catch this in action, even though I'd already done it. So I used up an entire shaker of cinnamon pretending to do what I'd already done, in the spirit of being who I already am—a "normal" guy with a house, a kid, a wife, an ant problem, and a life that doesn't revolve around being insulted by Perez Hilton or having my drunken phone messages leaked by my actress ex-wife and posted on TMZ.

Normalcy established, the trailer was completed and it looked great. Still, the process reminded me of everything I'd learned about people whose lives get used for reality TV, and I wondered: Am I making a big mistake? Who's in control of how I will ultimately be presented? I trust these people, they are good people, they are, like me, "normal" people with jobs, kids, spouses and the like. It's not them I'm worried about. What I'm worried about is an industry that makes a product out of people's life stories. What I'm worried about is becoming a caricature of myself in pursuit of some fleeting bit of fame I don't deserve any more than the next guy anyway.

Nevertheless, I decided to go on with it. In Toronto the filmmakers introduced me to Bennie Saunders, whose claim to fame has to do with having been on three separate reality shows, all aired on Canada's Life Network. The filmmakers wanted me to sit down with Bennie and talk with him about his experiences while they shot footage. I arrived with both of the producers and a cameraman. The neighborhood was working-class, with small, brick, row houses pressed together. Bennie's house seemed to be the smallest of them all. It was a decrepit bungalow with a living room the size of a postage stamp. We sat down on a creaky, stained futon, the cameraman pointed his lens, and Bennie started talking.

Turned out Bennie had asked his wife to marry him on reality TV (on a show which follows people about to pop the question). Then Bennie got married on reality TV (on a game show where couples compete to set up weddings for each other, and the prize is a honeymoon in Thailand). Finally Bennie and his wife had a child on, you guessed it, reality TV (on a show called *Birth Stories*). All of which happened more or less because he picked up the phone and called in. It was that hard. What's Bennie got that I don't? Well, he's a talker. He emotes. He loves to go on about his feelings. He's a yoga instructor, a school bus driver, and he plays drums and sings in a rock band. He's like the Egly family—eccentrically nonthreatening and always willing to play along. He's perfect for Peep.

But the more Bennie talked, the more I started to feel uneasy. The flimsy futon couch we were sitting on reeked. The house was a mess. There was no sign of his wife or his child. Bennie was twitchy. He talked about lining up to be in the studio audience of late-night talk shows. He talked about working as an extra in Hollywood movies. He talked about applying to the *Guinness Book of World Records* for having been in the most reality TV shows. He talked about wanting to do at least one more show, preferably something big like a *Survivor* or an *Amazing Race*.

When I finally got a word in edgewise, I asked him where his wife was. What happened to Lisa? Turns out that Lisa is gone. They've separated. But they're still in touch and Bennie hopes for reconciliation. How did perfect love caught on tape for three different shows lead to separation? Bennie started telling me about having seven children from several different women. One of those children, a teenager, came to live with him. The mother was unhappy. Ontario's Children's Aid Society was called in to investigate the situation. The teenager was returned to the mother. Lisa was pressured to leave as well, lest the Children's Aid Society take away the baby. She left unwillingly, but she left. That was Bernie's version of events. Whatever the story, it isn't a pretty one.

Bennie was starting to ramble angrily, so I suggested that we watch the shows he's been on. He popped in the wedding game show. It was your typical daytime cheese, the kind of thing that's probably being made right this second in twenty different countries. The competing couples choose each other's tuxedos, flowers, and wedding ceremony venues. What little drama there is comes out of the reaction the couples have to what's been picked out for them. On the show Bennie was beneficent: he's not crazy about the suit the other groom picked out for him, but who cares? It's not about the bow tie, it's about the love. Suddenly, back in his decrepit living room, I realized that Bennie was bawling. He was staring at the TV screen and crying his eyes out. This is the kind of thing that got him on all those shows in the first place. "Bennie, what are you feeling?" one of the producers blurted. I'd forgotten she was there. She wanted Bennie to look up. She wanted to be sure the camera caught the tears as they gurgled down his cheeks and dropped off his chin. Leave the poor guy alone, I thought. Then I remembered that tears were precisely what they were there to shoot. And anyway, we hadn't *made* him cry or manipulated him into crying, had we? So why did I feel guilty? Bennie looked up. Tears were still trailing down his cheeks. "I'm okay," he said. He said he was just overwhelmed by the beauty of that day. "Even after everything that's happened since?" I asked him. Bennie has no regrets about going on the shows. In fact, he revels in the experience, relives it over and over again. Why wouldn't he? On reality TV, Bennie is perpetually a good guy in love. On reality TV, life is good to Bennie.

Finally the producers called an end to the interview. Bennie, now fully recovered, immediately started trying to pitch me and the producers an entire reality TV show starring him, Bennie Saunders. Maybe something about his band? They've got a new singer. They're up and coming. They're going to be big. Or how about his family? All those kids and different mothers? It's crazy around Christmastime, he assured us. He'd actually filmed footage of his family with an eye toward pitching a reality show. Suddenly the producers perked up. "Can we get that footage?" they wanted to know. "Of course," he said. But, he reminded us, he was still holding out for something big. Like *Survivor*. Bennie followed us outside where the gear was being loaded into the trunk of a car. "Wait, wait!" he called, suddenly remembering that he'd forgotten to do something important. He ran back inside to find his camera. He needed a photo of all us together. He needed to document yet another potential television appearance. I put my arm around Bennie's shoulder. We both did our best to smile.

chapter five

Breaking the Seal: Gossip, Grooming and the (Secret) Allure of Peep

A man who lacks judgment derides his neighbor, but a man of understanding holds his tongue. A gossip betrays a confidence, but a trustworthy man keeps a secret.
—Proverbs 11:12–13

I have a postcard I've been meaning to send. It's nothing special, just the skyline of the city I live in. The city at night, lit up and revealed, but also secretive and hidden. This is where I live. This is where we all live, perpetually caught between revelation and exposure. We go about our business, figuring that most of the time, almost all of the time, nobody notices. We're counting on it, in fact. We're counting on the fact that whatever our kink, fetish, habit, or peccadillo, there are many of us and we're all doing it. So who's going to notice me?

But we want to be noticed. We live in cities of millions. Surely in the midst of these giant hives crawling with people there's someone out there who's willing to pay attention to me, even if just for a minute. Or maybe not. Which is why I have a postcard I can't decide if I should send. On the front, a simple city scene of the kind any tourist might buy. On the back, my secret.

What I wrote on that postcard is between me and Frank Warren. Warren is the Maryland-based artist who presides over an empire of secrets, more than 100,000 confessions sent to him from around the world. From whom? He doesn't know. About what? About anything and everything. Warren's dominion is PostSecret and he is a high priest of Peep. He has millions of followers, supplicants, converts, and even breakaway sects to his credit. He's taken one of the oldest human traits—to keep and tell secrets—and turned it into a global phenomenon, a transnational entertainment mini-dominion that's as simple and complicated as the primal need to admit the truth. PostSecret is candid, disturbing, and wildly entertaining. If you're looking for the front lines of Peep, here it is. Just be careful. Reading the thousands of secrets written on postcards and anonymously sent in to Warren is the Peep culture equivalent of doing crack. You'll find yourself going back again and again. You'll bookmark PostSecret.com, buy Warren's four book compilations of secrets, attend his many campus events as he crisscrosses the country talking about the power and value of unburdening. But you still won't be satisfied. You'll want to know more. "Ever since I discovered PostSecret I look out for secrets," writes an anonymous contributor to the site. "On street corners, lamp posts, faces, dollar bills too. I need to be reminded that everyone has secrets and that I can be open to being there when someone needs to let one go. I am trying to be the kind stranger I've always wanted to meet."

The "kind stranger" or the addicted consumer of a phenomenon that turns the secrets of others into Peep culture entertainment? Entertainment, though, isn't the right word for a blurry picture of a mother and daughter, with these words on the back: "I'm not going to cope when my mom has lost her battle with cancer. I'm going to kill myself. I hope there is an afterlife." Or this text pasted over the faces of two college girls: "The first night I shared a room with my black roommate I locked my suitcase." Not all the secrets are so portentous. On the back of a postcard showing vintage seventies cops sporting handlebar moustaches: "I call the cops on all the parties you don't invite me to."

I reach Frank Warren at his home in rural Maryland where he stores the hundreds of thousands of postcard secrets people have entrusted to him, and where he pores over the thousand or so cards he gets each week, trying to decide which ones should appear on the Web site, get a place in a future book, or be included as part of a show in an art gallery. I imagine him in his house, reading secrets, filing secrets, uploading secrets. Secrets, secrets everywhere. Is one of them mine? In a way, they're all mine. And yours. A shared humanity of secrets splashed across the screen, global and local, personal and political. I imagine Frank putting secrets in vaults, in safety deposit boxes, burying secrets in the backyard, following his own private code of Peep storage. The reality, of course, is more prosaic.

"I keep them all and I keep them in those big bins you can buy at Home Depot," says the soft-spoken artist. Warren tells me that the project started in 2004 when he passed out invitations to submit anonymous secrets on postcards for an art project. "I thought that would be the end to the project, but the idea was spread virally, and now it has a life of its own. . . . I feel as if I've stumbled upon something full of mystery that I do not fully understand."

Who could understand it? I ask Warren: Why are so many people drawn to PostSecret?

"Some of the reasons people come initially might just be curiosity," Warren says. "But you can't look at these secrets without them resonating with you personally. You can recognize your secret on a stranger's postcard. Each secret is very individual, but the emotion and the feeling and the experience ties us into a commonality."

This notion of a commonality is at the heart of Peep culture. Over and over again we see the collective, shared urge to watch and be watched. When Peep seems to matter most is when it is about an (almost) anonymous us, a commonality of blurred but nevertheless specific people who could be us. Frank Warren tells me about "the search for authenticity, people desiring to see what's real, what's below the surface, what's been hidden." He also tells me several anecdotes about people who have been moved by PostSecret to in some way confront and deal with issues in their lives. He tells me about a woman who wrote out six secrets to send in, but ended up leaving them on her boyfriend's pillow for him to read and consider. On the Web site, I find another such anecdote:

> I wrote and drew up a postcard for PostSecret. I put it in an envelope and sealed it, but I couldn't find any stamps. Not wanting it to be found by nosey family members, I shoved it between my mattresses and forgot all about it. Yesterday my friend dropped something between my bed and my wall, and pushed my bed out of the way to get to it. In the process, the top mattress came partially off the bottom one, and the envelope was there, and it had torn open. She read it. "I WAS ABUSED BY MY BABYSITTER." We talked about it for a while and the whole story behind my secret came out. I've never told anyone before, and I was so glad to get it off my chest. Together, we ripped up the postcard and burned it. I feel freed.

Anonymous confession. A cry in the wilderness. A tree falling that everyone can hear. Oh, sure, we have life partners, family members, priests, therapists, judges, journalists, and even various incarnations of God to hear our confessions, to expose our secrets to. But they all come with an agenda. Warren has no agenda. He just has us—his faceless mass of readers. We are both the source of the secrets, and the consumers. We are Peep culture and, as such, we are in no position to judge. Like Warren, we come to listen, learn, laugh, and, at the end of the day, line up for our turn.

"As the human population continues to grow, so does our sense of loneliness," says Warren. "You'd think it would be just the opposite—but with population growth comes more and more isolation. So hopefully PostSecret allows you to carry a greater sense of empathy. I really do believe that all of us have a secret that would break your heart if you just knew what it was."

◻ ◻ ◻

Should we all know each other's secrets? How many times can our hearts break for strangers on a Web site, for their bad luck and bad choices? Talking to Warren you get the sense that despite the fact that he has profited personally from the secrets and is now making a very decent living off of book sales and speaking engagements, he genuinely views himself as mainly a trustee. People trust him with their secrets, and he has to live up to that responsibility. At the same time, his success as an accumulator and curator of other people's secrets inevitably sends a message to others who may end up being far less scrupulous. The success of Warren's project tells us that secrets are valuable commodities; secrets can be harnessed, captured, and used. And so it's no surprise to discover that commercial culture is out there desperately trying to figure out how to harness the power of something like PostSecret to enhance brands and connect people to products.

A copycat site I visited, called SharedConfession.com, is festooned with ads and dominated by rants (sample confession titles: "I Hate Bums" and "I Won't Vote for the Black Man or the Woman"). The difference between PostSecret and its copycat commercial brethren is the difference between an embarrassed, regretful revelation of racism ("I locked my suitcase") and a frank, defiant pronouncement of intolerance ("I won't vote for the black man"). It's the tone and purpose that makes all the difference. It's the difference between crassly getting people to say anything, the more the better, and carefully choosing individual voices that resonate with the notion of revelation and forgiveness, with the possibility of community in an anonymous age.

SharedConfession is not alone in trying to jump on the se-crets bandwagon. Well-known, "interactive," reveal-your-secrets campaigns have been rolled out by giant corporations in recent years. *The Gargoyle*, a book by Andrew Davidson, published by Random House, has a complicated plot revolving around a callow, promiscuous fellow whose life changes dramatically after he is badly burned in a car accident and becomes physi-cally abhorrent. *The Gargoyle* has it's own mini-confession Web site, BurnedByLove.com, on which readers are invited to share a story of love "burn." "Thank you for reading and/or submit-ting your most intense story," says the site. "Now, read the most intense love story ever." A modest entry into the world of Peep culture marketing. Far more expansive are Unilever's Dove Real Beauty campaign, and the Kimberly-Clark Corporation's Let It Out campaign, attached to Kleenex. These are expensive, high-concept, public relations exercises at the cutting edge of twenty-first-century marketing.

"Kleenex® brand provides lots of ways for everyone to let it out™," announces the Let It Out Kleenex Web site. "From inspir-ing you through our commercials, to taking our good listener and blue couch on tour around the country, to giving you a way to participate right here at this site, most people believe releasing emotions more freely is healthy. We hope you've enjoyed creating your own blue couch moments." The introduction teeters into the nonsensical, but that hasn't stopped thousands of people from dropping by and "letting it out." Most of the people are anony-mous. "Milwaukee" writes: "My boss is such a miserable person who has very little self esteem that she has to put others down all the time to make herself feel good. She is so rude and jerky to everyone. I can't stand her. I wish she would quit and leave the company." Is this disparate human beings connected to a shared truth? For we silent lurkers, it's an opportunity to revel in one person's whiny, helpless anger. Peeping other people's secrets doesn't always connect you to deeper truth and foster meaningful community. Moreover, strange things happen when corporations underwrite online sharing. Writes "Underdog of the world": "I am 16. I am a sophomore. I am a rape victim. It happened this year, by a guys I thought was one of my friends, and to make it worse it was at My church. He said he needed to talk and i trusted him. Well i think you know the rest. My life change, my friends changed, my schools changed, but most importantly i changed. I have no one to talk to about it and i wish i did. I also wish i wouldn't have trusted him." That's her story. Kleenex helpfully writes under it: "Find Similar: Rape."

On the Dove Real Beauty Body Image Forum, roughly 14,000 women have left comments. Writes Bangzoom1118:

> I still struggle with my body image issues. I have such few stretch marks from the pregnancies, which I consider to be a miracle. People cannot even see them because they are in places always hidden by clothing (even hidden by a bikini). But I can't help it . . . the little tiny bit of cellulite that I will probably never get rid of still irks me . . . the tiny little imperfections that no one probably notices but me, even if I am wearing a swimsuit . . . they all still bother me so much. I see those airbrushed photos of models and celebs and wonder why my skin does not look like that, but then remember that I am not airbrushed!

"I am not airbrushed!" could be the slogan for these forums. But I'm not sure it's even true. Frank Warren, who in many ways and through no fault of his own instigated this kind of campaign, sees this incarnation of Peep culture as a baring of souls that inevitably leads to connections and greater human understanding. Forums like Let It Out, Real Beauty, and SharedConfession.com make the opposite also feel true: there's a sense of ghostly diminishment in the revelations, a sense of stories and lives being airbrushed and harvested. Who are the people who offer up their secrets to these sites? To what end are they being encouraged to share their secrets? I wonder if the companies themselves know exactly what the relationship might be between Peep culture confession and what they are selling. They know that people want to be noticed. What they might not know is that this longing to be noticed has to do with the collapse of the kinds of communities and neighborhoods that we used to rely on to provide us with intrinsic, effortless, recognition of our existence as human beings. These sites cannot replace community, of course, which is why so much of the material that gets posted seems angry, embittered, petty, vindictive, and even hopeless. The emotion and anger you find on these kinds of forums is real, but it's also disconnected from actual people and situations. This is Peep as a global gossip factory, gossip disconnected from corporeal community, gossip floating aimlessly through cyberspace, never knowing what it's there for and who will be spooked by it. All these people, ghosts in the machine of Peep ("Find Similar: Rape"). How will it all end? "There's no way to turn it off," Frank Warren tells me when I ask him about the future of PostSecret. "My wife fears the secrets will chase us down even after we've retired. Maybe that's my secret: I hope the secrets never stop coming."

◻ ◻ ◻

The secrets might stop coming. Already the very idea of having a secret is starting to feel outmoded. Why hoard a secret when you can use it to get money, attention, friendship, or community? Today, in part thanks to the progression from the well-meaning spirituality of PostSecret to the awkward hucksterism of Kleenex's Let It Out campaign, Peep is becoming a business. The business model, however illusory, seems to revolve around the idea that what people want is instant therapy, ongoing, online, primal-scream communion. What we want is someplace where our secrets can be scrubbed, wrung out, and air-dried outside for all to see. Dirty laundry made clean. Gossip gone global.

The move from well-intentioned art project to somewhat

confused marketing campaign is now giving rise to the next stage in the evolution of Peep culture as it pertains to secrets: the deliberate design of systems that revolve almost entirely around the dissemination of personal information.

One of these systems is Twitter, the social networking site that lets you answer the question "What Am I Doing Right Now?" in 140 characters or less. Seeking more insight into the intersection between global gossip, global profit, and the potential for online community, I visited the creators of Twitter in their spacious, downtown San Francisco factory turned office. There I found the founders, Jack Dorsey and Evan Williams. Rumpled and tattooed, they looked more like they were fronting a band then running a tech-development company. And like any band on the cusp of mainstream success, they bragged to me about their growing appeal. They told me that the number of Twitter users was tripling every month. (Citing the need to keep the competition at bay they won't tell me the exact number of users, but when I first talked with them in the summer of 2008, industry pundits estimated that there were half a million Twitterers. Half a year later that number was estimated to have grown to over six million users.)

I immediately asked the obvious question: Why would someone want to Twitter? Evan Williams put it this way: "The question 'Why are we interested in this stuff?'—'Why is this entertainment?'—could be flipped on its head when we ask, 'Why is fictionalized, non-real entertainment, normal entertainment, interesting?' People are in the world and that's real." According to Dorsey and Williams, Twitter's appeal is its ease of use, its instant accessibility, its short bursts of seemingly unimportant chatter. "We became addicted very quickly," Jack Dorsey said, explaining how the concept, once implemented in a test version, immediately took hold with everyone in the office. Why is Twitter addictive? "It's connection with very low expectation." Dorsey talked about using Twitter to achieve greater rapport and understanding with his family. He described one night when he Twittered the 700 or so people who get his messages, telling them that he was in a bar drinking whiskey with co-Twitter-creator Williams. "It's funny because I actually started drinking late in life, at like twenty-two or so. So my parents who live in St. Louis never really knew that I started drinking. I was with Ev and we were drinking whiskey and I decided to Twitter about it. And my Mom was like, 'I knew you drank cider sometimes, but whiskey?'"

Twitter is all about revealing the tiny secrets you keep from those who know you best. It works because of its constancy and consistency. After a while you stop thinking about what you're revealing and who's on the other end, reading about your mundane life. "You're writing to a wall," said Dorsey. "And whoever reads that wall interprets it as they will. So there's a sense that you're just putting information out there, there's not so much weight to what you're writing, there's not as much of an audience with Twitter."

What he means is that while there *is* an audience, it's not as obvious or apparent as doing something like reality TV or even blogging. No one's going to stop you on the street and say, "Dude! I read you on Twitter!" Twittering feels like you're talking to yourself. ("Heading out of the house now . . . don't forget to lock the door . . . heading to the subway . . . grab a coffee on the way . . . no, no time for coffee . . . running late . . . damn, there's that tickle in my throat again . . . am I getting a cold?") Plus, with less sense of audience, there's less sense of performance and so, unlike reality TV, there's a greater aura of unmediated truth-telling. It's a purer, more instantaneous form of Peep. I'm reminded of something Frank Warren told me: "The nature of authentic soulful secrets is very compelling. They seem to be inexhaustible. Every day I receive new surprises." Commentary about the weather merges with musings on life and links to blog posts and major announcements about work, relationships, and even health. "It's very easy to get a greater context for someone's life," Jack Dorsey explained. "I've learned so much about people that ordinarily I wouldn't ask."

By randomly clicking on the first person I saw on the Twitter site, I discovered the life of Bridget Schumacher of Buffalo, New York. ("Bio: dancer. baker. teacher. student. soon to be a librarian. *smiles*"). I signed up to follow her, which meant she received an e-mail telling her that I'm now among those getting her feed. I get her feed via text message or by logging onto the Twitter Web site. I'm not that dedicated to Bridget's activities so I chose to follow her exclusively online. At the same time I also wanted to experience the feeling of being followed. I started Twittering and hoped to catch on. Several months went by and I was stuck at twelve followers. Bridget, who signed up to follow me after I signed up to follow her, has hundreds. Julia Allison, the New York socialite made momentarily famous by the celebrity-gossip blog site Gawker.com, has 1,300. Tech entrepreneur Jason Calacanis has 28,000 followers, Fast Company tech cheerleader Robert Scoble has 27,000, and blogger Scott Beale has 12,000 followers. So what was I doing wrong? For one thing, I posted once or twice a day, and everyone above, including Bridget, seemed to post at least ten to twenty times a day. Plus, my posts were boring. They were about writing or the weather or links to my blog, which was probably also pretty boring. Still, I Twittered on and slowly, very slowly, broke the twenty and even the thirty mark. I was on my way to half a hundred! Who are the people who signed up to follow me? That I can't tell you. My thoughts went out into the world and disappeared.

But of course they didn't really disappear. Though we Twitter without much sense of an audience, that doesn't mean that what you put out there isn't getting noticed.

"Everything that you send goes out over the phone," noted Dorsey. "So the information has been sent to different places and Google and Technorati index it, so when you mark yourself as public you are really committing yourself to being in the public eye." Here Williams jumped in: "Basically you shouldn't Twitter about your cocaine habit."

We laughed, but, well, at the time I kind of wished I'd had a cocaine habit to Twitter about. Everyone else seemed to have a swirl of gossip and activity around them. I was struggling with that dreaded box of 140 characters, desperate to find that single sentence to put out there. Something that someone else might care to know. Then I remembered what Evan Williams told me when I asked him why people think that others might want to read their Twitter updates. "It's no more presumptuous than making small talk," he said. Dorsey added: "I follow people I don't know because I find them interesting." What makes someone interesting on Twitter isn't their big ideas. It's the little tidbits, the minutiae of the day to day. The very stuff I hesitate to put out there, figuring no one cares, is what might make me interesting to other Twitterers. But why should I even bother with Twitter? Wouldn't I be better off just picking up the phone and calling a friend? When I put that question to Williams and Dorsey, they looked at me with sympathy. I just didn't get it. "You're not reducing face-to-face time," Williams told me patiently. "You don't choose to stay in and do Twitter. It's like those spare moments on the Web when I'm doing another task I switch over to Twitter for literally fifteen seconds. There is no fewer face-to-face, no fewer phone calls, there's more awareness of other people in my life and maybe that even leads to further conversation with some people."

Somewhere between gossip and everyday life lies the realm of what makes us interesting. PostSecret is the big reveal, while Twitter is the small chipping away at the block of stone that is your life. Both ultimately are about deriving a sense of community and commonality through sharing the details—your details or other people's details, people who are as likely to be strangers as they are to be the neighbor next door. Before leaving Twitter I drop in on Bridget: "My goal is to tackle three of my to-do list items before I need to head across campus for the afternoon.

Here we go." "Off to surprise my nana w/ huge family dinner: 14 children, 14 grandchildren and a bunch of family dogs :) Even out of towners are here!" "Trying to figure out why my bed was in the middle of the room when I woke up this morning. Rough night sleep?"

◻ ◻ ◻

If you go to the photo sharing site Webshots.com (or any other similar site) and enter the search phrase "breaking the seal" (hey, don't look at me like that, it was my friend's idea), up will pop some thousand-plus photos of random people about to go to the bathroom. So, okay, I think to myself: the "breaking the seal" theory. It goes like this: Peep is addictive, and once you start it's hard to stop. For better or worse, it's easy to forget that you are essentially converting your (or other people's) private moments into public announcements. A service like Twitter, or the many Web sites where you can instantly confess, rant, or otherwise up-load videos and photos, makes the process of forgetting that much easier. Once you "break the seal" you can't stop yourself from do-ing it again and again and again. Our mass digital culture makes it easier and easier to confess, reveal, and connect. And the more we reveal, the more it seems okay to put anything and everything out into the world for public consumption. Like heading for the bathroom when your bladder is full, you start doing it naturally, without thinking. Making your mundane secrets public turns out to be pretty addictive. It even feels, in some counterintuitive way, oddly natural. Once you start, why stop?

But here's the problem: not all of us want our secrets re-vealed. Not all of us want to offer up our lives to a global mael-strom of Peep gossip. More and more of us are getting caught in the culture of Peep unwillingly. The more that secrets, how-ever mundane, become an instantaneous, unending source of currency to be exchanged for attention, catharsis, and even

community, the more likely it is that anything you do in public or
even in (semi) private could automatically show up on someone
else's feed. (Consider, for instance, the case of Olympic champion
swimmer Michael Phelps who took a bong hit at a University of
South Carolina house party only to find pictures of the momen-
tous occasion circulating in cyberspace three months later.) In
other words: Hey, if I don't have a cocaine habit to "tweet" about,
well, maybe you do. When we're not shaming ourselves, it seems
we're gleefully shaming others.

Like seismic tensions suddenly and unexpectedly buckling
some random corner of the earth, sometimes this fluctuating energy coalesces into an outburst of populist worldwide mirth at the
expense of a particular person being singled out for no particular
reason. The April 2003 global shaming of portly Quebec teenager
Ghyslain Raza is widely considered the first example of the viral
video phenomenon. It can also be seen as a breakthrough moment in the history of Peep culture: the first global shaming of a
single human being for the sole purpose of the amusement of the
entire world.

While alone at school, Raza recorded a video of himself en-
ergetically swinging a lightsaber and pretending to be a Star Wars
character. Unfortunately for him, his classmates found the video
and, kids being kids, they promptly circulated it amongst each
other and then posted it online. The result was the perfect storm:
a video that anyone anywhere could instantly understand and
laugh at. A fat kid huffing and puffing as he battles imaginary Je-
dis or Vaders. Everyone knows Star Wars and everyone knows fat
kids. Put the two together and you get something as accessible as it
is divorced from its origin as a moment of adolescent cruelty. The
video first appeared on the Internet on the evening of April 14,
2003. About a month later, one U.S. blog featuring the video reported that it had been downloaded 1.1 million times. By October
2004, another site dedicated exclusively to the video reported that
the two-minute clip had been viewed seventy-six million times.

Today, five years later, Internet commentators agree that the Star Wars Kid video remains the most-watched clip in Web history.

And yet few know how this story ends. Follow the trail of global Peep back to its local source and you'll often find confusion, angst, regret, and despair. Raza, confronted with chants of "Star Wars Kid! Star Wars Kid!" whenever he so much as peeked his head into the hallways or lunchroom, dropped out of school. Lonely and housebound, he turned himself over to Montreal psychologists who diagnosed him with depression. Raza ended up with a private tutor, barely able to leave his house without people on the street wanting to talk with him about being the Star Wars Kid. He eventually sued the three teenage perpetrators who, of course, said that they were just playing a prank, not trying to ruin anyone's life. Finally, in 2006, the case was settled out of court.

But of course it's not over, not for Mr. Raza who will carry the humiliation of that two-minute moment with him for the rest of his life, and not for the next Star Wars Kid whose goofy antics will go global. After Raza, there's the Numa Numa guy who posts himself dancing crazily to a Romanian pop song. There's the Dancing Cadet, caught jerkily gyrating to dance music on a hidden camera planted by his roommate. Both young men end up taking the sudden attention pretty well. They're being made fun of, but they realize there's an opportunity to profit from their emergent fame. For instance, Turkish "jurnalist, music and sport teacher [sic]" Mahir Cagri was hired as pitchman for a now long-gone dotcom after bloggers started sending millions of people to check out the unintentionally hilarious Web site of this random guy. A real life Borat, Cagri's page starts with "Welcome to my home page! I kiss you!" before going on to announce his love of "sport, swiming, basketball, tenis, volayball, walk [sic]." Then there's Jay Maynard, who was so proud of the cool costume he made himself—"a skin-tight, electroluminescent bodysuit resembling the outfits from the movie Tron"—that he decided to put it on and model it for his Web site. Millions of hits later and his geeky suit and pudgy physique were momentarily famous. Maynard loved the attention: he did as many interviews as possible and made an appearance on *Jimmy Kimmel Live*.

But others were not so happy, including Little Fatty, a Chinese teenager who became an icon when pranksters started inserting this pudgy fellow's face in various digital-collage mashups. Qian Zhijun was sixteen years old when someone took his photo attending a traffic safety class. The photo circulated online and Chinese Internet users became weirdly engrossed with manipulating the oval face of this man-boy. Suddenly Qian, now dubbed "Little Fatty," was appearing on movie posters for *Pirates of the Caribbean, Harry Potter, Austin Powers,* and *Brokeback Mountain.* Celebrities and politicians were sporting his chubby cheeks, not to mention Buddha and porn stars. When Qian found out that he was an Internet joke, he was shattered: "It was as if I had been struck by a thunderbolt. I felt really humiliated." Eventually he came around: "At least this makes people smile. I like it when they put me on the body of heroes, such as Russell Crowe in *Gladiator*. But I hate it when they place me on the shoulders of naked women or when the touch-up job is terrible." Like the Numa Numa guy who initially reported depression and not wanting to leave the house before eventually seeming to accept his new position as an accidental global entertainer, there's a sense that, well, the cat is out of the bag so what choice is there but to grin and bare it? Both end up launching official Web sites that predictably fail to capture the spontaneous, feverish energy of what was interesting about them in the first place.

In South Korea, Little Fatty's equivalent is Dog Shit Girl, a college girl who refuses to clean up after her dog when he does his business on the subway. A photo is taken and posted to a blog and the next thing you know the entire country and various parts of the world are virulently condemning the girl to the many deep pits of hell. Her name and address are revealed online and the girl, deeply embarrassed and even afraid, drops out of university and eventually issues a public apology to the country.

❏ ❏ ❏

Around the same time that Dog Shit Girl was making her debut as the poster girl du jour of Internet embarrassment, sites exclusively dedicated to shaming were coming into being. The progression from PostSecret to Let It Out to Twitter normalized the sharing of secrets. Following a similar path, we now have the move from amateur shaming to Web sites and even businesses entirely devoted to the idea of catching other people doing bad things and making those bad things permanently public. The summer of 2005 saw the launch of HollaBackNYC, inspired by one woman who photographed a vulgar fellow on the subway. Today there are at least fourteen sister sites dedicated to indirectly confronting men who harass women on the streets, including versions in Chicago and San Francisco. There's even a HollaBackAustralia. These kinds of sites represent a kind of Peep culture evolution. They seek to do on purpose what the woman who posted Dog Shit Girl's image to a popular Korean Web site did by accident. Their goal is to induce shame and make an example of individuals who act badly, stupidly, or idiotically. Catch him in the act and put him on a Web site for posterity and maybe he'll think twice about flapping his gums about how hot you are and what he'd like to do with you.

Since HollaBack, the concept has proliferated, to say the least. Sites like WomanSavers.com, TheBadBoyfriendClub.ning. com and Dontdatehimgirl.com are active with lists of guys and girls accused of being psychopaths, liars, abusers, and cheats. Writes Sporty25 on Dontdatehimgirl: "Women beware of this great looking, sweet talking, Christian man who lives in Texas. I met him several years ago and he is a person who will lie to your face. He gained access to several online accounts and screwed up my credit plus paid a few of his own bills. I trusted him and this is what happened. . . . Be careful girls!!"

The rise of the shaming site isn't limited to relationships between the sexes. Where there is contention, where there are strangers regularly coming into contact with each other, there is shaming. For instance, the frustrations of the daily commute have created a whole host of sites dedicated to shaming reckless, drunk, or just plain careless drivers: PlateWire.com, Above-AverageDriver.com, Irate-Driver.com, BadDriving.com. Then there's parking: MyBikelane.com, Caughtya.org, Youparklikeana**hole.com, Iparklikeanidiot.com. A *Wall Street Journal* article tells the story of Chris Roth, who fell afoul of several other motorists and was discussed in depth online. "This man needs his license revoked," wrote one poster, who accused Roth of cutting in and out. Another charged him with driving on a shoulder and having the audacity to "flip off" an old lady who wouldn't let him cut in. Eventually, Roth found the critiques when someone put a comment on his MySpace page telling him to check out PlateWire. But what he found there went way beyond simple complaining. The information available about him included his license-plate information (a perhaps ill-considered vanity plate reading "IDRVFAST") as well as his full name, cell phone number and link to his MySpace page, plus epithets describing him as a "big jerk" and a "meathead." "There is no accountability," the thirty-seven-year-old Mr. Roth of Raleigh, North Carolina, told the *Journal*. "You can just go online and say whatever you want whether it's factual or not." Though he admits that he speeds and gets impatient behind the wheel, he also brushes aside the anonymous posts critiquing his driving: "Who are they to decide what is safe or not?"

"Who are they?" indeed. Or maybe the question is "Who are we?" Many of the shaming sites are started, then quickly abandoned after a few threatened lawsuits. Or they're left to die the death of fewer and fewer posts. But the overall notion of creating Peep culture entertainment out of the embarrassing and/or antisocial antics of others is here to stay. Your problems, their problems, it's all amusement for the masses, regardless of whether or not the people involved are willing participants or even guilty of the indiscretions they are accused of.

Peep, as a form of disembodied entertainment more like TV than filing a police report, creates overlapping narratives, impressions, and emotions, not considered judgments. For some, it's funny and entertaining (even more so because it's "real"). But for those who find themselves in the spotlight, the results range from unfortunate to life-threatening to surreal. When a Chinese student was accused online by a husband who believed the student was having an affair with his wife, the student's phone number and personal details quickly appeared alongside the accusation. Soon after, vigilantes actually appeared at his house to mete out justice, despite the fact that the student denied ever having the affair. (Well, what else would he do?) How about the saga of high school teacher Cristina Mallon? Her impromptu cheer routine done in front of her humanities class was caught on cell phone video by one of her students and posted online before you could so much as yell, "Go Tigers!" Tens of thousands watched the YouTube video and ensuing news reports. The English teacher and cheer coach quickly resigned before, presumably, she was fired for looking stupid and embarrassing the school.

The perfect example of the progression from amateur random acts of shaming to professional shame-meisters scouring the globe looking for quality shame material comes to us courtesy of Oklahoma City's Johntv.com. The brainchild of Brian Bates, a self-proclaimed video vigilante, Johntv is "one Oklahoma man's effort to target, expose and impact street, organized and forced prostitution." Basically the site consists of videos Bates shoots, showing him catching johns and prostitutes in various sexual acts. There's a lot of swearing, threatening, scrambling for clothes, blurred-out body parts, and cars hurriedly pulling away. Is Brian Bates saving women from sexual exploitation? I really don't know. What I do know is that he looks like he's having a great time pointing his camera into the back seats of cars. Why wouldn't he? Not only is Bates judge and jury of everyone he decides to shame—as he told the *Los Angeles Times*, if you get caught by the cops, you pay a fine, but "if you get caught by me, you get a life sentence"—he's also profiting handsomely for his work as a full-time shame-hound. He sells his videos to news and talk shows for $250 a clip (I originally heard of him while watching one of those "Most Shocking Videos Ever" shows at my parents' house), he gets paid to appear as an exclusive guest on Maury Povich's tabloid TV show, and he uploads all his videos to YouTube where he gets hundreds of thousands of hits and clears more than $70,000 a year. It's on YouTube where the Bates-administered life sentence plays out over and over again. As he puts it: "There's no reprieve, no probation. People will be hitting that video on Google searches as long as you live." Here again we see the progression from amateurs using shaming and secrets haphazardly to professionals harnessing the potential of the secret to systems that can deliver profit. Will there be more people who seek to use other people's lives and secrets as the source for their for-profit feed? Of course there will.

So who governs our Peep culture outbursts, and stops shaming and gossip from becoming a source of global entertainment with the potential to ruin people's lives (whether they deserve it or not)? The answer is nobody. Consider the story of Tim Halberg, a California wedding photographer who got sick of his newspaper disappearing from his driveway. So he stayed up all night waiting for the paper to arrive, then attached a note saying "I'm watching you! Don't ever steal my paper again." Then he waited to catch the thief, who turned out to be a neighbor in his fifties, still in his bathrobe. The neighbor picked up the paper, read the note, put the paper back and walked away. Halberg caught the incident on video and decided that rather than confront the neighbor, he'd post it to YouTube. After reading about the story in a newspaper, I went to watch the video, which had by then been viewed around 16,000 times. Then I fell into the Peep rabbit hole and watched video after video featuring bad neighbors stealing newspapers, endlessly hosing down their walks for no reason, letting their dogs bark crazily, videos labeled "neighbor trespassing" and "our weird neighbors." I didn't make it over to Flickr where there are plenty more of the same, plus entire areas dedicated to people who talk too loudly on their phones in public places. Most of this shaming material doesn't do much good in terms of actually solving a problem one might have with a neighbor or a bad driver or a prostitute turning tricks next to a school or a serial cheater bouncing from woman to woman and leaving misery in his wake. Sorry-Mom.com, with 40,000 unique visitors a day when I dropped by, is in the don't-date-him ilk of shaming sites. Each one- or two-sentence condemnation of a sleazy sex partner comes accompanied with a huge picture of the supposed perpetrator, complete with large black bar across the eyes and nose. This creates the sense that women are actually going to be able to identify these miscreants when they sidle up to them at a party. But the truth, of course, is that unless you have an uncanny ability to remember chins, these unnamed individuals remain safely anonymous, functioning more like generic pictures of deadly car accidents shown to teenagers at driver's ed class than mug shots of escaped convicts.

In this Peep age of cyber gossip, truth is determined not by one's ability to trace a story back to a reputable source, but by how many people indicate interest through linking, downloading, sharing, and otherwise participating in the narrative. In the age of Peep, also the age of the cell-phone camera and the instant upload, shit happens. And anyway, why shouldn't bad drivers get their comeuppance? Why shouldn't bad neighbors be exposed? Why wouldn't a teacher acting like an idiot get what's coming to her? The authorities can't be everywhere all the time, and from my own experiences with a bad neighbor and his three pit bulls, I know it takes a tremendous amount of effort to get anything like a satisfying response from police or bureaucrats. Putting a few incidents online might not do much, but it might make you feel like you're part of something, garner you some support from others struggling with a similar problem, and, hey, give people a chuckle while they while away the work day. If nothing else, peeping your problem, suspicion, or outrage is guaranteed to make you feel less alone.

◻ ◻ ◻

Before the Industrial Revolution, people lived in small towns centered around agrarian pursuits that were, by necessity, collective in nature. They lived in large, extended family groups, and they tended not to move around very much. They were born into rigid class and social tiers, with very little chance of changing their position in society. Everyone knew everyone, and everyone knew exactly what was expected of them. Most people didn't read, and relied on the stories told to them by elders and authority figures to accumulate their information about the world. "Together," writes scholar Sylvia Schein in the book *Good Gossip*, "these factors—the credibility of oral information, the strict codes of behavior, as well as immobility and closeness of the relatively small communities—gave gossip great potency. Gossip was often accepted as truth, and, given the strict codes of behavior, gossip could destroy people's reputation and their position in society."

Gossip functioned as a kind of communal policing. At a time when everyone lived in relatively close quarters for the purposes of survival, and there was little if any mobility, you couldn't hope to get away with much. If you deviated from social norms you would be noticed and gossiped about. If you persisted in your behavior, you could suffer everything from community approbation and religious censure to punishments like whipping or banishment. You were never alone, which meant you never had much time or reason to feel lonely. This was often repressive, but it also served to define your place, status, and role in the world. As scholar Aaron Ben-Ze'ev writes, gossip satisfies "the tribal need, namely the need to belong to and be accepted by a unique group."

In preindustrial society, gossip reinforced group standards, protected the community from those who might weaken its bonds, and kept shit disturbers in their place. Gossip—talking idly about other people's personal affairs—turns out to be a powerful force for the maintaining of convention and social order. Gossip also gives us a way to compare ourselves to others. What are they earning, what are they buying, what are they doing in the bedroom? In this way, we attain a greater understanding of aspects of our own lives that we are too repressed or too afraid to bring up in everyday conversation.

Gossip had such an important function in preindustrial community that some scholars have even suggested it may have been the initial impetus for the development of language. British evolutionary anthropologist Robin Dunbar makes this argument in his book *Gossip, Grooming and the Evolution of Language*. The way Dunbar sees it, primates developed a way of living in groups largely to protect them from predators. "Baboons, macaques and chimpanzees are more terrestrial and prefer the more open habitats on the forest edge. Here the risk from predators is much higher. . . . The species solve this problem by being larger than the average primate and, more importantly perhaps, by living in unusually large groups."

Large groups cut down on the risks of attack. But group life needs rules and regulations, a way to live together that will prevent constant fighting which could undermine the benefits of communal society. As we all know, getting along in large groups is difficult even if, as Dunbar writes, "sociality is at the very core of primate existence; it is their principal evolutionary strategy, the thing that marks them out as different from all other species."

We primates love our big social groups, we even need them for survival. But we have a problem getting along in them. For one thing, there always seems to a bad apple or two hitching a free ride in the cart. Dunbar discusses the work of Swedish biologists Magnus Enquist and Otto Leimar, "who pointed out that any highly social species faces a considerable risk of being exploited by free-riders: individuals who claim a benefit at your expense on the promise to return it later in kind, but in fact fail to do so." The Swedes showed that the larger the group, the greater chance that free-riders will appear and be successful. "In large and dispersed groups, the free-rider can always keep one step ahead of discovery. . . . It takes time for the whispers of his unreliability to filter across from one individual to another within the group." What's a self-respecting bunch of apes to do? The answer is gossip.

The primates living in these large groups spend a very long time grooming each other. They groom each other far more than is necessary for the act to be about mutual health and hygiene. The grooming is, in fact, about establishing relationships. Grooming feels good. It takes a lot of time. It is a way of excluding free-riders who, not having put in the large amount of time it takes to groom and be groomed, are shut out of the community of alliances. Grooming, for Dunbar, is an early form of gossip, a way of signaling who is in and who is out, who, in fact, does not belong, or is not wanted because they buck social convention. "Perhaps language evolved not so much to keep track of your friends and acquaintances as to keep track of free-riders and coerce them into conforming. . . . Gossip may have evolved as a mechanism for controlling free-riders."

Once a means of living in large groups in relative harmony was worked out, the monkeys and apes became dominant. Their numbers grew and they had more free time. They began to evolve. They developed language. Language allowed the burgeoning neo-humans to extend their social networks and become even more dominant and efficient:

> Language allows us to exchange information over a wider net-
> work of individuals than is possible for monkeys and apes. If
> the main function of grooming for monkeys and apes is to build
> up trust and personal knowledge of allies, then language has an
> added advantage. It allows you to say a great deal about yourself,
> your likes and dislikes, the kind of person you are; it also allows
> you to convey in numerous subtle ways something about your
> reliability as an ally or friend.

The average human, Dunbar and others have suggested, lives in a "community" of about 150 people, which is to say that about 150 people actually know who you are. This is three times the size of the group that your average chimp lives in. How did this number come to be the standard? Dunbar theorizes that 150 is "roughly the number of living descendants . . . that you would expect an ancestral couple to have produced after four generations at the kind of birth-rates conventionally observed in hunter-gatherer and peasant societies. . . . Five generations takes you back to grandma's grandma, or as far back as anyone can vouch for particular relationships." In other words, the human brain evolves to allow us to remember and recognize and live in communities of 150 or so people that we collectively can identify and place. Language, which we use to express social knowledge and gossip, has allowed us to triple our group size. Like our ape ancestors, we lived securely in our preindustrial villages and communities because we had a mechanism to distinguish freeloaders and pretenders from family members and productive members of our society. That mechanism was gossip: Everyone knew everyone and, most importantly for our sense of self, everyone knew us.

Human beings are hardwired to gossip, shame, and expose. One researcher studied daily conversation and concluded that 80 to 90 percent of human conversation is about "the immediate social world inhabited by us and the people we know." When we talk, we talk about people. Our capacity for big ideas may well have been a by-product of our need to have a better way to socialize, to find out who is friend or foe, who's in or out. Before industrialization and urbanization, gossip worked because everybody knew everybody and there was nowhere to go, no next town or online community to reappear in as a totally different person. Even if the gossip wasn't true, it acted as a censure for others to beware that kind of activity lest they become the next victim of the community's attention. In his book about reputation and the Internet, Washington DC law professor Daniel Solove notes that shaming used to be a relatively effective means of policing. It was gossip solidified into public opinion. Ancient Romans would brand the forehead of the criminal with the letter corresponding to their crime. In 1674 Salem, Massachusetts, Hannah Gray, accused of being bawdy and slutty, was sentenced to stand at the meeting-house with a note on her head that said: "I stand here for my lascivious and wanton carriages." This kind of shaming would set the stage for Nathaniel Hawthorne's 1850 novel *The Scarlet Letter*, a high-school standard that tells of a seventheenth-century Boston woman branded as an adulterer, forced to perpetually wear the letter A, and shunned by the community.

Shaming doesn't work very well anymore. Our societies and communities have changed. We live in an anonymous society of single-family dwellings, lonely car commutes to work, and tenuous social connections that we have to work harder and harder to maintain. And we are transient—we move from place to place quickly and easily, shedding identities and pasts, endlessly re-inventing ourselves. We cannot be shamed because there is no single inescapable community that knows us, gossips about us, and watches us for signs that we are acting in ways contrary to the accepted standards of society.

As Robin Dunbar writes:

> In traditional peasant communities the world over, everyone

lives in everyone else's pocket. They have to, of course, because houses are crammed together and walls are like paper. But more than that, people want to: community is a genuine community, a co-operative whose members share the same problems of day-to-day survival. They are also bound by ties of kinship, at the very least through one sex and often through both. Modern industrial conurbations often lack that sense of community because they have been created anew out of nothing . . . [people living there] have no social ties, no common history behind them. Their networks of friendship and kinship may be stretched far out beyond the confines of the housing estate, a problem that is exacerbated by the high rates of mobility that force people to move long distances in search of work.

As a result, we are desperate to be noticed by our friends, families, and authority figures. We are so desperate that we actively seek out the trappings of shame as a way to set ourselves apart from the anonymous, easily ignored mass. We actively seek out ways to be known as low-brow, bawdy, and slutty. We brand, tattoo, and pierce ourselves, desperately trying to be noticed as criminals, rebels, gang members, and social outlaws. We do so because we can't count on our community of 150 to tell us who we are, whom we should trust, how we should live. Nobody knows us and we don't know anybody, so we need to send out signals about who we are that can be instantly understood, signals that are able to indicate both our uniqueness and our potential openness to alliances with similarly unique people. We pick and choose from an array of communities—pop cultural, online, religious, fetishistic—that we think will best tell the story of who we are, situate us in a community that will both affirm our need to be part of the group, and still afford us ongoing opportunities for exposure and reinvention.

We live several different lives all at once. We are one thing at work or school, another thing with our families, and another with the handpicked members of communities we've adopted

to set ourselves apart from the mundane, everyday life that di-
minishes our specialness. All these overlapping, fragmented
communities no longer reign in bad behavior. There's no cohe-
sive social network to say "that's not the way you conduct yourself on a date, young man" or censure a neighbor for stealing a
newspaper. We are many different people living in many different
milieus. As a result, we are responsible to almost no one. We can
get away with a lot more.

Our ability to morph and disappear is as much a curse as
it is a cure. Everyone's a shape-shifter. So who do you trust? The
arrival of Peep as a primary cultural pastime suggests how much
we long for the kind of cohesion and recognition we used to be
able to get from the tribe. PostSecret's Frank Warren talks about a
desire for commonality. The creators of Twitter talk about knowing more about people, feeling closer to them. The HollaBack
and Don'tdatehim sites are an attempt to bring social propriety
back to the community milieu. But, as with many of these kinds
of sites, the stories are usually posted anonymously, and rarely
include anything like identifying characteristics; so you end up
participating not in meaningful acts of public shaming with the
potential to reign in behavior, but in the dispersal of informa-
tion-as-entertainment: unsubstantiated, disembodied, passed on
as prurient tidbit, however harrowing it may be. This is the longing for community hitched to the horse of Peep culture and flayed
all the way into town. This is the need for community turned
into its opposite: various shaming sites futilely flailing against
a raging whirlpool of rudeness while inviting more rudeness as
post and counterpost circulate. A neighbor puts another neighbor on YouTube, eschewing face-to-face discussion in favor of a
cyber-policing that ultimately serves to further fragment what
little semblance of community we have left. Though our intentions are often heartfelt and instinctual, when gossip goes Peep,
community as we once knew it pretty much disappears, replaced
by global and transitory nodes that demand our active, constant,

participation in reshaping our identities.

Peep tries to fill the gap. We wish gossip still worked. We wish there could be ways to keep people from being total assholes and being rewarded for their antisocial, hateful, hurtful behavior. We wish we could be recognized as whole, holistic, intrinsic human beings, not members of professions, people with pop-culture kinks and particular pastimes or fetishes. At the same time, we have no interest in returning to societies where people were put in stocks and branded because they didn't believe in the right god in the right way, or slept with someone they weren't supposed to. We want the unstated rules that govern traditional community, but we don't necessarily want those rules to apply to us. This, in many ways, is the conundrum of modern society and emerging problem of Peep: we yearn for community but lack the willingness to be hampered by the structures of community. We want what the apes had, but we aren't necessarily willing to put in the work, to spend two hours a day grooming (getting to know) the neighbor.

Robin Dunbar concludes his ruminations on how gossip might have led to language and contributed to human evolution, by noting, "We are Pleistocene hunter-gatherers locked into a twentieth-century political economy." We are still instinctively doing things the way we might have done them in our tiny communities a thousand years ago. We are still looking for recognition from the tribe. But we're also trying to fit into the puzzle of a twenty-first century life that revolves around the fluid anonymity of cash. Peep gossip is a way to address our need for tribal approval and our need to see ourselves within the crisscrossing infrastructure of an electronic world centered around the logic of global capital and its visible corollary, mass-media fame. In this way, a community of sorts develops. It's an anti-community, a displaced digital community with endless local nodes. It revolves around personal revelation and even shame, it promises connection and sharing, and it utterly lacks the means to connect us to the people in our day-to-day lives. Instead it connects us to a widespread

Peep culture of billions, all seeking the ape-old feeling of giving and getting attention. In the absence of true communities of
individuals who live a shared life of mutual dependence, the best
we can do is try to artificially create the feelings that these communities provided. And so we cyber-groom; desperately trying
to fit into a tribe that doesn't exist anymore.

◻ ◻ ◻

With neither old-style community nor new-style shaming to rely
on, Peep culture, the bastard love child of gossip, continues to
get weirder and weirder, further and further removed from the
rules of civility and probity that still govern most face-to-face
interaction. Students shame their teachers, teachers shame their
students, neighbors shame their neighbors, corporations invite
people to shame themselves, and professional shamers troll the
streets, looking for video opportunities to cash in on. The result
is the increasingly ghoulish specter of shame-for-fun intertwined
with for-profit systems that encourage us to shame ourselves and
others. The bizarre story of Mitchell Henderson, a seventh grader
from Rochester, Minnesota, shows just how strange and removed
from what was once considered normal behavior all this can get.
A few years back, a depressed and disturbed Henderson took a
.22-caliber rifle down from a shelf in his parents' bedroom closet
and shot himself in the head. His family mourned and his classmates flocked to the young man's MySpace page where they left
condolences and remembrances, many of them resonant of the
twisted logic of the adolescent set. Wrote one poster: Mitch is "an
hero [sic] to take that shot, to leave us all behind. God do we wish
we could take it back." From there, Mitch's page was linked to
MyDeathSpace.com, a particularly bizarre manifestation of Peep
that finds news reports, obituaries, and whatever else its administrators can archive regarding a person's death, and links them to
the deceased's MySpace page.

Before we get back to Mitch's story, let's linger for a minute on MyDeathSpace—an online community as macabre as it is addictive. I spent several hours on the site, roaming between death notices and MySpace profiles, some festooned with commemorations, others left eerily static. For instance, the site of Melody Corona who, according to DeathSpace, died in her sleep at age seventeen of a Xanax overdose, shows a vibrant young woman—in one photo she playfully flips us the bird—and her own introduction to her life: "THE name is Melody Sunshine Corona. <-- m'hm THAT is my real name, ASKKK ABOUTT ME!! I am only but 17 years old;; but dont judge me by my age, or at all, i grew up fast, if you dont like it "ohhh f*ckin well. i was born && raised here in San Antonio, TX. i no longer attend school;; but im goin for that GED." Her mood is listed as eccentric and the quote above her profile picture reads: "Sometimes it's good thing to have fake people in this world, helps you find out who your real friends are." Melody's real friends have probably long since stopped visiting this eerie digital waxwork. But the rest of us—lurkers looking for the next momentary Peep thrill—well, we'll keep coming.

In fact, we apparently kept coming to Mitch's MySpace page too. A reference to a lost iPod on the page's long list of remembrances titillated some of the people who came via MyDeathSpace to peer in on the proceedings. They latched on to the notion that the seventh grader might have shot himself over a lost iPod and brought that idea to a message board devoted to juvenile pranks and mayhem. Pretty soon, passive Peep entertainment became global malevolence. A picture of an iPod on Henderson's grave was posted to the same message board. Henderson's face was Photoshopped over an image of swirling iPods. His MySpace page was hacked and Henderson was given the face of a zombie. There was even a YouTube video that reenacted Henderson's suicide and included a smashed iPod. The joke went so far as to include crank calls to the Henderson household. When Mitch's dad answered he'd hear, "Hi, this is Mitchell, I'm at the cemetery" or "Hi, I've got Mitchell's iPod."

In the age of Peep, we spread rumor, shame, and gossip like margarine. Plentiful and tasteless, we apply a thick coat of it to everything and anything. Caught in the layers of gooey, whipped oil and permanently preserved, the mundane indignities of everyday life continue on forever, even after our lives have ended. Once we've broken the seal on that giant-sized vat, we don't seem to know when or if we should ever stop. Random pranksters expose the fractured morality of the entire of concept of turning otherwise forgotten moments into a mass-produced spread that covers every surface, melting into the nooks and crannies, coating our teeth, tongue, throats, and bellies, no matter how hard we might chew or how desperately we try to make ourselves disgorge. Connection without expectation creates community without meaning. Night falls on our secrets, and, all alone in my city of millions, I decide, after all, to tear up my postcard.

Watching the Detectives Watching the Neighbors in the Golden Age of Surveillance

Our society is not one of spectacle, but of surveillance. . . . We are neither in the amphitheater, nor on the stage, but in the panoptic machine, invested by its effects of power, which we bring to ourselves since we are part of the mechanism.
—Michel Foucault, *Discipline and Punish: The Birth of the Prison*

Perhaps the greatest challenge now is the possibility of all the citizens surveying each other. It's the kind of thing you can do surveying your neighbor in the backyard.
—Jennifer Stoddart, Privacy Commissioner of Canada, 2008

It was another busy afternoon in SpyTech. I watched discreetly as a young man inspected cameras hidden in teddy bears and clock radios. A chatty fellow wanted to see miniature voice recorders, even though, as he loudly proclaimed, he wasn't planning on buying anything. A woman came in with an elaborate rented apparatus that needed repairs. Her dog had chewed through a wire, putting an abrupt end to a student art project involving cameras affixed to pets. Finally Ursula Lebana, the owner of this midtown Toronto business, managed to break away from a returning customer on the phone who wanted to buy a cell-phone signal jammer (illegal in Canada, she told him) to take my questions. I started out by asking her how things have changed since she opened Canada's first "spy" store back in 1991.

"People who came into the store at that time were quite shocked," Lebana told me. "They never realized that cameras were that small. They said, 'Oh my god, that's scary.' And 'Isn't it terrible to monitor the nanny, where's the trust?'"

But seventeen years later, business is booming.

"Now people say, 'Oh, I want a hidden camera,'" said Lebana, who has since opened SpyTech locations in Ottawa and London, Ontario. "They are more willing to use them now. They're more familiar with it. I'm even getting repeat customers—a girl came in and she had her first baby so now she's monitoring the nanny like her father did sixteen years ago, which is nice."

Cozy stories of intergenerational nanny monitoring aside, there are lots of ways to characterize the ongoing revolution in surveillance technologies and attitudes. "Nice" isn't one of them. But on second thought, maybe Lebana is onto something. In the almost two decades SpyTech that has been selling miniature cameras, micro recorders, and software spying packages, we've gone from fearing Big Brother to wanting to be him. Where's the trust? There isn't any. But don't worry. There's a new world of ubiquitous, self-directed surveillance to make sure we all play nice.

Surveillance is conjoined to Peep culture. Both practices share the idea that seeing all, knowing all, divulging all, is a good thing. Peep emerged from the breakdown of traditional community life and the rise of mass electronic entertainment as a replacement for communal society. Surveillance also emerged from the breakdown of traditional life, and is likewise made possible by technological advances. It's hardly surprising, then, that surveillance and Peep are inextricably intertwined. Here's how it works: An ever increasing amount of the entertainment we encounter daily is derived from other people's lives—from YouTube videos to reality TV, to tabloid exclusives. This material is made possible by the widespread practice of surveillance. Where would all those cheesy Shocking Videos of Wild Women from the Midwest reality TV shows get their material if not for convenience-store security cameras? Meanwhile, the more surveillance is seen as an aspect of mainstream entertainment, the more we incorporate its practices and ideologies into everyday life and, in turn, create our own Peep culture. It all starts with surveillance. If we want to understand Peep culture, we need to understand the way surveillance is spreading from the lobbies of banks to certain crime-ridden street corners, to all street corners, to our own bedrooms, cars, offices, and even day-care centers. Without surveillance, there would be no Peep. And without Peep, it's doubtful that Lebana's SpyTech and an entire industry of prying technologies would be doing such great business aiding and abetting people's need to know everything about everyone around them.

❏ ❏ ❏

"We are selling more than we did ten years ago," Lebana tells me. "Of course," she adds, "prices have come down." Ten years ago, a teddy bear cam cost $1600. Today you can take home your cuddly bear cam for $275, walk away with a pinhole camera for $69, or, if you like, spend a few thousand dollars on a complete, ongoing, permanent surveillance system. "Now people buy more," says Lebana, "and always have it there."

A quick look around the store (and online) supports Lebana's claim. Surveillance cameras are cheap and mainstream. Giant-sized electronics purveyor TigerDirect is selling a "Hi Res Color Outdoor Security Surveillance Video Camera" for $170.99. I can get an "indoor dome camera" for as little as $48.99. I can even get a "color indoor/outdoor camera" for a mere $60.99.

"We say to people, 'See if your spouse is cheating,'" Lebana tells me, explaining her sales pitch. "Because once you put a hidden camera in your house you can find out what's going on. Very popular is our semen detection kit, that's for cheating spouses, you use that on fabric, underwear. It's been around for three or four years now. People come in and ask for that. If you call the police and say someone is vandalizing your property, what can they do? They can't stand outside twenty-four hours a day. So now you have a way to protect yourself, and I think it's a very good thing for people. Cameras are becoming smaller and smaller. They are hidden in smoke detectors, they have motion detectors. We have now a gum-stick camera the size of a stick of chewing gum, [and] the Zippo lighter camera—the quality isn't the highest, that's a gadget for fun."

Lebana didn't start SpyTech almost twenty years ago because she thought there would be a growing market for "fun" gadgets. She started SpyTech because she was running a small business and her employees were stealing from her. She looked into ways to catch the perpetrators, "and I thought that was very interesting, many people in business have these troubles. And I thought if I would have known these products existed I would have used them many times." Lebana, a woman with a keen sense of commerce, plunged into the burgeoning surveillance business. Today she tells me that looking back she not only would have used personal surveillance technologies to monitor her employees, but also her nanny. "Because I had small children and I was divorced. So one of the main things was to have people monitor what the nanny's doing when they are not home, and also to find out who is stealing from the business."

In talking to Lebana, two prevailing themes emerge: the increased availability and ease of use of surveillance technologies, and the ongoing need to protect yourself in a world of instability and hidden threat. The sense of uncertainty and anxiety that pervades our society and makes us feel like we need to protect ourselves with surveillance products is, not coincidentally, also increasingly pervasive in our (Peep) culture. Again we see the symbiosis between surveillance and Peep: the more we watch and record, the more we capture moments of intense drama, and the more those "real life" moments of drama are going to end up as Peep culture entertainment in the form of sensational video clips, photos, broadcasts, and blog posts. The more this dramatic, wildly entertaining material is broadcast, disconnected from its original context and removed from any kind of perspective, the more we think we need to be under surveillance for our security and protection. So it's easy to see why surveillance and Peep are fast becoming best friends forever.

"We have a lot of neighbor problems now," Lebana tells me. "People are more impatient, more aggressive. Sixteen years ago when we opened up, the neighbor problem was loud music and barking dogs, that was basically it. Now it's death threats, it's vandalism, it's nails under the cars, all kind of strange things, and of course [when] the police come you have no proof who did it, but if you have a hidden camera then it's easy. It's very easy to get the evidence."

Lebana recounts the story of a woman who came into the store complaining about someone ripping up her flower beds in the middle of the night. She wanted to find out who was doing it and the police told her to get a camera. "So she stuck a little camera in the window and recorded what was happening. And she saw it was the neighbor. The next day she did the same thing, it was the neighbor again. And she was very upset because she thought they were good friends. We have many, many different stories like that, things going on, it's just unbelievable."

The stories Lebana tells me aren't about catching murderers, jailing pedophiles, or even deterring shoplifting. They're about ugly neighbors, questionable employees, and domestic harassment. There's a story about a woman threatened at home and work. Death threats are stuck to the door of her apartment. The woman comes into Lebana's store asking for help. With the assistance of her brother-in-law, she installs a camera in the hallway of her apartment building to see who's coming to her door. The camera provides a view of the hallway through the peep hole in the door. But the threats continue to show up. So Lebana sends over a technician to install a hidden camera in the exit sign above the hallway. "The next time it happened she recorded on her

VCR what was going on," Lebana tells me, "and she called me, extremely upset. She said she caught the person who was doing it, and it happened to be her brother-in-law. You never know what's going on."

"You never know what's going on." That's the mantra of surveillance in the Peep culture age. Protect yourself because the world is a strange, dangerous place and if you don't look out for number one, no one else will. "Ninety percent of the people who monitored the nanny were not happy with what they saw," Lebana assures me. "As soon as the parents left the house the nanny became a different person, not looking after the kids or the baby very much at all." What's the nanny up to instead? Flipping through magazines, watching TV, stealing, and maybe even abusing the kids she's supposed to be protecting.

Lebana's spiel on the danger of nannies reminds me of a clip I saw on CNN.com, a "news" story in which a mom with a nanny cam rushed home from work after seeing the nanny roughly handling her infant twins. When I dropped by, the story, titled "Nanny Cam Shows Rough Handling," was in the "most viewed" category. The cornerstone of this news report is a short clip of two seven-month-old twin babies being swung by their sleepers onto a couch, where they promptly slump face-down and are left to their own devices. The story might very well have been a commercial for Ursula Lebana's SpyTech. It featured very little information and plenty of "shocking footage," plus, of course, an interview with the teary mom who, luckily enough, was watching the nanny cam via live feed at work and was able to rush home and fire the nanny before . . . well, the kids weren't actually in danger, they just weren't being treated very lovingly. The camera shows them as plump and sedate and destined for what seems like a pretty cushy life, despite the ungentle treatment—in contrast to the many children who starve to death before their first birthday all over this planet. But that's irrelevant. Kids at risk! Fire the nanny! Protect yourself! And don't forget to stick around to see what's coming up next. The message of the story is clear right from the start: people can't be trusted; protect yourself.

In the meantime, the older kids are running wild on the Internet. For this, Lebana sells an array of programs that let you monitor your child's every key stroke. Well it only makes sense. Lebana says: Parents should monitor what their kids do on the Internet. With all the pedophiles now, we've been pushing it— monitor your teenagers. Of course eight to ten years ago now the press would say, 'That's terrible,' but fifty years ago all these problems didn't exist. When kids brought their friends home and there was a bad apple you kicked him out. Now they are doing all these things on the Internet and it's the same thing, you want to screen out all the bad things for them. These kids don't know, they're not that smart yet, and I really think it's very important for the parents to know what's going on.

For every danger Lebana cites, we can think of several high-profile cases that the type of monitoring she peddles might have prevented. In terms of keeping an eye on what your kids are doing online, the obvious case to cite is that of thirteen-year-old Megan Meier, who committed suicide after forty-year-old Lori Drew down the street sought to amuse her daughter, an acquaintance of Megan, by using MySpace to impersonate a hot boy. Mom (with a little coaching) used her hot-boy alter ego to flirt with Megan, then abruptly broke off communication, suggesting in a final message that "the world would be a better place" without her. Already an unhappy, self-conscious teen on antidepressants, Megan hung herself later that day. (The incident, I should note, immediately became Peep-style entertainment when, in another instance of weird double-Peep post-death shaming cruelty, a prankster created a Megan Had It Coming blog which claimed to be by one of the dead girl's classmates. The posts included lines like "Killing yourself over a MySpace boy? Come on!!!! I mean yeah your fat so you have to take what you can get but still nobody should kill themselves over it.")

"It's not people only catching other people doing bad things to them or their business," Lebana assures me. "It's people protecting themselves. We had one case of a bad, bad divorce, very bad blood going back and forth, and the poor guy got arrested several times by the police, his wife accusing him of coming over and beating her up, harassing her, threatening her. He was in jail for a few days. So now he put up a camera in his place, in his room, sitting there watching TV with time and date on it, so the next time this happened the police came over and he said, 'I've been here all night and I've got the proof' and he showed them it. Then the police went over and arrested the woman. So you can protect yourself."

In the absence of community, there is more order but less common ground. Crime in general drops, particularly violent crime. (Despite ongoing hysteria about mass murderers and serial killers, violent crime continues its decline in Western societies.) But smaller insurrections, like stealing from your employer, pretending to be someone else online, or running another car off the road in a fit of road rage, seem to be increasingly endemic. As a result, more and more people are taking matters into their own hands. We vigilantly protect our turf because, well, it's all we really have to call our own at a time when the idea of a shared space, a community commons, has all but disappeared (which is a factor in why we're so angry, even if we aren't quite able to articulate the sorrow at our loss). If someone veers into our lane or lets their dog piss on our tree, we want to know about it. Not only that, we believe we absolutely have a right to know about it. The age of Peep is the golden age of surveillance. Surveillance makes Peep possible, and Peep makes surveillance increasingly permissible. Whether it's surveillance we undertake on our own initiative or surveillance undertaken by police and governments on our behalf, under the auspices of Peep culture, surveillance is protection, deterrent, babysitter, and an ongoing, cheap, and plentiful source of entertainment all rolled into one.

◻ ◻ ◻

Almost every day, surveillance cameras spring up in trouble-spots and bad neighborhood clusters, domed mushrooms pushing their snouts out of shadowy, forgotten crevices. They are everywhere and we've stopped noticing them. An ABC News/*Washington Post* poll conducted in July 2007 found that 71 percent of Americans favor increased video surveillance. Good thing, because in the United States, land of the free, there are an estimated thirty million public and privately operated surveillance cameras creating four billion hours of video a week.

Tacoma, Washington, and Baltimore, Maryland, are largely credited (in the mid-nineties) with being the first large cities to use surveillance cameras as part of their crime prevention plan. The idea was, at the time, to identity particularly crime-ridden areas and put cameras up in them. Cheaper than feet on the street, this was a supposedly effective method of capturing crooks or at the very least scaring them off. No wonder the concept quickly spread. Soon places like East Newark, New Jersey (population 2,000 souls) were responding to what one writer described as "a single violent incident" by installing sixteen rotating surveillance cameras watching over every street in the nine-block borough. The sleepy town of Lyons, New York (population 4,300 and described on its Web site as "the seat of Wayne County and a meeting point between miles of lakeside vistas") is another place that got into the surveillance act. Lyons now has a single camera keeping a watchful eye on its main street.

After September 11, 2001, what was a growing, though still optional trend, became a must-have solution. Cities were provided with billions of dollars to install surveillance systems and improve "homeland security." Both Baltimore and Chicago upgraded their systems considerably with the cash. Chicago had some 500 cameras at the end of the nineties but now has 2,250 cameras in its "Homeland Security Grid," which the Department of Homeland Security helped finance with a $5.1-million grant. Another $48-million grant from Homeland Security is helping the city create a 900-mile fiber-optic grid linked to a $43-million operations center constantly monitored by police officers. Chicago is now using a sophisticated IBM video analytic system that automatically detects abandoned bags and possible suspicious activity, such as a car continually circling the Sears Tower.

Meanwhile, Baltimore has also used federal grants to finance its originally modest camera system and $1.3 million "Watch Center." The cameras are connected to the state's existing highway-monitoring cameras, and the plan is for five counties in Maryland to connect with the city's surveillance system.

Smaller cities are also getting into the act. Urban areas that have added surveillance to their arsenal over the last five or so years include Richmond, California; Spokane, Washington; and Greenville, North Carolina. Minneapolis–St. Paul has 80 percent of its highways under watch courtesy of 2,350 pole-mounted cameras that record footage of intercity traffic as well as key entrance points to the metropolis.

Naturally, New York City and Washington DC are at the center of efforts to upgrade surveillance systems. Washington has a secure command center that allows officials to view twenty-one streaming video feeds from 4,775 surveillance cameras, projected across three screens and monitored at all hours. The plan is to connect these cameras to 5,000 more cameras already in place in the city, including 3,500 cameras in and outside public schools, and cameras currently maintained by the Metropolitan DC police. There are critics of this plan, but, as Councilwoman Muriel Bowser (representing a relatively affluent northern area of the city) puts it: "There's not a meeting or a community that I go into that doesn't tell us how cameras have positively impacted public safety in their neighborhoods."

In July 2007, New York City officials unveiled the "Lower Manhattan Security Initiative," a surveillance plan modeled after

London's "Ring of Steel." The plan includes license-plate readers, automated roadblocks and 3,000 new surveillance cameras,
adding to the 250 already in place. In the spring of 2008, police
acquired a new surveillance weapon: a ten-million-dollar surveillance helicopter that patrols the skies above Manhattan and
allows police "to see and recognize a face from two miles away,
peer inside a building from three to four miles away, and track a
suspect car from twelve miles away."

It's fitting that many U.S. cities are taking their inspiration
from the United Kingdom. The UK leads the Western world in
police closed-circuit television (CCTV) camera use. There are
something like one million publicly operated cameras nation-
wide, watching town squares, highways, and busy shopping
strips. Throw in the private CCTV cameras and you get four
million plus cameras. You also get some pretty crazy numbers,
including the estimate that there is one CCTV camera for every
fourteen Britons and the estimate that the average UK citizen will
be caught on 300 different cameras while going about his or her
day. And all this happened pretty quickly. As one reporter wrote
in the late nineties: "By the end of 1997 more than 450 British
towns had comprehensive street surveillance in place, up from 74
only 3 years earlier." Far from being a hotbed of anti-surveillance
agitation, citizens are by and large sanguine about surveillance.
In fact, after 9/11 and the London Tube attacks, the UK intensified its CCTV program. A Home Office initiative called the Safe
Cities Program was formed, that has since doled out hundreds of
millions of pounds in grants for cities to implement CCTV anti-
crime projects.

Market research firm iSuppli estimates that globally the
surveillance-camera business will be worth $9 billion by 2011, a
near doubling of the industry that did an estimated $4.9 billion in
business in 2006. Clearly American cities aren't the only ones inspired by London's total surveillance infrastructure. Even where I
live, in relatively sedate Canada, a country that remains free from

the scars of terrorist attack, a country that features a declining crime rate and, as Michael Moore made clear in his documentary *Farenheit 911*, where even people in the big city sometimes forget to lock their doors, we've got cameras in our club district, and we've got cameras just a ten-minute bike ride from my house at the intersection of Bathurst and Queen. Meanwhile, in the summer of 2008, while I was working on this book, 10,000 cameras were being installed and activated in Toronto's subways, streetcars, and buses. When the Toronto Transit Commission revealed its surveillance plans, citizens shrugged and went about their business. It took the London, UK, nonprofit group Privacy International to register a complaint. A Canadian Broadcasting Center (CBC) radio producer who attempted to do a radio piece on the police surveillance cameras installed in Toronto's club district told me that he gave up on the project because all the bright-eyed young people he interviewed under the giant, domed cameras were universally positive about the watchful presence of authority. Though nowhere near the UK and U.S. numbers, police surveillance cameras are in use in at least fourteen cities in Canada. In Canada, as in the United Kingdom and United States, polls show general widespread support for surveillance cameras. An Angus Reid poll found that 69 percent of respondents think the devices are necessary, while 21 percent disagree. Sixty-three percent of respondents believe the need for safety trumps individual privacy rights on the topic of surveillance cameras, while 20 percent think individual privacy rights should always come before safety concerns.

Stéphane Leman-Langlois, a University of Montreal criminologist, conducted focus groups in a crime-ridden downtown Montreal neighborhood where CCTV cameras had recently been installed. He was trying to take the pulse of residents regarding how they felt about the cameras invading their space. Not wanting to influence them, Leman-Langlois simply asked residents to discuss their feelings on safety and security. The problem, as

Leman-Langlois tells me, was that the cameras were almost never mentioned unless he directly asked people what they felt about them. They didn't notice them, they didn't think about them, and, if asked, they either dismissed them as irrelevant or cautiously welcomed them, so long as they didn't lead to reductions in the number of actual police patrolling the streets. "The only conclusion about the perception of surveillance," Leman-Langlois ultimately concluded, "is that they don't perceive it. They don't see it as surveillance at all."

In other words, nobody is worrying about surveillance. In fact, the prevailing attitude is that people actually want surveillance.

Okay, saying that *nobody* is worrying is a bit much. There are lots of people worrying. There are think tankers, academics, government appointees, politicians, lawyers, art collectives, and as many paranoids of the polis as you can shake a stick at. It's just that they are on the fringe of North American and, to a lesser extent, Western European opinion. Again and again people make it clear that first and foremost they want to be safe. And if takes surveillance cameras and other surveillance-like applications to keep them (and their property) safe, then go for it.

There are limits, it's true. But even the limits seem to have limits. Polls that take the pulse of America suggest that support for surveillance remains high, even when that surveillance includes what were once considered blatantly illegal domestic interceptions of communications without a warrant, in direct violation of the country's constitutional protections. A 2006 poll reported that 70 percent of respondents "would not be willing to support governmental monitoring of the communications of 'ordinary Americans.'" On the other hand, an almost equal number—68 percent—agreed that monitoring would be fine if it was only directed at "Americans the government is suspicious of." These numbers were evident in the summer of 2008 when the issue of domestic spying returned to Congress, and few noticed or cared. As Congress wrestled with demands from the Bush White House for an extension of domestic spying provisions that the *New York Times* described in an editorial as largely "unnecessary and a threat to the Bill of Rights," the citizenry were elsewhere: worrying about high gas prices and a faltering economy, watching Tiger Woods win yet another U.S. Open, and debating which blockbuster summer movie comic-book character—Iron Man, Hulk, or Batman—could kick the most ass. By the end of summer, a Democratic Congress had approved "the biggest revamping of federal surveillance law in 30 years" and given a widely unpopular lame duck president everything he wanted, including immunity for phone companies that cooperated in the illegal National Security Agency domestic wiretapping program that the White House set in motion after 9/11.

How will it all end? San Francisco's Adam Jackson might give us a clue. After moving into an apartment in the rough Tenderloin neighborhood, Jackson stuck a webcam out his window, set up a Web site, and invited people to log on and watch his intersection. The idea, of course, was for everyone logging on to act as a kind of group neighborhood watch, willing and able to call the police. Two cameras and a microphone recorded twenty-four hours a day, and there was even an adjoining chat room so that people could talk amongst themselves while waiting for moments of excitement. Here we see precisely how surveillance merges with and encourages Peep culture, and vice versa. Though some in the community were pissed off, Jackson's persistence led to the inevitable success of his home surveillance/entertainment system: clips posted to YouTube of fights, car chases, and break-ins swelled the initial small audience to over 500,000 viewers. Now Jackson is planning to take it to the next level—his new site, Ourblock.tv, will provide anyone who has a good view of an intersection with the technology and platform to set up cameras to monitor his or her own street corner.

◻ ◻ ◻

I trailed my wife across the screen. She was heading east at roughly eleven miles per hour. Her latitude was 43.6549307685 and her longitude was 79.4143996015. I watched as a black dot slowly tracked across a Google Map. That's my wife, I thought. She's heading to work, moving briskly through the west side of downtown Toronto. And then she stopped. Why did she stop? A problem with the device? On screen, it's saying that power is 100 percent and GPS accuracy is "excellent." Nothing wrong with the device. She's just—stopped. I stared at the blip on my computer screen. It reloaded and produced her new location: same as her old location. Minutes went by. It's a red light, I thought. But now it's too long to be a red light. So she's run into someone she knows at a red light and they're chatting. No. Accident, I thought. She's been struck by an open door, by one of those arrogant drivers who never thinks to check for bikers before swinging out of his SUV. Yeah, accident. She's been run over by a truck. I grabbed the phone and started dialing her cell. It was five minutes and her dot hadn't moved. Then it moved. She moved. I put down the phone. She's proceeding east again. She's gaining speed. She's clipping along at twelve miles per hour. I felt weirdly elated. She's fine! She's on her way to work! I watched the dot travel along College Street, make a turn, and park itself at, yes, her place of employment. She's arrived, I thought. She's okay.

After a while, my relief turned to annoyance. Why did she stop? What was she doing? I was annoyed that I knew where she was, but not why she was there. Suddenly I was filled with the desire to want to know everything there is to know about the whereabouts of my wife and my child. I'd only been using the device for a day. But the experience of tracking my wife to work was proving itself to be totally addictive. Every hour or so I logged back on and checked on her. She's still there. Still at work. Where else would she be?

When she came home from work, I coyly inquired: "So, how was your trip to work today?" She coyly responded: "Good. Why?" She knew I'd been watching. "I noticed you made a stop," I said in what I figured was my best nonchalant voice. "Oh, did you?" she said. "I was wondering if you'd notice." "I did," I said. "You stopped for five minutes at College and Manning." "True," she said. She wandered off to the kitchen to get a drink. "But," I said, following her, "why did you stop?" "Guess," she said. I guessed. I guessed again. I kept guessing until I was all out of guesses. "Nope," she said. It was driving me crazy. I really wanted to know. The bank, the grocery store, the Starbucks, the American Apparel—all came back with a defiant nope. Finally I remembered another spot along that strip: "The bakery?" My voice came out pleading, begging. "Yup," she said. "I stopped for a tuna sandwich."

She bought a tuna sandwich. It was 12:07:37 when she stopped and 12:12:32 when she started rolling again. That's how long it takes to buy a tuna sandwich. That's how long it takes me to get paranoid. A tuna sandwich. Four hundred dollars of real-time tracking technology to track my wife buying her lunch. She doesn't usually buy lunch. She usually makes lunch. She did it for me, for my benefit, to give me something to look at while I tracked her to work. Lesson one of tracking your loved ones: They will toy with your mind just because they can. Lesson two: tracking makes you paranoid. It turns the ordinary into a big deal. Suddenly you want to know—you think you should know—things that you never got to know before. You didn't know because you didn't think you could know, even if every once in a while you really did want to know. Sure, there are those moments when a loved one isn't answering at work or cell and you think, so where are they? Answer: they're at the bakery getting a tuna sandwich. On rye? On whole wheat? Suddenly you need to know.

My wife was carrying the GPS Snitch in her bag. It's made by a Calgary, Alberta, company and it retails for $399. Brendan

Cook, executive vice president and cofounder of Blackline GPS, the company that makes the Snitch, tells me that the product has multiple uses. It's primarily meant as a preventive device you can hide in your car or boat. You can set the Snitch to send you a text message or e-mail if your vehicle leaves a predetermined perimeter, or if it moves at all. If it's on the move, you'll have no problem tracking it. In one case, a fellow in Miami, Florida, emerged from the shower to find an alert on his cell phone: his motorcycle was on the move without him. He called the police, gave them the real-time location of the bike, which he was tracking online, and seventeen minutes later they had apprehended the thief. There aren't many more stories of how customers are using the Snitch. It's only been on sale for a year, and only recently been available in major Canadian chains like Future Shop. Future Shop is owned by the U.S. chain Best Buy and Cook hopes that the Snitch will soon be sold at Best Buy. In the meantime, U.S. customers can buy the product through specialty shops and online. Cook says that for competitive reasons, he can't divulge exact figures, but the company is approaching 10,000 in terms of the number of units sold. Not a bad number, when you consider the cost of the thing. What else might people be doing with their GPS Snitch? Cook has no shortage of hypothetical uses for the Snitch: for instance, if you're worried about your elderly mother wandering off and getting lost, you could put Snitch in her handbag. If you want to watch over your kid while he's off at school, how about Snitch in his backpack? Snitch also has a social element, Cook tells me. You can invite people to track you. They'll get their own login on the company Web site and can do their own searches. The company also has a deal in place with BlackBerry: you can track your Snitch via your BlackBerry, and you can also share your location with others who install the program Blip, which not only lets you share your Snitch location via BlackBerry, but also lets you track other people who have a GPS-enabled BlackBerry smartphone.

"What about spying?" I ask Cook. I can slip the Snitch into

a car or a handbag and track someone without their even knowing, can't I? "We don't want to see users operating outside of the law," responds Cook, noting that Snitch is marketed exclusively as a personal security and social networking device. But of course Cook can't deny that people could use the device in that way. "We don't want to know in terms of company liability. Technology always has a good and bad side to it, a baseball bat can be used to hurt someone or to play a game. People can use things in a good way or bad way, it always comes down to that. There's a dark side of technology, but for us the benefits far outweigh those risks. As these technologies become more pervasive, it's going to be anyone's product that could be used for darkness or for good."

So what happens if someone calls in and says, "Hey, I found your device in the glove compartment of my car—is someone tracking me?" "It's sort of a double-edged sword when we have someone calling in who says they've found a device in their vehicle. We can't tell them who it belongs to. We can turn off the service. But we need to do to make sure we're not doing that illegitimately either. There's identifying information on the device, so if someone says they are being tracked without their knowledge we have the ability to identify the device."

At the end of the day, the company will do what it can, but its first priority is to protect the buyer, not the person being tracked. Cook urges people to be transparent: he says if you're going to track, say, your teenage daughter when she goes out for the night in the family sedan, you should tell her. Everyone will feel safer and be happier that way. But my own experience using Snitch makes me wonder. Technically the product is a wonder. It works great. But tracking my wife, knowing her physical location at all times, makes me nervous. I'm not feeling happier, and I'm not feeling safer. I'm feeling like the distance between what I know and don't know is greater than ever. I want video. I want to see her. I want to know exactly what she's doing when she's doing it. This isn't a matter of distrust or jealousy. It's a matter of a little knowledge making me want a little more knowledge. Snitch enables me to track, but there's not much I can do about what I see. I could call her cell phone to make sure she's all right, but she never answers her cell phone anyway. I could call the police or the paramedics, but what would I tell them? "My wife was biking to work and she stopped for five minutes and, well, I'm pretty sure she's been run over by a truck?" I'm reduced to pleading with her to tell me where's she been when she gets home from work. Spying on your wife (even with her full knowledge and consent) isn't all it's cracked up to be. By the end of the week, I was a nervous wreck, thinking about all the things that could happen to her as she moved to and fro, biking, walking, taking the bus, and otherwise going about her perfectly safe, everyday life.

Snitch is part of a growing trend toward "location-based services." According to William Clark, a researcher at the technology consulting firm Gartner, about 43 million people worldwide will use location-based services on cell phones in 2008, almost triple the16 million from 2007. Gartner sees big money ahead for products like Snitch, Loopt, and other services that take advantage of the predominance of GPS in handheld devices like the BlackBerry smartphone and the iPhone. The revenue generated is expected to go from $1.3 billion in 2008 to $8.1 billion by 2011. One example of many is the iPhone application WhosHere, that lets you connect and chat with everyone signed up for the service who is geographically near you. As of January 2009 it already had over 200,000 users. Similarly, in early 2009 Google launched a feature called Latitude that allows users to have their location pop up on Google Maps wherever they may be. You invite people to track you and they can do so on the iPhone, the BlackBerry, and a whole bunch of other devices. There are, in fact, so many new "geoapps" that there's already a service that broadcasts your location to all of them at once, helpfully sending our your location instantly to everything from Facebook to Twitter, to a variety of other, nascent services like

Outside.in, Loki, and BlogLoc (automatic updates of your physical location to your blog). So if you do it right, you can basically set up your phone to instantly track you all the time. Lest you be wary of such specificity, another service, Fire Eagle, saves you the trouble of bouncing from site to site, telling each one where you are by providing location updates to all at once. It also lets you decide if you want people to know exactly where you are or just generally where you are (a neighborhood or city). Also, and I'm not sure if this provides comfort or more confusion, you can manually input a location even if you're not there—as Tom Coates, founder of Fire Eagle, explains: "You have to have the ability to lie about your location."

In the very near future, millions of people will start reflexively monitoring themselves, their loved ones, and their property (including their pets). Add in the explosion in use of personal surveillance equipment like the kind Ursula over at SpyTech sells, and you've got a picture of a North American civilization in the full sway of a domestic surveillance renaissance.

This ongoing renaissance takes many different forms. My wife and I recently had dinner with a couple who have an eight-month-old son. The baby is in day care, because the couple both work full-time. They specifically chose a day-care provider that offers a surveillance component—a webcam over the play area. So now they can log into a password-protected site whenever they want to and watch their kid go about his day. Day-care surveillance is another growing phenomenon that may soon become de rigeur as parents become more and more wired. According to the president of WatchMeGrow, a U.S.-based maker of day-care surveillance systems, over 400 day care providers in the United States already have such technologies in place. While we ate, I asked the couple how they had made the decision that their day care absolutely had to have a webcam. Turns out that Mom works in mental health with, among others, convicted child abusers, many of whom had themselves been sexually abused as children. She's seen the horror and the harm, and doesn't want anything like that to ever happen to her kid. Having the webcam is just one more bit of insurance. How do they use the camera? They check it often, as much as possible. Another couple with a child told me a revealing anecdote about how much people want to use this kind of service: the day-care provider actually had to send out a request to parents to log off. So many people were logging on for the entire day, that the bandwidth was being used up and other parents weren't able to check in on their little ones. Anyway, back to dinner. One time, Mom tells me, she noticed that when the other kids were sleeping, the staff weren't playing with her little boy, who, as the youngest kid and on his own unique sleep schedule, was wide awake. She talked with the day-care director about what she saw, noting that this was the one time of the day that her kid could have the full attention of the staff and get individual stimulation. The day-care director agreed with her, of course. But on the other hand, I thought to myself as she told the story, it's also the only time of the day that the generally underpaid, hard-working day-care staff get a bit of break. It's understandable that they aren't rushing to play with the one kid who won't go to bed during their brief hour of relative peace and quiet.

Domestic surveillance, when it isn't making us paranoid, can also make us judgmental. In many cases, there's no right or wrong to a situation, just one's ability to interpret it in a certain direction. Relatively new parents are going to see things exclusively in terms of the well-being of their child. That doesn't mean that what they see isn't valid, it just means that, as with all kinds of surveillance, the actual situation is in the eye of the beholder. Partial information makes it easy for us to make assumptions. We don't have the full story. The world isn't wired for sound, video, and satellite tracking twenty-four hours a day. Not yet it isn't, anyway.

After a week, I was exhausted from Snitching on my wife's

travels. It takes a lot of mental energy to watch someone you love go about their day. I've got a vivid imagination. Anything can happen. Anything can be happening. The truth is, I was happier not knowing. What's the saying? Ignorance is bliss.

❏ ❏ ❏

However, ignorance is a dumb way to do business. Nowhere is the need to watch and be watched more prevalent than in the workplace. The rise of industrial capitalism and wage labor brought with it an obsession with watching the workers. Are they slacking? Can they be made to move quicker? Productivity is the name of the game, and productivity is not going to happen by closing your eyes and not wanting to know. As the twentieth century dawned, so too dawned a new age of employee-employer relations would be defined by the American Charles Taylor, who developed the notion of "scientific management." Note the way the rubric of science was invoked. This is the proper way to go about things, the scientific and orderly way to turn secrets and gossip into indisputable knowledge which can be acted upon and used to improve any given situation. Both Taylor and his counterpart, fellow assembly-line enthusiast Henry Ford (whose theories also have a moniker: Fordism), ruminated on and implemented methods to improve worker productivity through the division of labor and the close observation of exactly what the workers were doing and how they were doing it. When thinking about how these masters of industry went about improving productivity, I'm always reminded of the work of Eadweard Muybridge, an Englishman living in San Francisco who, in 1877, developed a whole new photographic method at the behest of the rich former governor of California, Leland Stanford. Stanford hired Muybridge to determine whether or not all four of a horse's hooves leave the ground when the animal is in full gallop. In these relatively early days of photography, Muybridge developed an ingenious system of twenty-four cameras electronically triggered when the horse galloped through wire stretched across a track. His photographs captured each separate motion a horse made in the process of a single gallop. He proved that horses do indeed leave the ground for an instant, and in doing so he changed the way we understand our ability to look at the world around us.

We are the horses. Today the rise of a workplace Peep culture that demands constant observation, that demands and compels the revealing of secrets even as those revelations make us all feel somehow more lonely than we really are, is largely complete. In 1987 experts put the number of clerical workers having their computers monitored at between 20 and 40 percent. By 2005, it was reported that "more than two-thirds of US firms now engage in electronic monitoring." A 2005 survey by the American Management Association and the ePolicy Institute found that 36 percent of companies monitor workers on a keystroke-by-keystroke basis; 55 percent review e-mail messages, and 76 percent monitor Web sites visited. Workers can expect to have their keystrokes recorded, their surfing histories examined, and their e-mails scrutinized. If they are in possession of company cell phones, they can expect to have their calling patterns monitored and their whereabouts examined and compared to receipts. And in all cases, should their activities prove to be not in the interest of the company, they can expect to be fired. Indeed, in just one case of many, a veteran worker was fired by the New York City Public Schools after cell phone records indicated he was cutting out early from work. Workplace monitoring is all the rage even if you don't work in an office environment. Freelance-for-hire Web site Odesk.com requires that those bidding on jobs install the Odesk software on their computer. This "proprietary work-management software records random screenshots, keystrokes, mouse moves, even webcam images—and then sends these electronic tattletales back to contractors." New York city cabbies are currently suing the city for ordering mandatory GPS units to be installed in cabs, an order that they claim is unconstitutional, an invasion of their privacy, and a potential portal into a murky world dominated by trade secrets the cabbies have no desire to give up. (But why should there be secrets when there can be clarity and revelation? This lawsuit neatly mirrors a mass strike of Cleveland cabbies in the 1920s after it was ordered that all cabbies in the city had to be fingerprinted by the police.) Glenn Derene, a reporter writing for *Popular Mechanics*, notes that giant corporations increasingly rely on a handful of companies who specialize in electronic monitoring of employees. "These programs and machines are constantly scanning every packet of data moving across a company's network, sniffing for suspicious patterns and keywords while logging any events that could prove to be a threat. Companies that use software such as Guidance's Encase and competing products from Deepdive, Paraben and Kroll Ontrack employ security professional . . . who have the proper codes and permissions to look into almost anyone's workplace computer." Another commentator writing about workplace monitoring notes that theft and fraud cost American stores $41.6 billion in 2006, an all-time high. Employee activity accounts for a full half of that total. So can you really blame the employers for wanting to know what their employees are up to? The article goes on to describe New York–based grocery store Pathmark's use of a product called Storevision that installs up to 120 cameras in the stores and allows higher-ups to log in via webcam to check out what's happening in the stores in real time. Even the vegetables are being monitored: over one hundred cameras watch over operations of Michigan's Chase Farms, which not only lets them monitor workers but also provide customers with "video updates" of their orders.

As we've already seen, surveillance in the name of security encourages and legitimizes Peep culture. Well, guess what? Surveillance in the name of productivity functions in much the same way. The more we're used to being watched in the workplace, the more we're likely to incorporate similar techniques into our domestic lives. And, as always, the more cameras there are pointed to quasi-public areas like grocery stores, malls, and offices, the more likely it is that something crazy, weird, and exciting will be caught on camera to be sold to the highest bidder or find its way onto any number of Web sites.

Surveillance is never just the cold-blooded methodical record of what went on. It's always open to interpretation, to human foible, to the weaknesses, desires, hopes, dreams, and egos of the people behind and in front of the camera. Behind the urge to efficiency and the surge in workplace surveillance are people. Flawed, mercurial, unpredictable people. In the course of researching this book, a fellow from Los Angeles currently studying for an MBA at a UK university got in touch with me. He told me that he was going to recount a story from his past, a story he hadn't told anybody else. I got the feeling he was groping toward some kind of understanding of what strange forces might have caused him to do what he did. This gentleman asked me not to identify him by name or use the name of the company involved. When you hear what he told me, you'll see why.

I'll call him Rich. When Rich was twenty-four he worked for a production company in Los Angeles. The company had around one hundred employees. Rich was the only IT guy at the company. As he put it, "I was in charge of anything with a plug." Among other things Rich was asked to do was back up the company e-mails, particularly the e-mails of his two bosses, who were getting upwards of 1,000 messages a day and worried about losing their laptops and subsequently all their correspondence. Anyway, Rich, who at this point had been working at the company for about a year, was backing up e-mails when he noticed a message concerning him. The e-mail, from one boss to the other, suggested that they should fire Rich. "So I saw that and I got really pissed off," Rich told me. "They had always said, 'Everything is fine, everything is fine.' So I did a search through all the e-mail for my name. And I saw it was coming up quite often, some cases it was great, but in many cases it was bad, bad attitude." Rich starts to feel paranoid, as if, he tells me, his "job could just disappear." To calm his paranoia he began reading more and more e-mail. "Once you cross the line, why not read all this stuff? I'm reading personal e-mails between the bosses, about other people in the company, so it was, like, very strange." It got stranger. Rich soon started reading the e-mails of all the employees in the company, and not just the ones that pertained to him. "I started reading other people's e-mails, coworkers', about dating and stuff. The world I was seeing in these e-mails was totally different from the reality sitting around me. In the middle of this I had a coworker who was about three years older and I had a massive crush on her and we were flirting via e-mail and one day I sent her a really risqué message." The comment was a mistake, Rich tells me, a serious misread of their relationship. She stopped talking to him and also complained to her boss about the message. "Then on the boss's e-mails I find this e-mail chain saying that the IT guy is going beyond his role, and her supervisor said, 'I can understand it because of the way she dresses.' And then it went up to the next guy who said, 'I don't think the supervisor is adequately address-ing the problem.' And then the bosses are laughing their heads off and one of them said, 'You know he could really do much better.'"

In little ways, Rich started to flaunt the power he had over everyone else in the company. He sets up computer terminals for new employees before he's even been told they are starting. He warns another employee that he's about to get fired. He uses his access to advance his career and impress the bosses, and to control situations he is threatened by. "I was dating a girl in the company and I would read her e-mails and I would see other guys in the office pursuing her, and I would use that preemptively. On Friday I'd be like, 'Hey let me show you a new spot,' so she wouldn't go to happy hour with the guy hitting on her." I asked Rich what it felt like to have the power to penetrate the private correspondence of others without them knowing. He told me it was addictive, almost impossible to stop. "It was like a reality show, because, I mean, it's natural that when we perceive that things affect us and they're out of control we tend to want to control them if we can." Rich discovered, among other things, that an important figure in the company was surreptitiously looking for another job: "So I sat there for months watching this guy search out jobs and on the other side I'd read the next level up and they'd say 'Oh god, I think he's looking, we have to give him more money, but when I asked the recruiters we know they said he wasn't in touch.' Which was funny because he was in touch with them."

But Rich wasn't enjoying his privileged position. In fact, it was stressing him out. He couldn't sleep. He was drinking too much. He was getting more and more anxious as he saw his name bandied about by the bosses via e-mail, one boss hating him, the other defending him. Did Rich ever think that what he was doing was wrong and that he should stop? "We're conditioned to respect people's privacy, so initially it felt like such a big step into this place of moral ambiguity. But once you start doing it—. I remember one time at a conference this IT guy told me he had everyone in this company's e-mail forwarded to him and he used tags and he said he was using it to get ahead and always know what was coming. Even if you don't want it to impact your behavior it does. You get really paranoid and hypersensitive; there's this self-monitoring that goes on; you can respond a certain way and see what they write to someone else, so you can see how they see you, which is an incredibly powerful thing. But once I got away from it, when I look back I have these very convoluted memories of drama. I do remember trying to stop but it was almost one of those thing where I've already done it, why would I stop?"

Things started to come to a head when Rich encountered some quasi-legal accounting practices that the bosses didn't know about. "The accountants were going back and forth about some money they had lost and you get the tone that this may not be the most legal thing to do." Rich was really starting to lose it. His time at the company was drawing to a close. "You end up with this accurate appraisal of the situation but you can't say anything to anyone so you have to carry it around on your own. And it's very much one of those situations where once you open yourself up to knowing something you can't un-know it, it's going to have an impact on your behavior, what you do and how you do it."

Rich left the company and no one was ever the wiser. But Rich knows what he's done, and how it's changed him. He's a bearer of other people's secrets, and that comes at a cost. Who can he confess to? Who will carry his secret around and, in that way, absolve Rich of a "crime" that seems increasingly prevalent, even commonplace?

"It was a big lesson never to do it again. I've had the opportunity on many occasions since, and it's just not worth it. I had a girlfriend whose actions became very erratic and she'd use my computer and I had access to her e-mail and one day I loaded up her e-mail box but it was almost this immediate response where I got really anxious and nauseous. I opened her e-mail box and I was like, 'at some point you have to draw a line,' and I didn't read them. Once you enter that world you're basically giving the information power over you, it can really influence your way of seeing reality. I told the girl and she was like, 'You know I read your journal once and I wasn't happy that I did.'"

All our lives we feel watched. But that sense of being overseen gives us no comfort. We're watched by doctors, teachers, officials, the tax man. And they in turn are watched. And those who watch them are watched. Secrets are revealed, but nobody talks, and we remain alone on an increasingly crowded planet. Efficiency always breaks down when it comes in contact with humanity. As with the totality of the Peep culture phenomenon, surveillance never seems to show *only* what is needed, or *just* want it is wanted. It infiltrates our world view and entices us to go further than we intended.

❏ ❏ ❏

We'd like to believe that the rise of surveillance, precursor and now enabler of the rise of a full-scale Peep culture, is temporary. Surely our rampant use and overuse of surveillance technologies is only momentary. Surely it, like Peep culture generally, will soon play itself out. After all, the United States, founded by rabble rousers and persecuted religious minorities, has traditionally been a country resistant to government incursions into the lives of others. In the past, Americans have not been very interested in things like the census, passports, and national identification cards (coming soon to Britain and already in wide use in a variety of European countries). It wasn't until 1930 or so before the government could confidently say that 90 percent of the births in the country were actually being officially noted. Before 1914 there was no such thing as a U.S. passport and it wasn't until the 1950s that American citizens actually had to show the passport before being allowed to reenter the country. When the U.S. military proposed the fingerprinting of its soldiers in the mid-1910s (for identification purposes), there was a public outcry that prompted the *New York Times* to beg for people to temper their outrage: "The world, like the army, is full of cruel wrongs and bitter insults for those who look for them, but why manufacture more out of nothing—or of easily tolerable things like having one's picture and fingerprints on record?"

Similarly, the U.S. public has traditionally been wary of anything resembling a national identification card. The 1935 Social Security Act establishing the Social Security number system was virulently attacked by both the Right and Left, as pundits worried out loud about people being forced to wear ID tags and the government establishing a system of "snooping and tagging." The *Boston American* warned: "Your personal life will be laid bare, your religion and the church you attend will be listed. Your physical defects will go down in black and white. . . . Your union affiliation will be stated . . . even your divorce, if you have one, will be included."

The Social Security number system was implemented, of course, but not before laws were put in place controlling who can ask for your number and what they are allowed to do with it. At any rate, with Hitler prowling Europe and the rise of Stalin in the USSR, the priorities of the day quickly shifted. In Germany and the USSR, the government was controlling every aspect of people's lives. The fascist and communist police states were the complete opposite to everything America and its allies stood for. A war was in the offing and no matter how hard the United States tried to stay out of it, when the country did finally join in, the prevailing tone was a moral one: Fight for freedom or risk enslavement to totalitarianism. These stark contrasts were best expressed in George Orwell's futuristic novel *1984*. Published in 1949, the book became as close a thing to an instant classic as there will ever be. People immediately hailed the book as a visionary masterpiece, an enduring warning against the all-knowing, all-seeing state. The book was also an obvious reaction to the legacy of the Nazis (who harnessed the computing power of IBM to track down even Jews whose parents had converted to Christianity before they were born), and the picture of life gradually emerging from the Soviet Union. Britons loved the book, and so did Americans. As the original reviewer of *1984* wrote in the *New York Times*, "It is probable that no other work of this generation has made us desire freedom more earnestly or loathe tyranny with such fullness." Throughout the Cold War, Americans would hold the view that surveillance was something that totalitarian foreign powers (generally ones of a Communist persuasion) did. Surveillance was considered the repressive tool of alien nations where citizens were forbidden from saying out loud how miserable they were.

But the fall of the Berlin Wall and the breakup of the Soviet Union changed the collective perception of surveillance as something "they" use to control and repress. A new evil was emerging: fundamentalist terrorists. Americans, most famously suspicious of authority, so stubbornly individualistic that the country still lacks the state-overseen universal health care that is a given in every other Western democracy, began to embrace surveillance as a damn good idea. Conventional wisdom has it that 9/11 was behind this shift. Suddenly, even the tapping of citizens' phones without a warrant was found by the majority to be a good idea. It's hard to believe that such a consensus could have been achieved even in the Cold War fifties, let alone the sixties of Lawrence Ferlinghetti and Dr. Martin Luther King (both dangerous Americans to the FBI) or the seventies of Vietnam and Watergate.

Obviously the attacks on U.S. soil by foreign-born terrorists made us rethink just how much we were willing to give up to feel safe. And obviously the idea that the enemy is hidden inside us, as opposed to bristling with nukes just over the border, gave internal surveillance a credibility it never had before. But look carefully and you'll find that surveillance of people on U.S. soil by American authorities was widespread and prevalent in the years leading up to 9/11. Cities like Baltimore launched their CCTV camera programs a good six or seven years before the fall of the Trade Centers. Employee monitoring didn't skyrocket because of 9/11. Rich didn't feel entitled to peep on his coworkers via surveillance of their e-mails because of the "war on terror." Something was in the air well before those ill-fated planes took flight. Books about Big Brother USA watching its citizens are coming fast and furious. Titles like *The Right to Privacy* by Ellen Alderman and (none other than) Caroline Kennedy (1997), *Invasion of Privacy* by Louis R. Mizell (1998), and *Surveillance Countermeasures: A Serious Guide to Detecting, Evading, and Eluding Threats to Personal Privacy* (1994) were all written well before 2001. The privacy/surveillance panic culminated in the millennial year of 2000 with two books both called *The End of Privacy*, one by Reg Whittaker and one by Charles J. Skyes, plus Clay Calvert's *Voyeur Nation* (2000). All published before 2001, and all offering everything from sober to hysterical analysis of our loss of freedom as a result of the intersecting spheres of government and corporate monitoring of private citizens.

According to a block-by-block survey conducted by the American Civil Liberties Union in 1998, New York City already had almost 3,000 surveillance cameras trained on public spaces well before 2001. And guess what? It was 1999 when the city council of Everett, Washington (population 100,000) voted to spend $200,000 to buy eight surveillance cameras to monitor their downtown. And it was in the years before 9/11 that the FBI spent something close to $10 million building their own e-mail intercept system, Carnivore. (The FBI later admitted to using the technology about twenty-five times between 1998 and 2000 before scrapping it for cheaper, easier-to-use systems.) An article written in Manchester's *Guardian* in 2000 started out by proclaiming, "Governments all over the world have suddenly become embroiled in controversy about electronic surveillance of the Internet." From there the piece named names, exposed secret international cooperation, and indicted countries as diverse as the United States, Netherlands, France, and Australia, all of them enthusiastic about finding covert ways to increase their digital monitoring powers in defiance of the stated preferences of elected officials and national constitutions.

This stuff was already happening. We were already ignoring it or even approving of it. Sure, blame 9/11. That's the easy way out. But are the customers flocking to SpyTech because they think their neighbors are nuke-wielding nutcases? David Lyon is head of the Surveillance Project at Queens University in Kingston, Ontario. In 1994 he wrote a book called *The Electronic Eye*, which, as he tells me, deals with the "sociologically interesting, politically questionable, and ethically challenging question" of "how personal material gets processed." The British-born Lyon has been studying surveillance for a good twenty years. Until recently his work was pretty much only read by similar-minded lefty academics. But lately there's been an explosion of sociological and criminological research in surveillance—whether or not it stops crime (mostly it doesn't, but that's a whole different book), how it works, how it effects people's perceptions of their communities, how it intersects with issues of race and class. Lyon has found himself sought out by the Canadian and British governments, as well as various private think tanks and nonprofit organizations, to share what he knows about surveillance. When I sat down with the lanky, soft-spoken professor, my first question was an obvious one: "Is it all just because of 9/11? If the twin towers were still standing, would we be so willing to incorporate more and more surveillance into our daily lives?"

"I come down very much on the side of 'it would have happened anyway,'" Lyon tells me without hesitation. As far as this veteran of surveillance research is concerned, everything we are seeing now was well underway before Osama bin Laden became a household name. But surely, I say, 9/11 had an effect? "September 11 accelerated it," Lyon agrees. "And it gave an opportunity to all kinds of fields. The biometrics industry was not in good shape before 2001. By September 12 biometrics just went ballistic and the kinds of questions, critical, doubtful, that were being asked about biometrics somehow were muted. [September 11] was a huge impetus to generally military-industry-based surveillance technologies."

Similarly, University of Iowa–based thinker Mark Andrejevic writes in his book *iSpy* that while, yes, "the war on terror is a historically unique formation," it is "perhaps no more destabilizing and threatening than the combination of the cold war, the Vietnam war, and the forms of international terrorism that characterized the early 1970s." He goes on to argue that what makes the "war on terror" feel different is that it takes place in the "digital enclosure," his term to describe "the creation of an interactive realm wherein every action and transaction generates information about itself."

The digital enclosure, Andrejevic writes, is "a place in which submission to monitoring becomes an increasingly pervasive part of everyday life in all its facets." This, again, is a kind of "it would have happened anyway" argument—the "digital enclosure" was already in place in 2001, and, as the *Guardian* exposé and the FBI's Carnivore program show us, the almost reflexive monitoring of that enclosure was already becoming commonplace early in the new millennium.

Okay, so we know where the shift didn't come from (though 9/11 undeniably helped, particularly by shoving anyone skeptical or critical of surveillance technologies out of the room). So where *did* it come from? Lyon links two phenomena together. First he talks about what he calls "responsibilization": "The whole shift from government responsibility for the disadvantaged to making the individual responsible for him- or herself regardless of the circumstances. That's a crucial shift. That has to do with the decline of state welfare and, in criminology, the responsibilization of the local citizen. It's not the police responsibility, it's your responsibility, you've got to protect yourself."

Alongside this, Lyon talks about the rise of surveillance as part of everyday life—a commercial adjunct that at once encourages and makes possible today's Peep culture. "This stuff is everywhere," Lyon tells me. "The TV culture is tremendously important, that idea that we deserve our fifteen minutes of fame. The fact that people want to act up in front of surveillance cameras, want to be on YouTube, seems to be to be something we dare not forget: we are thinking about the screens on which personal data are running across all day long, but at the same time our goal is to ourselves be on the screen. People desire to be on the screen."

◻ ◻ ◻

For David Lyon, television encourages surveillance and surveillance encourages televised Peep culture, and it all happens in an expanding vacuum of "responsibilization"—the strategy of encouraging people to fill the gaps in, say, the surveillance network, by setting up their own surveillance networks to watch their kids, spouses, neighbors, employees, and properties. For Lyon, this tautological and increasingly inescapable system works well, at least in part, because of just how good surveillance looks on television. On TV, surveillance protects you, catches bad guys, and keeps you wildly entertained (convenience store shoot-outs, high school cat fights, elevator sex caught on tape, world's wildest police chases). As art history professor Branden W. Joseph writes:

> Television and the surveillance camera form two of the system's most emblematic poles. If surveillance, by optical means or otherwise, is the means of entry into the system, the manner in which the information is provided or more typically, unknowingly, extracted for aggregation, the television screen (and now the computer monitor), is the system's primary outlet, the interface through which the audience receives the information by now processed and targeted as a particular view of the world.

And just what is that "particular view of the world"? Whether it is through nightly news, reality TV, or scripted dramas, the media at large depict widespread individual, corporate, and governmental surveillance as indispensable to our safety, security, and good times. News broadcasts reaffirm the efficacy of surveillance by making its imagery a nightly staple. After the news, any number of dramatic, scripted television serials add to our sense that criminal masterminds roam the streets, and only the conviction of a few good cops with, thankfully, an unlimited budget for high-tech surveillance gadgets, keep horror and anarchy at bay. Reality TV adds to the mix and helps keep us off balance (and sometimes even genuinely frightened) by blurring re-creations and fictions with news and surveillance footage to create highly effective, at times bone-chilling, verisimilitude. In all cases, we are repeatedly exposed to the same two ideas: 1) it's especially enjoyable to watch people do things on camera when they don't know they are being filmed; 2) the ability to secretly watch and record people is an essential tool to maintain law and order. Conflate these two ideas and you've got Peep culture. Surreptitious watching is not only prime-time mainstream entertainment, it's good for you, too! Secret recording not only catches bad guys, it opens up a potential portal for us to access the media universe we're otherwise excluded from. Who knows? We might be on TV right now! But unlike the hapless protagonist of *The Truman Show*, we won't be angry about it. We'll love it and wish it never had to end. Only the bad apples amongst us average citizens fear surveillance. They're the ones who aren't playing by the rules. They'll get caught, probably while we're watching. Stay tuned. It's inevitable. There's nowhere left to hide.

There's always been an element of Peep in hysterical news reports about crime that, for at least the last hundred years, have gone well beyond what the public needs to know about a particular incident. Newspaper publishers figured out long ago that crime sells like nothing else (especially in the era before global celebrity and the ensuing ratings success of celebrity crime). In her book *Froth and Scume: Truth, Beauty, Goodness and the Ax Murder in America's First Mass Medium*, Andie Tucher traces the invention of what she dubs "mass voyeurism" all the way back to the penny presses of the 1830s. To be exact: 1836, the year that, as Tucher tells us in a 1985 *New York Times* article, "James Gordon Bennett, determined to make his *New York Herald* the best-selling penny newspaper in the city, achieved this goal with help of a lurid and exhaustive coverage of the ax-murder of a prostitute." Bennett was perhaps taking his lead from an 1823 edition of the *Illustrated London News*, which spared no expense in chronicling a particularly nasty murder scenario, using five illustrations, including several of "the scene of the murder" and the "pond in which the body was found."

When Charles Dickens's character Martin Chuzzlewit, from

the novel of the same name, stepped off a steamer from England into the New York harbor, he was immediately accosted by a mob of newspaper vendors: "Here's this morning's New York Sewer. Here's this morning's New York Stabber. Here's this morning's New York Private Listener. Here's the New York Peeper. Here's the New York Plunderer. Here's the New York Keyhole Reporter, cry the street vendors, promising juicy tales of the 'last Alabama gouging case; and the interesting Arkansas dooel with Bowie knives . . . the Sewer's own particulars of the private lives of all the ladies that was there.'"

Ah, crime and sex, sex and crime. When famous orator and moralist Reverend Henry Ward Beecher was brought to trial in an 1875 adultery case (he was exposed by free-love proponent Victoria Woodhull as a hypocrite, after she revealed that he was having an affair with a member of his congregation), nearly every U.S. newspaper covered the trial and some printed daily transcripts. The first newspaper edition carrying news of the deadlocked verdict hit the streets fourteen minutes after it was announced.

Things were just getting going. By the 1920s, papers were able to incorporate the widespread use of photography into their product. Now sensationalism could hit new heights or, depending on how you look at it, sink to new lows. One paper, the *New York Evening Graphic*, pioneered a technique we'd see later on television. They called it the "composograph" and it featured staged scenes—some involving staff members of the tabloid—reenacting events such hangings or medical operations. But, of course, real was still preferable. In 1928 Tom Howard brought a miniature camera taped to his left ankle into a New York penitentiary electrocution room to capture the moment that 2,200 volts of current shot through the body of notorious murderer Ruth Snyder. The resulting photograph, grainy and ghostly, was splashed across the front page of the *New York Daily News* under the single-word headline "Dead!" The paper sold one million extra copies that day. The next day the *Daily News* printed a similar picture under the headline "Funeral Held." (Sixty years later, *60 Minutes* would go one step better when it showed footage of Dr. Jack Kevorkian assisting a chronically ill patient to end his life.) Writes Clay Calvert, excoriating voyeurism in America in his book *Voyeur Nation*: "Regardless of precisely which era—penny press, yellow journalism, or jazz journalism—one pinpoints for the origin of modern-day, reality based electronic voyeurism in the United States, it should be clear from this brief history that sensational, mediated voyeurism . . . is not new."

With the public's appetite already well developed, early TV immediately plunged into the dramatics of—what else?—law and order, criminals and their pursuers. Westerns like *Gunsmoke*, which started on radio then ran on CBS TV for a solid and astounding twenty years (1955–75) are the forerunners of the cop show to come. Matt Dillon is U.S. marshal for Dodge City, Kansas, during the wild West days of the 1880s. He has to preserve law and order, but, like Lieutenant Caine of *CSI Miami*, sometimes it all gets to be too much for him. As the series evolved, viewers were increasingly permitted access to his emotional life, to the painful reality of endless gunplay and declining morality. Viewers could see, right before their eyes, the lawman evolving from a stereotype of brawny reassurance to a figure of fascination, not least because, as an authorized killer, he was only one step away from criminal depravity himself. "We made him a man with doubts, confused about the job he had to do," CBS vice president Hubbell Robinson said of the character. "He wondered whether he really had to do that job."

The western blended into the cop show, and the cop show sought to achieve emotional pull by depicting not one-dimensional characters but complex portraits of "real" people dealing with the "real" horrors of crime, poverty, and life on the street. The technique, early on, was to focus on "truth" through the re-creation of actual events, thus avoiding censorious accusations that TV writers were conjuring up hellish scenarios and giving people sick ideas. Plus, as the penny press of the previous century had demonstrated, truth sells. So *Dragnet* was "based on the actual case files of the Los Angeles police department." The show focused on the meticulous police work necessary to collar a criminal. Sound familiar? *Dragnet* is the obvious precursor to today's breed of technique-obsessed cop shows, programs that eschew gunplay for the "reality" of computer searches and lab tests. As in those shows, Jack Webb, as *Dragnet*'s Sergeant Joe Friday, wants "just the facts, ma'am," as he deals with catching a child beater, tracking down stolen white rats injected with a deadly plague, and breaking up a high school porno ring.

 Dragnet isn't the only show claiming to be rooted in fact. The 1959 program *The Untouchables* featured Robert Stack as mob-busting federal agent Elliot Ness. The show used a documentary-style narrative approach to its storytelling technique. Particularly interesting was the use of radio personality and columnist Walter Winchell as voice-over narrator. His authoritative voice, connected as it was to news and real events of the day, gave the show its air of gravitas and immediacy while allowing it to push the boundaries of what was permitted on network television, in the name of authenticity. Wrote a reviewer in *Variety* at the time: "Violence and sex become legitimate qualities of adult fare when the story is realistic and believable, and that's the charm of the quasi documentary technique with a series that bases more or less on fact."

 In other words, the formula works. Fact is better off as fiction. Or is it that fiction is better off couched in fact? "There are eight million stores in the Naked City," ends the first cop show to be shot on location in New York City. "This has been one of them." *Naked City* ran from 1958 to 1963. A show aspiring to similarly seedy authenticity, *77 Sunset Strip*, also launched in 1958, with a pilot called "Girl on the Run." The program featured the antics of a nineteen-year-old sociopath who combed his hair before murdering his victims. He so intrigued watchers that he became a staple on the series. *Kojak*—played by the bald Telly

Savalas from 1973 to 1978—started with a three-hour pilot based on the brutal 1963 "Career Girl Murders" of Manhattan's Upper East Side. The pattern of adapting a real story and providing audiences ways into the interior lives of terrifying main characters (cops, criminals, or, increasing and most fascinatingly, both at the same time) whose lives are dominated by violence and fetish, has now been firmly established. Bad guys watch victims, cops watch criminals, and we get to watch everyone from our not-as-safe-as-we-might-think position on the rec room chesterfield.

The eighties and nineties strove for more realism, more emotional pain, more gore, and of course more sex and violence. Shows like *Hill Street Blues* and *Cagney and Lacey* bore witness to emotional depths of their characters, but eventually we ended up back where we started: police dramas focusing obsessively on procedure, on the reassuring power of surveillance technology and methodology to reign in the unpredictable bad apples aimed at destroying the happiness of innocent people. These are shows in which, as red-haired, slow-talking Lieutenant Horatio Caine of *CSI Miami* might say, "we let the evidence tell the story." The evidence inevitably includes some gained by surveillance. And surveillance inevitably leads to amazing feats of computing in which tattoos are delineated, license plates are divined, and the fuzziest, grainiest image yields a wealth of useful clues. Not only that, but there are countless plots in which the wrongdoers themselves use video as a way to relive their crimes for entertainment and/or to send a message taunting detectives. Video plays a double role for the (still largely male) evildoer in these stories: video is the reason he does what he does (so he can record it and make it real), and it is his undoing (the sound of a train in the background leads to a certain neighborhood; the quality of the light suggests a certain abandoned factory; the timbre of the microphone leads to a certain product which can only be bought in a certain store which keeps meticulous records of who purchased what, and so on and so on). These shows show all, for our own good—they are part soft porn, part snuff, part western, part surveillance, and part reportage, always careful to use a "just the facts" approach that somehow justifies night after night of young pretty women found with their throats slashed and their panties missing (after all, this really happens). A mere three months to the day after Anna Nicole Smith died, *Law & Order: Criminal Intent* gave us what television newspaper columnist and funny man Vinay Menon described as "the sordid details of her short, unhappy life in a bid to entertain anybody who awoke this morning and thought, 'Gosh, why hasn't television devoted more time to this important story? . . . Enter detectives Wheeler (Julianne Nicholson) and Logan (Chris Noth). And brace yourself for more tawdry voyeurism masquerading as an analogous deconstruction of a topical celebrity tragedy."

CSI, Law and Order, Without a Trace, Dexter, and more to come, all use interconnected surveillance techniques to solve crime. This too has a kind of culmination in the form of the television show *24*, a secret-agent series featuring operative Jack Bauer, who always seems to have exactly twenty-four hours to beat the shit out of the terrorists and find out where the bomb is planted. But Jack Bauer is no hapless Inspector Smart. He's aided by pinpoint satellite technology. Bauer can find out almost instantly on what floor of the building the hostage is being kept, how many are in the room, what they are doing and saying, and who he's going to have to torture to get the information he needs to save America. Not to read too much into this kind of thing, but it seems like we're living in a time when we need to believe in Jack Bauer and his vision of doing whatever is necessary. We need to believe in Horatio Caine and his vision of evidence as inevitable truth-telling. These are the moral underpinnings of a morally ambiguous Peep culture that privileges watching over intervening for the conjoined purposes of security and entertainment.

◻ ◻ ◻

Television continues to be influenced by the true-crime report-ing of tabloid journalism. But today journalism is just as likely to be influenced by television. If you are allowed to fictionalize murder and mayhem as entertainment or public service, then surely you are allowed to show the real thing. There's a reason the nightly news is now so much more exciting than it used to be. Car crashes, police chases, thefts, fires, beatings—any and all of these things are likely to get caught on surveillance tape. How many times have you watched a bleary feed show a few shadowy figures waving a weapon at a convenience store clerk? And if the clerk goes down fighting? Even better! Wars, natural disasters, and economic shifts affecting millions might be in the offing that evening, but if your local outlet has footage of a good robbery or car chase, you better bet they are going to lead with that. Several studies have shown that the nightly news features shorter and shorter segments of random moments of violence; it's a parallel world where most citizens of North America aren't living in some of the world's safest, most affluent communities but in veritable war zones of crime and punishment.

There seems to be a never-ending stream of footage show-ing real people in real danger. While Eric Kliebold and Dylan Harris were prowling the halls of their Columbine, Colorado, high school looking for jocks, cheerleaders, and black kids to shoot, the Denver NBC affiliate was inviting students trapped in the school building to call the station and talk about their feel-ings live on air. Some students did. One student was actually put on the air before the station changed its mind and decided that America was not yet ready for prime-time, real-time audio foot-age of an actual killing. Ironically, Columbine High School al-ready had surveillance cameras installed in its hallways. Portions of the footage would eventually make it to the Net, as would the home videos the duo made that show them ranting, raving, and brandishing their weaponry before heading off to the school.

Law-and-order factual programming, not unlike the scripted

stuff, is in love with the hidden camera, the surveillance camera, the amateur video camera. Not only does this material compel our attention in a way that no other kind of footage can—because it seems real, unmediated, natural—but it also comes cheaply. So it is that entire nights of entertainment can be derived from *America's Most Wanted*, *Cops*, *American Detective*, *Top Cops*, *FBI: The Untold Story*, *True Stories of the Highway Patrol*, and *World's Scariest Police Chases*. On the Animal Planet channel there's even *Animal Precinct*, featuring animal-cruelty investigators rounding up horse abusers and cat killers. Even MTV found a way to make this work, with their show *Room Raiders*, in which participants are kidnapped—bundled out of their living spaces when they answer the door, regardless of what they're doing and what they're wearing (producers pray that their comely young volunteers will arrive at the door dripping wet from the shower, in nothing but a towel). Next, experts go through the living space of each participant. They comment on clothing brand choices, search the computer for porn, and I think they even occasionally employ some of SpyTech's semen detection fluid. Meanwhile, a member of the opposite sex watching from a separate location is trying to decide if he or she should date this particular kidnap victim or move on to one with less (or more) porn and sex toys hidden in the closet. The popularity of these kinds of shows, as well as the predominance of reality shows like *Big Brother*, which rely on ubiquitous hidden cameras, tell us, as German culture critic Ursula Frohne puts it, "that we are on the threshold of a transition from the bureaucratic-institutional tactics of surveillance to the medially staged spectacle of the individual's total surrender to the media's regime of the gaze."

Which is to say that in the age of Peep we don't fear Big Brother, we clamor to be subjected to Big Brother. In fact we want to be Big Brother. We want to have his infinite, all-seeing, and, more importantly, all-broadcasting gaze transmit our every whine, gaffe, complaint, and ill-considered pronouncement. We willingly surrender to the "regime of the gaze." We don't just want to watch, we want to be watched. We want to be on the screen and why wouldn't we? Fame, fun, and reward beckon. Only the guilty evade the spotlight, a precept that seems to drive celebrities and politicians to an inevitable tearful chat with Larry King after every revealed infidelity or stint in rehab.

The shows beckoning us to watch and potentially be watched are everywhere. And the most popular and enduring of them are the law-and-order shows in which we see real people being arrested, pursued, waylaid, and interrogated by real law enforcement officers. They are so prevalent and so much a part of our culture that it's hard to remember the genuine horror that greeted reality TV franchise *Cops* when it first aired. "On the one hand, it's absolutely captivating, raw and unpredictable, a bubbling boiler of excitement," wrote then *Los Angeles Times* critic Howard Rosenberg. "On the other hand, the camera assumes the disgusting role of hanging judge by prematurely filling the screen with the faces of numerous suspects swept up in drug busts, some of whom may turn out to be innocent." Then, as now, guilt and innocence are just a pretense to watch and be watched. Mark Fishman, associate professor of sociology at Brooklyn College writes of *Cops* that its "cinema verité style invites voyeurism. It does not solicit tips, and offers no pretense to catching criminals." The message of all this isn't that these people are bad, guilty of crimes; it's not "don't do crime." In fact, it's the opposite: crime is entertaining; the camera will always show crime; one way to get in front of the camera is to do crime. Crime is entertaining, entertaining people are famous, famous people are the pinnacle of Peep society!

America's Most Wanted and its global copycats seem to be about catching the worst of the worst, but the show's over-the-top hype, it's foreboding tone, bordering on the ridiculous, its close-ups of the tearful victims and survivors, and more than anything else its cheesy yet ominous re-creations of crimes (harking back to the composographs done by the newspapers in the 1920s) suggest that its real mission first and foremost is entertainment. Ultimately what these shows sow is anxiety. In a Peep culture era, that anxiety becomes the need to know. And the need to know becomes the need to be seen. Entertainment, surveillance, police work, and pure, prurient voyeurism blur. If there's anything like a culmination to this ongoing blurring, it's found on the UK show *CCTV Cities*, an almost unbearably earnest reality show that's like a cross between *Cops* and *The Office* (except that it's all "real"). The show, set in an actual CCTV control room in a British city, shows us your average CCTV camera operator twiddling the dials and zooming in on crimes, tragedies, and possible miscreants. As they zoom, they talk about their feelings: "We're just here to help"; "it's a good feeling when at the end of the day you can help someone." To break up the tedium of their asinine observations there's plenty of appropriately grainy video footage and on-the-street action in which the police and emergency services follow up on the tips sent their way by the camera operators. Drunks are rescued, criminals are apprehended, and nothing goes unseen or unpunished in the big city.

Despite appearances, the typical law-and-order grainy digital video image doesn't help us prevent crime or come to grips with the role of violence in our lives and societies. But the widespread broadcast of these images does attune us to the idea that there should be a camera present, a way to record what happens in case what happens turns out to matter. If something does turn out to matter, then it seems there can suddenly never be enough footage. We sit in our darkened room, our tongues hanging out, demanding more. Consider the 1999 murder of television presenter Jill Dando, host of *Crimewatch UK*, described as "the first major network television show in the UK to use CCTV footage as key material in a program structured around the idea that the public would identify criminals." Dando made a career out of urging viewers to take a good look at tapes of bad guys and call in with tips. Think of the victims and act bravely to put a killer behind bars. But then, in an awful and ironic twist, better off on *CSI* than in real life, she became one of those victims. CCTV footage of her shopping on the day of her murder became one of those tapes. Over and over, British television showed a seemingly carefree Dando going about her shopping routine. The footage had no relationship with what was to come—the thirty-seven-year-old Dando was shot in the head outside of her house, in what remains an unsolved murder. As one perplexed scholar notes, "The impotent imagery of Dando shopping just before her murder potentially reminded us that there will always be a mass of surveillance footage available of each of us, but very little of it is doing its ostensible job of protecting us from anything." Nevertheless, "somehow it seemed as though it was necessary to address Dando's murder via the form of television watching that she had helped to pioneer." This is what we do in the age of Peep culture. For better or worse, we make images of everything and everyone. And, again, for better or worse, we show those images. The pictures exist, and they compel us to see them.

In February 1993 in Liverpool, England, two-year-old James Bulger disappeared from a shopping mall. He had been with his mom, but she lost track of him. A few days later, the surveillance footage came out. Widely broadcast around the UK and the world, and particularly on *Crimewatch UK*, the video showed two older boys holding James Bulger's hand and leading him out of the mall. This accidental footage reveals a touching scene: two boys seemingly helping another, much younger boy. To see it is to be perplexed by it. What does it mean? How can it mean anything? Why did we have to see it over and over again when, really, if it showed anything it showed a kind of inverse scenario, the opposite of what eventually did occur? (The ten-year-old boys eventually admitted to taking Bulger down to the nearby train tracks and killing him.) The footage lives on, to be shown and repurposed and reimagined, the ghostly afterimage of a Peep culture that forgets nothing. As British writer Blake

Morrison ruminates in his book on the Bulger murder and the trial of the two boys:

> And now, in court and on the news, the video compilation of security stills plays in endless detail for us all. 15:38:55, James alone outside the butchers. 15:40:24, Denise searching. 15:41:29, James on the upper floor, close to two other boys. 15:42:10, Denise still searching. 15:42:32, the still that froze a million hearts, James's hand—raised in trust—in the hand of Jon Venables, Robert Thompson leading the way. 15:43:08, the three boys leaving the precinct. Forward, and back, stop, rewind, review, pause, freeze. Forward and back, forward and back, as if we watched it often enough the picture might change and James be there again, safe by Denise's side.

❏ ❏ ❏

There's a hypnotic beauty to surveillance images, regardless of what they show. At SpyTech I spent $250 on a weatherproof surveillance camera complete with night vision. I drilled a hole in my garage and mounted it pointing out so that it oversaw the alley behind the house. Now, on my computer, I could watch the alley twenty-four hours day. I could even take pictures and record video. For a while I had it set to record five seconds of video and snap a still picture every time it sensed motion. But an astronomical number built up, of video clips showing cars driving past and people walking their dogs. I was spending an hour a day watching and sorting these mundane images. I decided to limit myself to just watching when I feel like it, occasionally taking a still picture of the alley if something interesting happened.

Nothing interesting happened. Not even close. The alley, one of hundreds like it in downtown Toronto, is in a neighborhood in transition. When we first moved in, there was more squalor, but in the last couple of years gentrification had taken over. About four years ago someone broke into our garage (more like I forgot to lock it) and took a few items of no value. I once saw a strung-out transvestite running down the alley with a bag of stolen tools. That's about it. To be honest with you, the alley isn't really dangerous or scary. My primary concern are the people who let their dogs do their business in front of my garage and don't pick up.

But back to my surveillance, which now consisted of checking in on the alley whenever I thought of it during the course of my computing day. I watched the alley in the morning, I watched the alley in the afternoon, and, my favorite, I watched the alley at night before I went off to bed. It was hypnotic. I got to know that patch of neglected space the way I know my own face. Over and over again I pondered the interlaced cracked concrete, a maze of atrophying asphalt that slopped to the metal cover of the sewer grate. The tufted patch of weed just tall enough to sway in the breeze. The quality of the light, gray on gray, no matter the time of day, darkness perpetually threatening to take hold. The alley is not a pretty place, but it was fascinating to look at. I'm not going to claim that I became obsessed with looking at it, but I did think of looking at it much more than I ever thought I would. Every time I sat down at the computer, as a matter of fact, I methodically opened the camera feed and spend a few minutes with the alley. My wife said it best. Staring at the screen one evening she said: "Nothing ever happens, but I can't stop looking at it."

University of Montreal criminologist Stéphane Leman-Langlois has a theory about the relationship between our Peep culture's increasingly intermeshed relationship with surveillance and overall societal impressions of what crime is and where it comes from. He tells me that the obsession with surveillance encourages police in general to focus on the visible at a time when visible crime is steadily in the decline. "It's a pretty significant change in the sense that police started in the last forty years to look into things like spousal abuse, an area where people started going into people's houses, not because they wanted to, but because the law says they have to. Another area that gets more police, very little policing but more than it used to be, is white-collar crimes and things like the environment, very minor policing but it used to be zero. But if you start centering again on the visible through CCTV, you are going to forget about all this stuff because it's not visible." Interesting to note that for the most part, televised law-and-order programming also focuses on the visible: car chases, drunks, drug dealers, fights. When was the last time you saw a police officer on *Cops* busting someone for identity theft or elder abuse?

This return to the visible mirrors what Leman-Langlois sees as an overall "culture shift of perceiving crime more and more in terms of insufficient surveillance." As he explains it, we come to see crime as actually "caused by insufficient surveillance. So we used to be trying to figure out the root causes of crime, but now we are saying people are committing crime because no one is watching. The criminals wouldn't be doing this if the cameras were there."

Think of the English town of King's Lynn, a small burg with almost no crime. Yet in the nineties, with *Crimewatch UK* and *Cops* ruling the airwaves, it became one of the first places in the world to install a comprehensive surveillance system. One scholar describes this phenomenon as springing from "the perceived need for surveillance." If there is crime, if there is even going to be crime (of course there's going to be crime), put up a camera and the crime will go away. Problem solved. That's the message television has been sharing with us over the last ten years. "On the news," says Leman-Langlois, "they call for help to the public: can you recognize this person? Or they show risky behavior: this is what happens, so you shouldn't do it. Or here's a pickpocket in action and in thirty seconds the police are going to jump him. So the message is: this video is very helpful for policing purposes."

Surveillance footage gone Peep and broadcast through the mass media is a lot like reality TV. It presents not truth but the appearance of truth, not reality but the aura of reality, not knowing but the feeling of knowing (or at least what it would be like

to know). The urge to know permeates Peep culture and connects phenomena like our burgeoning love of DIY surveillance
to caught-on-tape TV, *Room Raiders*, *A Shot at Love with Tila
Tequila*, and a photo of Tila Tequila taking out her trash. Writes
Mark Andrejevic:

> Detection has become one of the watchwords of popular cul-
> ture—not merely in the proliferating variants of shows like CSI,
> but also in the formats that offer to take us behind the scenes of
> the making of the video or movie, of the lifestyles of the latest
> pop culture heroes, or of the public image of a famous band or
> celebrity. The obverse of a culture of savvy debunkery—one that
> takes the performance of subjectivity as a given—is a culture of
> perpetual detection: a series of ongoing attempts to see behind
> the public performance, or at the very least to prove that one isn't
> taken in by it.

It's all connected, all part of the endless stream of Peep culture. And because it's all connected, it's all blurry. Monitoring
your business is entertainment, entertainment is law enforcement, and caught on tape is a potential opportunity. Here's a
relatively benign yet telling example. In January of 2008, New-
foundland computer store owner Dave McGrath captured the
theft of a $300 computer processor on his surveillance camera.
He notified the police, then put the segment up on YouTube. People all over the world watched the video more than 36,000 times.
And from the over one hundred comments it's clear that most of
the people watching did not tune in because they thought they
could identify the perpetrator. So why look at the clip? Or maybe
the question is—why not? We're used to thinking of this kind of
material as entertaining as well as socially useful and productive.
As the store owner told a reporter: "This is my spot, my area,
the cameras are on, we have signs saying the cameras are here.
If someone's silly enough to come in and do it, I think I have the
right to show it."

The right to show it. But what is *it* exactly and where do we draw the line? McGrath's video is just the tip of the online iceberg. There are entire sites—and sites within sites—dedicated to making surveillance footage available to us. LABankRobbers.org is one of a compendium of geographically ordered sites that posts luridly appealing surveillance footage of bank heists in progress. The aim is to capture the crooks, but the effect is pure Peep. From there, I search Google for "shocking surveillance video" and am offered an array of enticing clips including "kid gets hit in head with baseball bat" and "dog goes wild on a solider during a drill." We're just getting started. How about a video purporting to show U.S. soldiers in Iraq blowing up a dog? On yet another site I am invited to watch "domestic violence at its best" which promises an "angry boyfriend punching his girlfriend where the sun don't shine." There's also what purports to be a spy being executed, subtitled "This is disturbing, was the second shot really necessary?" Up next: "Classic School Yard Girl Fight," which has a rating of 3.57 out of 4 based on 61 votes. Then there's a guy smashing his testicles via skateboarding accident, a clip from a surveillance camera that captures a "cop urinating on private property," a "horrific highway pile" featuring "dead bodies all over the road," and "guy shot in the head gets loaded into morgue van (warning very graphic)." All of this material is derived from surveillance cameras or the ubiquitous presence of cell phone and digital video cameras that are being used like surveillance cameras to randomly film events as they transpire. All of the material has the grainy look and very real feel of an episode of *Cops* or *Rescue 911*. Quite a bit of it looks like the part on *Jerry Springer* where people are cued to slap each other and rip each other's clothes off while screaming bleeped-out obscenities. In fact, there's an entire Web site devoted just to clips of amateur fights. No, wait, I take that back. There are two Web sites devoted just to amateur pugilistic endeavors. No, wait, I see now that there are three, uh, four— okay, more than ten but probably less than 500 Web sites that collect and make available everything from schoolyard brawls to bar fights and knifings. And for the bean counters out there, ratings are high. Most of these clips have 10,000–20,000 clicks to their credit, more if they can claim that the fight is between "two hot chicks" and one of them ends up "with her bra totally torn off."

We are learning to instinctually pull out our cameras and capture anything and everything on video. The watching was already standard for us. Now we're extending our relationship with Peep by becoming not just watchers and the watched, but also content generators. In some of the schoolyard brawls I've watched online, I could actually see several different students in the background holding their cell phone cameras up to the action. As is usually the case with surveillance, no one intervened. That would have wrecked the show.

Jonathan Finn, a professor at Wilfrid Laurier University, has written a book entitled *Capturing the Criminal Image: From Mugshot to Surveillance Society*. When I get in touch with him, he tells me that he sees us as being in transition between "a photographic way of seeing [and] a surveillance way of seeing." What's the difference? A photographic way of seeing is more or less static, Finn explains. It's more like: take a picture, it'll last longer. We think in terms of memory, of making things last. In a surveillance way of seeing, nothing lasts, we're always moving on to the next image, "We're always," as Finn tells me, "monitoring." Finn says we're out there "hunting, we're going out there as hunters, always on the lookout for material."

We're not hunting for the great image that will resonate in people's minds and help us understand our place in the universe, but for the momentary thrill of the car accident or carjacking caught on tape. For Finn, the transition into the Peep culture age of ubiquitous surveillance creates "a frame of mind. It's a way of seeing and documenting events. It's infused into our daily lives to the extent that we're walking around looking for something to happen; you could be looking for criminals, funny moments, strange street signs."

We record not so much to keep ourselves safe, but because we're on the hunt. What are we hunting for? In part we're hunting for evidence of our own existence. We're hunting for a way to extend our senses and take part in a world of mass media that dominate our lives. The German Jewish philosopher Georg Simmel (who wrote presciently on individuality and modern society in the early twentieth century) mused about the relationship between the eye and socialization, theorizing that there is a unique psychological link that happens when human beings look at each other—an immediate, direct link that can only be established through the gaze. Marshall McLuhan famously wrote about the senses being extended by technology, even playfully calling one of his books *The Medium is the Massage*. (In it he wrote: "All media work us over completely. They are so pervasive in their personal, political, economic, aesthetic, psychological, moral, ethical, and social consequences that they leave no part of us untouched, unaffected, unaltered.") The widespread use of the camera to document anything, everything, and nothing suggests a desperate kind of replication of the primal gaze: it really did happen, I was really there, I saw it, I looked it in the eyes, and I bring you this video I shot as proof—proof not so much that something happened, but that I was there and that I exist. Look at me!

Are people actually doing extreme things so that they can upload their exploits and get seen? Are people breaking the law to draw eyeballs to their MySpace page? Of course they are. "Eight Florida teens have been arrested on charges that they beat another teen so they could make a videotape to post to YouTube." No this isn't the plot of a Larry Clark movie. It's the first line from an AP article reporting on an incident that occurred in Lakeland, Florida. I read the sentence and immediately went searching for the clip. I didn't find it on YouTube (which removes violent and pornographic images pretty quickly) but any number of media outlets around the world were happy to provide me with excerpts. I got to watch, along with who knows how many other thousands of people, one girl screaming and yelling and shoving another obviously terrified girl. Like the nanny cam story on CNN, there was no actual reason for me to be observing this footage, no public value in actually seeing it (as opposed to just knowing about it). I watched because it was there. Did these teenagers beat their peer for the same reason? Because the camera was there?

In Finland, of all places, a young man posted a YouTube video predicting that a massacre would soon visit the Jokela High School. The video was set to the song "Stray Bullet" and broke away from a shot of the high school to show a red-tinted picture of a man pointing a handgun at the camera. Lo and behold, seven kids and the school principal were shot and killed just hours later. Their assailant, a fellow pupil, also died after shooting himself in the head. Remember, the Columbine duo also made a tape before they set out, as did Cho Seung-Hui who gunned down thirty-three people at Virginia Tech. There's an interesting escalation here. The Columbine kids didn't do anything with their prerecorded ravings. Seung-Hui sent his to NBC. The Finnish kid put his up on YouTube. In all these cases, there is an incredible amount of documentation and detection, of behind-the-scenes media made exclusively for us to watch. This material is generated not just by the perpetrators by also by the victims, the authorities, and utterly uninvolved bystanders. It comes to us in the form of Twitter messages and blog posts made by frightened Virginia Tech students in lockdown, or as security camera footage from Columbine High School, or as the view through the news camera pushed against the darkened window. Despite the inevitable mass of footage, neither understanding nor prevention are achieved. Something else is at play here: Consider the moment in breakthrough LA gangsta movie *Menace II Society* (1993) in which the Hughes brothers give us young gangbangers who, after breaking into a store and murdering the shopkeeper, steal the videotape of their crime so they can watch it over and over again—the act and the video merging into a permanent state of semi-real, where only things caught on tape actually matter. TV as a way to be seen, as a way to be real. Surveillance as a way to get on TV, to enter Peep culture as not just the passive butt of the joke, but as the puppetemaster pulling the strings.

Maybe the Hughes brothers were inspired by a real LA incident caught on tape and forever ingrained in the collective consciousness. In 1991 a passerby with a video camera recorded policemen viciously beating hapless taxi driver Rodney King. Regardless of what may have prompted the beating, the tape took on its own life, told its own story, became real in a way that the eventual decision to acquit the officers of using excessive force can never be real. (As then Los Angeles mayor Tom Bradley said: "The jury's verdict will not blind us to what we saw on that videotape. The men who beat Rodney King do not deserve to wear the uniform of the L.A.P.D.") There are certain grainy moving images that, once recorded, take on a life of their own, become, in some unscripted but inevitable way, more dominant and true than anything we could have ever seen with our own eyes. The first plane slamming into the first tower, caught on camcorder by a stunned tourist. The grainy mall security cam image of preschooler James Bulger being led out of the mall by his ten-year-old, soon-to-be killers. The restrained, helpless Rodney King taking punches. These images, caught on tape as they actually happened, are evidence against the truism that we are safer watched by cameras. The cameras were watching when Bulger disappeared, when King was beaten, when the towers fell. If anything, these ever-present, disconcerting images leave us feeling more unsafe. So when the age of Peep demands more and more caught-on-tape sensational moments, it's not because we really believe we'll be safer if the camera is on. What we believe is that if we're on camera, we'll be less alone. Under the impartial "regime" of the camera's eye, we'll continue to exist even after we're grabbed by the arms and hustled out of the mall. We'll die, perhaps, but we won't disappear.

We're not afraid of the surveillance state. We're afraid of the gaps in our culture of surveillance. We're afraid of the dark spaces where our senses fail us. We fear the moments when, unobserved, unrecorded, and un-exhibited, we virtually disappear. It's for this reason that we have become so enthusiastic about Peep culture. In Peep we extend surveillance into our everyday lives. In doing so, we extend the camera's capacity to stave off our existential terror. The camera I'm pointing at the alley behind the house gives me a weird sense of comfort, though it's basically useless as a crime prevention tool. Looking at the alley without anyone knowing that I'm looking is addictive. It assuages something in me, some need I didn't even know I had. This isn't about my fear of crime. It's about extending my presence and challenging my fear of absence. In a postmodern society that turns everything into an endless recording, absence is the ultimate terror. We embrace surveillance because we're terrified of disappearing "without a trace."

Escape from the Castle: Privacy in the Age of Peep

> Much that is written about privacy is premised on the idea that privacy, once plentiful, is only now endangered. While privacy is endangered, it was hardly a staple in the past, when most people had little.
> —Janna Malamud Smith, *Private Matters*

We assembled in an upscale Italian restaurant on Toronto's tony College Street. Though we hadn't met before, all the others (except me) shared a common pursuit: they liked to strip naked, pose for the camera, and post those pictures to a series of Web sites with names like Voyeurweb and RedClouds. Their hobby was making amateur erotica.

They were a burly Buffalo bar owner and his wife; a gregarious couple from a small Canadian city; a foursome of avid posers and posters, all of them best friends, who drove in for the dinner from Michigan; and an upscale Toronto couple who looked like they just came from drinks at the country club. They were all older than me—in their mid to late forties and up—and could best be described as middle-class empty nesters.

Igor Shoemaker, the gangly, middle-aged proprietor of the Web sites Voyeurweb and RedClouds introduced the couples to me as they arrived. A German citizen, Igor lives in Amsterdam and operates his business with servers in Toronto, Vancouver, and Europe. He was in the city connecting with his Toronto office, and happily organized the dinner for me. As the couples straggled in, we shook hands, ordered cocktails, and chatted amiably about the Buffalo Sabres, the drive from Michigan, their plans for the rest of the weekend. It could have been any bunch of people meeting for a drink on a Saturday night, though there was a tension in the air, a sense of unspoken anticipation that emerged in occasional jocular asides—"Watch out for that one, she's a tiger!" The men talked photo equipment. The women talked about their kids. Drinks were served and someone pulled out a breast. A camera flashed. The night began.

We sat down to dinner and conversation turned to the reason we'd gathered—how they got into posing nude and why they do it. For the most part the ladies denied the erotic thrill and focused on the excitement of being watched and known. The thrill, they insisted, comes in finding out that so many men (and women) want to see them naked, still obviously think they're hot and sexy even as they approach and pass middle age. Their husbands nodded dutifully and talked about camera angles and lighting. It's a hobby, they insisted. It's not all we do, their wives announced, listing other pastimes ranging from volunteering to knitting. You see, we're not just perverts, they seemed to be saying. We're also regular people.

Across from me and to my right sat the Michigan foursome. They told me that they are attracted to the social aspect—they go to the parties, the dances, even the occasional resort holiday fomented on the Web site chat rooms. There's an active Michigan group that keeps the social events coming. They told me about the party rules—you wear a ribbon so that others know if they can take pictures of you or not. The color of the ribbon denotes your level of comfort with being publicly photographed and uploaded as part of the scene. The Michigan four pose with their faces fully exposed and are public about their participation. Others at the table keep their online faces covered or blurred; they fear, or at least have no interest in, being discovered by a neighbor, employer, or parent. I asked the wildest woman in the room—one of the Michigan four, the "tiger," known for stripping down at the slightest provocation—if she'd ever run into any strangers who recognized her from the many hard-core scenes she's posted online. This slight women in her fifties with frizzy hair and freckles smiled at me. "Sometimes guys recognize me on the street. I can feel them staring at me. They might not say anything. Or they might just smile. I know they know. Occasionally they might say, 'Didn't I see you on RedClouds?' Sometimes I pretend like I don't know what they're talking about, act like it wasn't me. It can be awkward."

It can be awkward, but at the dinner party everyone was in their element. To my left, a trim, bespectacled, casually dressed man in his late forties looked on as his wife, a toned and tanned woman with long, curly, burnished-copper hair (you might remember her from earlier in this book, screen name: Beauty), flirted with Igor. "I've wanted to meet you for so long," she purred. "You're our hero. You make it all possible."

Igor has made it possible for women of all ages, shapes, and sizes from across the world to post erotic images of themselves for online viewing by thousands, if not millions, of people. In the process, he's part of a distinctly twenty-first-century reinvention of the concept of privacy. This isn't some kind of hypothetical rebellion fomented by campus lefties. This is a widespread shift in how we think about privacy, sweeping through even the most conservative towns and lives. The RedClouds dinner made it clear to me how little this rethinking was about ideology or politics. The diners weren't seeking to make some deep point about sexuality. They were people who lived their lives on utterly conventional terms. But this was also a group made up of couples who had all decided, independent of each other, that there was a void in their lives they needed to fill by exposing themselves online.

They weren't doing it for money; though Igor offers cash prizes for the most popular photos, the rewards are relatively meager. They were doing it because they felt the urge. What's the urge? The urge is to escape from the isolating castle of contemporary privacy. The urge is to use private parts and private moments to break through barriers and connect to other fellow human beings. What Igor has made possible is an entirely new mainstream perspective on privacy. In this new perspective, privacy is a currency to be traded, bought or sold.

Plates were cleared and Igor ordered more wine. A light flashed and I realized that Beauty's husband was under the table, taking pictures with his digital camera. He resurfaced triumphant and showed me his conquest on the viewscreen. "Did she take her underwear off," I wondered out loud, "or did she not have any on in the first place?" The prim, blonde, Toronto country club lady blushed. Everybody chortled, fourteen-year-olds sharing a dirty joke in the junior high cafeteria.

❑ ❑ ❑

Anthropologists talk about "human universals," behaviors that all people have always exhibited throughout all time. One of the classic universals is, as anthropologist Donald E. Brown writes in his book *Human Universals*, "sexual modesty. . . . People do not normally copulate in public." Beauty and her coterie of even more explicit amateur models, and any number of "accidentally" leaked sex tapes, tell us that today more and more of us seem to be copulating *just so we can be seen in public*. So does that mean we're freaks, human beings unlike any who have ever walked the earth? Not necessarily. Think of it more as a cry (or moan) to action. Innumerable couplings that collectively testify to our natural desire to reclaim another human universal—our need to be known as individuals, not statistics and demographics.

We're alone all the time. We're alone on the bus, we're alone walking down the street, we're alone at the office and in the class-room, alone waiting in line at Disney World. We're tired of being alone, which is why increasingly we are barely hesitating to do whatever we feel we need to do to push out of solitude. In the extreme—though no longer all that extreme—people are delib-erately eschewing privacy by posing nude and uploading their sex acts online as a way to announce the singular primal fact of their humanity. Of course there are many more gradients to this push against solitude. From Facebook to webcams, from blogs to reality TV, we are actively involved in trading our privacy for community, shared meaning, and even cash and celebrity. We're willing to put ourselves out there, we're desperate to put ourselves out there, because we'd rather that people know we exist than sit alone in sprawling suburban bungalows lit by the blue glow of the monitor. This doesn't mean that we never want to have the right or ability to do things on our own, to do things unobserved by others. What this means is that a lifestyle centered around escape, distance, and buffer zones denies us a community that inherently knows who we are, a community that functions to reaffirm the simple fact of the existence of its members.

There's ample evidence that privacy is low on our list of con-cerns. One survey of Facebook users concluded that 90 percent had never read the company's privacy policy. Sixty percent of the users said they weren't concerned about privacy and 30 percent said they were somewhat concerned about their privacy. A more recent study explored the willingness of college students to vio-late their own privacy on the Internet. In a 2008 talk presented at the Security and Human Behavior Workshop in Boston, Carnegie Mellon behavioral economist George Loewenstein explained the results of a research study he had conducted with two colleagues. The researchers surveyed college students via e-mail, asking them to indicate if they'd engaged in misguided or even illegal activities. One group of students were told that they shouldn't worry about their privacy, nothing they said would ever get out.

Ironically, those students were less likely to admit to wrongdoing than the students who were given no assurances that their privacy would be respected, who, in fact, never heard a single word about privacy throughout the experiment. In the end, 25 percent of the students who were assured of confidentially admitted to copying someone else's homework. More than 50 percent of students who were told nothing about confidentiality said that, yeah, they'd copied someone else's schoolwork.

From this we can conclude that people do not naturally think of privacy, particularly when they are connecting online. They want to share, they want to be noticed, they want to mine their truth telling for the potential rewards of community. The more people feel like they are connecting with each other, as opposed to bureaucracies and institutions, the more frank they are willing to be. The same team did another experiment in which students were asked to take an on-screen survey enquiring about their performance of various "illicit" acts. One batch took the survey on an official university Web site, the other batch on a fun-looking Web site with the headline "How BAD are U??" looming over the image of a smiling devil. Students on the fun-looking site were found to be way more likely to admit to engaging in illicit activities, including the use of illegal drugs. So we can conclude again that people care less about privacy and more about connection. If we think we're exchanging life experiences, if we're feeling like we're tapping into our instinctual craving for meaningful social interaction and reaffirming our sense of (tribal) existence, we're unlikely to worry about our privacy.

A fall 2008 study by the Pew Internet & American Life Project found that only 49 percent of survey participants said they would be "very concerned" if online corporations who store data (like Google with its Gmail) shared their data with law enforcement officials without their permission. Only 63 percent of those surveyed indicated that they would be upset if the company continued to retain copies of files after the user had deleted them. In the United Kingdom, AOL surveyed a thousand online consumers about their understanding of privacy issues on the Internet. Eighty-four percent said that they were very hesitant to give up any personal details online. But 89 percent then went on to divulge personal details about their household incomes—"without any pressure or persuasion," says AOL. "Our research identified a significant gap between what people say and what they do when it comes to protecting sensitive information online," AOL Chief Privacy Officer Jules Polonetsky said in a statement. From this you can conclude, as AOL did, that people are stupid and need education on how to protect their privacy. Or you can conclude, as I do, that we want to connect, desperately, existentially, inherently. We're willing to reveal ourselves for little or no reason even against our own best interests if only that we might, for a moment or two, alleviate the loneliness we feel all around us.

❏ ❏ ❏

In 1604, the English court famously ruled that a "man's house is his castle." In Semayne's Case, the court wrote that "the house of every one is to him as his castle and fortress, as well as for his defence against injury and violence, as for his repose; and although the life of a man is a thing precious and favored in law; . . . if thieves come to a man's house to rob him, or murder, and the owner or his servants kill any of the thieves in defence of himself and his house, it is not felony, and he shall lose nothing." My privacy is key to my very humanity. As such, I should be allowed to do whatever is necessary to defend it (including sending my 'servants' out to get killed in my defense). But the court wasn't finished. They also wrote that "[i]n all cases where the King is party, the sheriff (if the doors be not open) may break the house, either to arrest or do other execution of the King's process."

Privacy, but only so long as you're a male citizen obeying the king's law and only so long as you happen to have a "castle" to

protect and "servants" to protect it. But the short, snappy home +
castle = privacy equation is so much easier to remember. A man's
home is his castle. Simple and appealing. In 1763 canny English
politician William Pitt (namesake of Pittsburgh) made a powerful statement reaffirming, extending, and fundamentally altering
the house-castle equation in a speech to Parliament: "The poorest
man may in his cottage bid defiance to all the forces of the crown.
It may be frail; its roof may shake; the wind may blow through it;
the storm may enter; the rain may enter; but the King of England
may not enter—all his force dares not cross the threshold of the
ruined tenement!" This kind of rhetoric about the sanctity of privacy is in direct contradiction to what the court decided back in
1604. But it reveals something fascinating regarding our passion
for a privacy we don't (always) want and maybe don't even need:
intended or not, privacy is inextricably tied up with owning stuff.
Even the poor man deserves some respect if he can manage to
scrape together enough cash to buy up a "ruined tenement." This
is a convenient, populist sentiment likely to please both the common folk (though they own very little real estate) and the well-off
(the more you buy, the more privacy you can expect). Couched
in the rhetoric of the people, who warrant privacy as much as any
landowner (provided they can afford it), it becomes an attractive
sentiment: No matter who you are, you deserve a little respect.
Even peasants have the right to protect their falling-down shack.

Not long after William Pitt addressed the English Parliament,
the U.S. Congress passed the Bill of Rights (1791), which amend-
ed the Constitution and promised that "the right of the people to
be secure in their . . . houses . . . against unreasonable searches
and seizures shall not be violated." What's reasonable and what's
unreasonable? Throughout most of human history, all but a very
tiny number of us lived together and pretty much shared everything. Privacy didn't exist. But as communal living was superced-
ed by law, order, bureaucracy, and the accumulation of capital, we
entered an era that put an increasing emphasis on privacy. After

all, your house, car, boat, and beachfront condo aren't going to be nearly as desirable and exclusive with half the planet crawling all over them. We must accumulate, and we're sure as hell not going to accumulate unless our stuff is ours alone, to use, hide behind, and otherwise patronize and protect as we see fit.

Privacy is becoming more and more connected to money and acquisition. The more you have, the more privacy you deserve to have. This growing trend and its inevitable contradiction (the more you have, the more interested others are going to be in you) led to what many consider to be the most influential law review article ever published in America. The article was titled "The Right to Privacy" and it was written in 1890 by two young lawyers, Samuel D. Warren and Louis D. Brandeis. In it they wrote that "instantaneous photographs and newspaper enterprise have invaded the sacred precincts of private and domestic life; and numerous mechanical devices threaten to make good the prediction that 'what is whispered in the closet shall be proclaimed from the house-tops.'" Apparently in the age of a hungry newspaper industry, "gossip is no longer the resource of the idle and of the vicious, but has become a trade." Gossip has it, in fact, that it was the trade in gossip—reports in a newspaper about Warren's dinner parties—that got the two lawyers thinking about this issue in the first place. The article basically concluded that there should be a law. The law should let people sue when their privacy is invaded.

Eventually such laws were enacted across the United States, again enshrining a home-castle type of mentality: what I do in my own private space is exclusively mine. (As opposed to what I do on the street, which is fair game for anybody.) But these right-to-sue laws constantly clashed with other laws and social imperatives, most particularly the state's right to investigate criminal activity and the state's right to regulate morality and social norms. Louis Brandeis went on to become a Supreme Court justice, where he famously argued against allowing the police to secretly tap phone lines. The 1928 case in question concerned a bootlegger—this was the era of Prohibition. The evidence against the bootlegger was acquired via phone tap. His lawyer argued that this violated his rights as a citizen and so the conviction should not stand. Justice Brandeis agreed, but the majority of the court decided that while, sure, your home is sacrosanct, the wires that carry your words out of your home are not. Brandeis thought this was ridiculous, writing in his famously prescient dissenting opinion in the case of *Olmstead v. the United States*:

> Subtler and more far-reaching means of invading privacy have become available to the government. Discovery and invention have made it possible for the government, by means far more effective than stretching upon the rack, to obtain disclosure in court of what is whispered in the closet. Moreover, 'in the application of a Constitution, our contemplation cannot be only of what has been, but of what may be.' The progress of science in furnishing the government with means of espionage is not likely to stop with wire tapping. Ways may some day be developed by which the government, without removing papers from secret drawers, can reproduce them in court, and by which it will be enabled to expose to a jury the most intimate occurrences of the home. Advances in the psychic and related sciences may bring means of exploring unexpressed beliefs, thoughts and emotions.

At the dawn of the twentieth century, it seems that the fledgling right to privacy was already under duress. Then again, maybe not. After all, to even have a discussion about what the state can and cannot know about you is progress, isn't it? Only a few hundred years earlier most people were just as likely to be executed by the whim of their rulers than afforded endless debate about their rights. Even today the bulk of the human population still lives in villages, tribes, and tenements, in extended family units where anything and everything you do will be seen and heard, judged and juried by your family and immediate community.

By that standard, privacy in the United States is hurtling forward. Forty years after the wiretap case, another landmark legal opinion took us even further down the road toward sanctifying the right to "privacy" as the right to do what you want in your own home unmolested (provided you have a home). The case took place in 1965 and it had to do with a Connecticut law banning all forms of contraception. The law had been on the books since 1879 but it had never really been tested in court because nobody had bothered to enforce it until Estelle Griswold (executive director of the Planned Parenthood League of Connecticut) and Dr. C. Lee Buxton (a physician and professor at the Yale School of Medicine) set up a birth control clinic in New Haven with the express purpose of getting arrested and challenging the law. The Supreme Court found in *Griswold v. Connecticut* that banning contraception is a violation of the right to privacy enshrined in the Constitution. (The Constitution doesn't actually mention privacy, but it's implied in the Bill of Rights, apparently, so there you go.)

This case was a major precedent for another contentious issue to come before the Supreme Court less than a decade later. In 1973, the Supreme Court's decision in *Roe v. Wade* legalized abortion. Again the issue is privacy: If we have the right to privacy, then we have the right to make private decisions about private matters. We can do what we want to our own bodies (provided there's no law against it) and making a law that limits our right to do what we want violates our constitutional rights. This kind of blurry, circuitous argument is open to all kinds of counter-arguments, which is why there remains the possibility that the court could change its mind and make abortion illegal—there's no law that actually legalizes it, there's just a law that says, well, it's not illegal because we have the right to make decisions about our own bodies and private spaces so long as we're not breaking the law.

The legal concept of privacy, which protects our private property (including our bodies), gives us the right to have protected sex without anyone interfering, but also hems us in by saying that we do not have the right to expect that a conversation we have with our sex partners over the phone will be private, because our words are passing through public airspace. Almost by accident we return to the castle: we're safe inside. We don't dare look out. We're better off with the window boarded over than we are exposing ourselves to the doings and deeds hiding behind the night's facade. Privacy has become something to hide behind. In private, we can use a condom, speak freely without fear of being recorded, and otherwise live our lives unobserved. But out and about in the world next door, your every move is fair game. As a result, the more privacy you have, the freer you are to go about your life undisturbed. How do you get privacy? You acquire more real estate. Since more stuff equals more privacy, it behooves all of us to expand our holdings as much as possible.

Most of us live in the equivalent of cubicles. We have and cherish our private space, but the necessity of going out into the world means we are constantly forced to put our rear ends on display. The conventional wisdom is that our ultimate goal is to close off the cubicle. We are cubicle dwellers but we want to be office dwellers, we want to be able to protect our backsides by shutting the door on the passing world with a reassuring, luxurious click. The rise of suburbanization (a by-product of the American Dream) set the stage for an obsession with privacy and personal space that was utterly without precedent in human life. As Mark Andrejevic writes in his book *iSpy*:

> Each household came to serve as the repository for a private set of appliances that displaced or replaced forms of collective consumption: the automobile displaced the trolley and train, the phonograph and radio the concert hall, and the TV set the downtown movie theatre. Thus began the trend toward personalization and individuation that eventually yielded the Walkman, the iPod, and the cell phone. . . . The trend continues that associated with 1950s suburbanization, which offered an escape from urban

congestion as surely as it served as a form of sorting, exclusion, and differentiation.

This is privacy not as a human right (the right to be left relatively alone by government and other social institutions) but as the basis for a social experiment that has transformed modern life and created a new human goal: exclusion. Twenty-first-century privacy isn't about human rights, it's about encouraging and privileging individual enclaves. In contemporary suburban society, privacy, "the right to be left alone should you so desire," has become "the compulsion to be left alone." Today we are taught to actively seek exclusion. The more you are able to shut yourself off from the world, buffered by a sea of servants, alarm systems, advisors, and electrified gates, the more of a success you are.

But being shut off from the world isn't all it's cracked up to be—not for the kids, the parents, or the vast, unseen infrastructure of nannies, maids, yard workers, dry cleaners, delivery people, and private security forces who are needed to make this kind of "privacy" happen. There are consequences to equating privacy with property and putting exclusion at the top of the list of achievements in our society. Scholar Amitai Etzioni writes in his book *The Limits of Privacy* that "social philosophers whose societies experienced . . . highly restrictive conditions did not concern themselves with the danger of legitimizing individual rights to excess." By this he means that the pioneering Enlightenment thinkers—from uber-capitalist Adam Smith to moral relativist David Hume—who sought to kick back against repression by imbuing the individual with sacrosanct rights, were unable to foresee what might happen to a society when it went too far the other way. Then again, who could ever have imagined just how much emphasis modern life would put on the individual's quest to live life unobserved and unencumbered?

As it turns out, our enclaves of private individualism are also havens of depression and anxiety. The more we protect our privacy (that is, our personal property), the lonelier we seem to get. The software of our society is telling us to barricade ourselves, to show the cruel world only a made-up face, a beauty-pageant grin. But our internal hardware is attuned to a different way of living altogether. Somewhere inside of us, we still live huddled together in caves, tepees, igloos, longhouses, grass huts, and wood shacks. We live hand-to-mouth, and we live on top of one another, extended families merging into other extended families, tribes, villages, shtetls, settlements in which everybody knows everybody, and going off on your own is considered a brave, possibly foolhardy act of spiritual communion, something you maybe endure once in your lifetime as a rite of passage, not something you do anytime you feel the need to "find yourself" or "have your alone time."

So from behind the barred walls of our castles we pop our antidepressants and log in online to chronicle the minutiae of our neurotic obsessions. We eagerly answer every survey, frantically rate and review our purchases, anxiously scan Frank Warren's PostSecret Web site for signs that others share our many problems, tell our shrink and our hairdresser everything, and make sure we turn all three locks and set the alarm system before we leave our apartment (you never know who your neighbors are, after all). Many of us are so desperate for attention, notice, and community that we're willing to blurt our secrets to the world. We're willing to accept at face value that anybody who pays attention to us—even people we've never met—and probably will never meet (including the paid employees of corporations)—are our friends.

When we share our private lives, we do so as a kind of unconscious protest against contemporary privacy's boxed-in ideology. What we're doing is groping our way toward some kind of digitalized version of our hardwired need for community. Unfortunately even the best of intentions is quickly co-opted. Many other interests have a hand in shaping our ever-shifting understanding of what privacy is and how it should function in capitalist society. To say that today there are myriad players with vastly different agendas is a massive understatement. Just about everyone, from upstart Web 2.0 tycoons to the old-style insurance companies and television executives working hand in hand with Homeland Security (result: ABC's *Homeland Security USA*, in which customs agents confiscate canned bat, cocaine, and a Swiss belly dancer's outfits), has a stake in advancing a particular perspective on what privacy is and how it should work. It's the average citizen who ends up getting caught in the middle of this push-pull process of reimagining privacy in the time of Peep.

◻ ◻ ◻

A while back, my father received a letter from his insurance company. The letter announced the company's decision to revoke his car insurance. He's not some wild-eyed, spoiled-brat teenager who just dunked his new Porsche in the country club's swimming pool. He's a middle-class, married professional in his sixties, living in the suburbs. What gives?

Dad called up his insurance company. They told him that they made decisions based on reports from a data collection company by the name of ChoicePoint. They told him he could call that company to request his dossier. He could then dispute any inaccurate information and the insurance company would re-evaluate their decision. Dad called ChoicePoint. They said they'd send him what they had on him. They sent him three different reports. One detailed his traffic violations. One recorded car accidents. One talked about his credit history.

As Dad told me about these reports, he became more and more incensed. One of the documents recorded that he had three speeding tickets in 2006. "That's between me and the Motor Vehicle Bureau!" he proclaimed. And anyway, he only remembers two. What's this third one? He can't remember the third ticket.

How's he supposed to dispute it if they don't even say where it happened? He's got three accidents listed on the report as well. "They were nothing," he assured me. "Fender benders and even less. Most of them didn't even involve an insurance claim. I wasn't driving. It was your mother." The report bore this out. Mom was driving. A zero-cost fender bender in 2008, an accident in 2006 (that ended up costing the insurance company five thousand dollars), and one all the way back in 2003 involving the old blue '96 Honda Civic that got passed on to me before I was forced to abandon it for dead at a gas station halfway between Ottawa and Toronto. On the phone, Dad was getting more and more pissed off. "That one that just happened; your mom was driving. I wasn't even there and there's no damage claim. How do they even know about it?" Dad's gotten himself really worked up now. "What right do they have to this information? They collect this stuff and then sell it, the fuckers! They're selling my private information and making money, and what do I get? Now my car insurance is going to triple!"

I pointed out to Dad that the vast majority of the companies that make his life comfortable and convenient collect data about him. Credit cards (which he has quite a few of, according to ChoicePoint), frequent flier miles, car loans, the mortgage on his house, the financing on his car, medical insurance, car insurance, and even Google. All conveniences that wouldn't exist if they couldn't record, and in many cases resell, every single thing he does through them. "That's different," Dad announced. "I let them do that, I say it's okay for them to do that. But this, nobody asked me about this."

Faced with ChoicePoint's irrefutable evidence, Dad felt powerless. They'd amalgamated data about him from various sources and produced a report that suggested that he wasn't a very good driver, that suggested, in fact, that his driving was getting worse. (Anyone who's taken a hair-raising trip to the mall with him might agree but that's—ahem—off the record and beside the point.) "I'm going to complain," he told me. Who was Dad going to complain to? The tickets and the accidents all happened because someone somewhere said they happened. He can't dispute their accuracy, only the picture that emerged when the dots were all connected. "I'm going to call the state government. The, like, human rights office or some shit like that." I expressed the opinion that Dad was unlikely to get very far with his complaint. The ChoicePoint material came with reams of paperwork about the rights of consumers. The bottom line is that in his case they followed procedure to the letter. There was only one avenue to complain if information was erroneous, or if it had been provided to people who shouldn't have had their hands on it. (Only those who have a legitimate reason to see the information for reasons of determining your apparent level of risk as a debtor or a driver, for instance, are supposed to get it.) You can't complain about the collecting of the information and the providing of the information to legitimate businesses who need it to make their decisions. I pointed out to Dad that unlike in Canada, Australia, and many European countries, the United States has nothing like a privacy officer or commissioner, a government-appointed position to oversee matters that effect our right to privacy. And even those commissioners don't change much in terms of how things like driving and credit reports get disseminated. It's capitalism, I told Dad. They get something they can sell and they sell it. "It's not capitalism," Dad said bitterly. "It's robbery. It's stealing."

My father's anger suggests the shifting nature of our sense of privacy in the age of Peep. So long as he perceived himself to be in control, so long as he felt that he could only gain, he was happy to reveal himself. Why not? I haven't done anything wrong and I couldn't care less if they are watching me for the purposes of providing me with better services. I will hole up in my castle and offer them little tidbits of information through the barred windows. But as soon as Dad discovered that the system wasn't working for him anymore, was, in fact, watching him—not to take care of him but to take care of its own self-perpetuating methodology, he was filled with rage. Now he wanted his information back. Now he cared that a private company could buy his motor vehicle records, his credit and credit card histories, and other records. Now, all of a sudden, some things should not be for sale, some things should not be permitted, there needs to be an agency or bureaucracy to prevent such indignities. Hey, someone snuck into my turret and cleaned me out!

But it's too late. Dad's life is public property, a treasure trove of information for sale that belies both the idea of privacy and the fantasy that we can somehow control the spread of data about us.

To prove my point, I decided to see what I could find out about Dad myself. How much of what ChoicePoint knows is actually "private" anyway? I set out to do a bit of online sleuthing. At Detectives.com I ordered a complete background search on Dad. It cost me $39.95. I also tried to order one on myself, to be fair, but apparently background searches on Canadians have to be farmed out and the price jumps to $289. Too steep for me. Cheapskate that I am, I decided to stick with Dad. For similar reasons, I passed on the site's offer to supply me with video surveillance of my subject for a mere $579. Next time. While I waited for my order to be fulfilled, I dropped by NetDetective.com to see what they offered. Turns out three years of online searches was a mere $29.95. That I could afford. I signed up. After all, NetDetective promised me "information on over 90% of the U.S. population."

They didn't disappoint when it came to Dad. His life was an open book. The combined report from Detectives.com and Net-Detective.com revealed his date of birth, his present and previous addresses (going all the way back to my childhood home in Ottawa, Ontario), the names of his wife and kids, where he worked and used to work, and a list of his various hobbies and interests. Here's a sample of what all of this looks like:

Cooking Enthusiast: YES

Length of Residence: 26 YEARS

Outdoor Enthusiast: YES

Occupation: RETIRED

Contributes to Charities: YES

There was also a list of his neighbors (I searched them too, since it's a flat fee), a discussion of his criminal record—I put plans of blackmail on hold when it turned out to be a speeding ticket—and the first four numbers of his social security number. I'm thinking it probably wouldn't be that hard to get the rest. Mainly the report focused on his finances: his income is predicted, the estimated value of his home is noted, the "presence of premium credit cards" is reported. I found out about his "Refinance Term in Months," his "Refinance Amount In Thousands," and even his "Refinance Lender Name."

This material, while less personally revealing than stuff I have on my Facebook page—including my political leanings and the answers to a lengthy questionnaire application I installed, which asks me, among other things, if I've ever been arrested and if I've ever had a one-night stand—is probably more useful. This is the kind of information you can use to stalk someone, to screw with their finances, to adopt their identity. It's also prurient Peep fun. For a flat fee, you can find out what your date makes and if he or she's ever been in trouble with the law. You can discover if your neighbor is renting or owns. It's pretty doubtful that every search done on these services has to do with checking the veracity of your own credit rating or searching for a long-lost relative. At any rate, there it is. Forty bucks, and Dad—utterly normal, hard-working suburbanite—is exposed to all who care to look.

I wasn't surprised by the information available about my father (though I was a bit disappointed that he didn't have wives in four other states and a host of hidden half-siblings he funnels money to via his second job as a Canadian Secret Service operative). There's a ton of information out there about anyone who participates in everyday normal life and has a job, magazine subscriptions, and car insurance. What we still might think of as private isn't even close. Our every move is being quantified and sold to interested parties. The private detective Stephen Rambam, a manic New Yorker who does "Privacy is Dead" seminars and made at least part of his name hunting Nazis, tells me that "now nothing is ever thrown away. Now you can store everything and the original is in digital format which means it can be indexed and cross-referenced. Artificial intelligence has gone through the roof. We've got six billion records just on people. If we can do that imagine the power of large governmental agencies. Everything you do is in some respect either directly or indirectly available." Rambam provides various examples of ways he uses random bits of information to determine who you are, what you are like, and where you are likely to be. "Everything is available online—from what types of books you like to read, it is child's play to extrapolate what your politics are. If you're buying a book by Chomsky you're not going to be voting for Bush." He goes on to note that if you're registered for social network Web site Dogster, you own a dog. If you're posting to chess maniacs, you play the game. "The bottom line is there is nothing that I can't learn about you. The basic building blocks of your character, your beliefs, your activities, your physical location, and now the holy grail of investigations which is your picture, all of this is available online."

Is Rambam upset about this turn of events? Not all that much. "The vast majority of this stuff exists for good reason. There's a credit report on you because lenders want to know if they should give you a half-million bucks for a house. In the U.S. I can check to see if my nanny is a convict and if my kid's bus driver was ever charged for DUI. I should have a right to know who my neighbor is and what their character is. Fifty, sixty years ago this wasn't important, you knew your neighbor, your father knew your neighbor's father. I grew up in a neighborhood, if my mother was looking for me and I was ten blocks away some ladies would lean out a window and yell 'Steven Rambam! Your mother is looking for you.' In New York City and Toronto the average person does not know who's living next to them. There has to be a means to determine who you're interacting with and do you want to interact with them." Plus, Rambam tells me, a lot of the material he finds online is put there by the people he's investigating in the first place. "The bulk of the really good stuff is self-created. I mean Twitter is just bizarre. I've broken workman compensation cases based on stuff they've put on YouTube."

Rambam is a realist and an opportunist. The stuff is out there for a reason: to advance the needs of capitalism and keep things moving along. The Peep material that isn't out there for a reason is often self-generated and, as such, ripe for the picking. If somebody is stupid enough to post a YouTube video of himself skateboarding while he's supposed to be laid up by permanent back pain, well, that's his fault isn't it? But it's also true that the credit ratings, court records, and surveys of our preferences that exist ostensibly to assist us are all the property of others—institutions and corporations that buy and sell the defining characteristics of our lives. My father's generation sees it differently, of course. Dad worked hard all his life for his suburban castle. He worked for his car, his house, his life insurance, his private stuff and, presumably, his right to privacy. And now it's all an open book. Moreover, that book is open to interpretation, interpretation that, with the click of a key, might very well leave him (horrors) taking the bus to get around. The homeless woman living in a bag in the park across from the White House has more privacy that your average homeowner. Her name doesn't come up in the NetDetective database and Stephen Rambam will not be able to use her online postings to determine her politics, sexual orientation, and, ultimately, her whereabouts. In contrast, Dad has become a cog in the machine operating his own life.

After talking with Stephen Rambam, he invited me to come

to the H.O.P.E. (Hackers On Planet Earth) conference in New York City. He wanted me to be his volunteer. His plan was to share the results of what he called my "digital colonoscopy" in front of a live audience. He would talk with my friends and neighbors, show surveillance footage of me picking my nose, and otherwise reveal every habit, peccadillo, and pastime of the human being known as Hal Niedzviecki. Warily I agreed to go to the convention. Then weeks passed and I started to worry. It's one thing to know abstractly that you don't really have privacy and maybe don't even really want privacy, but like a lot of people, I still count on a certain amount of anonymity based on the thought that, well, no one really cares what I buy, search for online, or make for a living. The more time passed, the more I disliked the idea of someone researching me and, worse, presenting that research to a live audience. Every time I went online I wondered: Just how much could Rambam find out? I didn't relish a list of my Google searches appearing on Rambam's PowerPoint presentation. "Recent searches include: 'Bed Wetting,' 'Anxiety Symptoms,' and 'Nude photos of ____' (insert name of hot movie star of the moment here). Hey, I would protest feebly, my cheeks burning. That bed wetting thing was for our two-year-old. The anxiety stuff was research for a short story. And that other thing, it was, uh—everybody does those searches. That doesn't mean I'm some kind of—. But my protests would be drowned out by laughter. I'd turn to look at the screen and see that Rambam had just posted my annual earnings.

I was feeling what Dad felt—a loss of control, a sense of impotent rage at being reduced. How did the system I thought I had all figured out turn against me so quickly? I never did get my "digital colonoscopy." Rambam grew impatient with me when I couldn't confirm that a planned television crew would be on hand to film the presentation. He moved on to another volunteer victim, leaving me both disappointed and relieved. Still, Rambam did me a favor. He helped me realize how easy it is to cling to outmoded ideas about the sanctity of individual privacy, even when we know better. Dad and I clung to those ideas because they are tangible and comfortable. We liked the idea that we had—or at least deserved to have—privacy, even when the truth is a lie and the idea is more valuable to the various corporations who adroitly utilize our private information in a hundred different ways than it is to us.

◻ ◻ ◻

Many institutions, entities, and corporations have come to realize just how willing we are to "share" in the age of Peep. They seek to "educate" us about protecting our privacy (which also protects them from lawsuits and other headaches, like too much intrusive government regulation). At the same time, they actively take the opportunity to turn our private information into the final frontier of capitalism, a kind of (de)personalized soul mining in which every one of our opinions on a product, every one of our address changes, every one of our family snapshots, is banked and assigned value. The goal seems to be to convince us of the utmost importance of our privacy even as they record and sell our every move.

A summer 2008 Senate committee investigation into online privacy found Microsoft associate general counsel Mike Hintze, Google chief privacy counsel Jane Horvath, and Facebook chief privacy officer Chris Kelly eagerly testifying about their efforts to help people retain their privacy. "Google supports the passage of a comprehensive federal privacy law," said Jane Horvath. "We believe that as information flows increase and more and more information is processed and stored in the Internet cloud—on remote servers rather than on users' home computers—there is a greater need for uniform data safeguarding standards, data breach notification, and stronger procedural protections relating to government and third-party litigant access to individuals' information." The giant Peep corporations fall all over themselves assuring us that our privacy is respected and that our secrets are safe with them. They have privacy officers, fund privacy conferences, team with privacy commissioners and schools to spread awareness, and employ scads of lawyers to make sure they're doing their best to uphold their side of the bargain. All the while they frame the discussion in terms of us keeping our privacy safe versus having our privacy taken away from us (by unscrupulous thieves or less-civic-minded corporations with no respect for the Constitution). But Peep culture shows us that the real debate is quite different. The real debate starts with the fact that privacy, as framed by corporations and governments, isn't much of a priority for us. We've learned a different lesson than the one that the privacy councilors and commissioners want us to learn; it's a lesson taught to us by the myriad celebrities and politicians who trade in their private lives and get the kind of attention most of us can only dream of. Pictures of twin newborns have a value; the story of your gastric bypass surgery and subsequent weight loss can jumpstart you into a new career; posing online nude can win you cash prizes and make you new friends. It's easy for corporations and governments to say that privacy must be protected and that they are committed to that. It's much harder for them to admit that many of us don't value our privacy nearly as much as the possibility of meaningful connection, convenience, and rewards like attention and even remuneration. I'll say it again: We desperately want to escape from the castle.

But that doesn't mean we want to be ripped off. The same September 2008 study by the Pew Internet & American Life Project that disclosed that less than half of us worry about data we store online being revealed to the government found that 90 percent of us would be very concerned if those online companies sold our personal files to others. We don't really care who peers in at our lives if we think that the peering will keep us safer, help us connect, or otherwise advance our interests. But we do care if we

think that someone is taking what we give away for free and selling it to the highest bidder without kicking a single cent back to
us. To paraphrase my Dad, that's not capitalism: that's stealing.

This couches the debate in a very different context. It puts
the onus on the various Web sites asking for our participation for
free to meaningfully compensate us for the information we are
currently giving away. Part of our escape from the castle has to
be a clear-eyed, unsentimental look at the different ways we can
utilize our ability to access this newfound, previously untapped
resource formally known as our privacy.

How much is your life worth in the age of Peep? How much
value is there in your routine? How much should I get paid for
letting, say, a grocery store keep track of everything I buy—everything my family and I put in our bellies?

To find out, I dropped in on Jason Pridmore, just putting
the finishing touches on a PhD thesis on the phenomenon of
loyalty points programs. When I spoke with him, Pridmore was
working at Queen's University, in Kingston, Ontario, under the
tutelage of none other than Surveillance Project founder David
Lyon. "What makes a research study of loyalty programs like
AirMiles part of the Surveillance Project?" I asked him. "When
I go into a classroom," Pridmore told me, "and I ask 'What is
surveillance?' the students think of CCTV cameras and the FBI.
They don't think of the mundane activities they do like when
they are buying something and the sales person says, 'What's
your phone number?' They don't think of that as surveillance.
Because surveillance has such negative connotations." Mild-
mannered Pridmore is no radical—he's teaching at a famously
conservative university and, like me, like most of us, he can't
resist the allure of a frequent flier plan and Facebook. But unlike
most of us, Pridmore wonders why we're so quick to use these
services, and so slow to consider their possible ramifications in
our lives and society. "I did a survey which concluded that there
is no correlation between whether people use loyalty programs

and have privacy concerns. People are so wrapped up in themselves that they don't really notice."

Surely they notice that they are pulling out a card every time they buy something with the aim of collecting enough points to get a reward. Of course we know we're doing something, Pridmore agrees. In fact, even though the loyalty programs generally seek to perpetuate what Pridmore dubs "the illusion of something for nothing," research has shown that "people are aware that they are modifying their behavior." In other words, you know you're driving out of your way to get to a gas station that will reward you with points. You know you are choosing one airline over another only because you've pledged "loyalty." But, according to Pridmore, what we don't really notice is what happens to the information we're allowing our loyalty program to collect. Where do all these mountains of data go and how are they used?

In his office, Pridmore pulled out two grocery store newsprint fliers. They were from the same store, covering the same week of specials. Except that one flier had a delicious grilled salmon with rice pilaf on the cover to advertise a special on salmon fillets, and one had a luscious ice cream pie on the cover, to advertise a good deal on frozen treats. According to Pridmore, the first flier was distributed in a neighborhood that had indicated a preference for healthy eating, and the other flier was distributed in an area that had statistically been more likely to go for the processed foods and calorie-laden treats. "What I suggest is that we end up seeing it becoming a reciprocal process whereby loyalty programs act as a means to gather information and that information then gets projected back onto those same individuals, so you see this cyclical process in which socio-economic factors become reiterated." Uh, can you say that in English? "If you keep getting these things it begins to reinforce who you are and what you are about." So it pigeonholes people and in many cases ends up acting as a proxy for assumptions about class and ethnicity.

Most of us don't think of this kind of activity as surveillance or privacy violation. In fact, we generally see the discounts and deals we get through participating in loyalty programs as a fair exchange. We give a particular company, franchise, or store our exclusive business, and in exchange we are rewarded for our loyalty with discounts or free products. We don't think about what the company might do with the stream of data we're providing them—a stream they don't much want to talk about and don't directly compensate us for. The information generated from our loyalty programs is sold to any number of gigantic companies and even government agencies. It is sold to information broker companies that seek to attach as many details to your name as they can legally acquire so that they can then sell that info all over again—to other databases, banks, marketing companies, private detectives, and more. In this way some of the biggest companies you've never heard of make piles of money and, in some cases, determine major issues in your life, like whether or not you'll get a job, a mortgage, or a good price on car insurance. Corporations like Equifax, Acxiom, infoGroup, and Dad's nemesis ChoicePoint (now owned by "Risk & Information Analytics Group" LexisNexis) store and trade the personal data of millions of Americans and billions worldwide.

Mark Andrejevic reports in his book *iSpy* that when he asked a cousin of his who works at "one of the nation's largest database companies" to send him a copy of the information the company had on file about herself (company rules prevented her from accessing and sending him his own information), "it was more than twenty pages long and included not only a list of all the places she'd lived, but the names of all her former roommates and all of the cars she'd owned."

The companies who trade your personal information run the gamut from fastidiously serving the needs of the insurance and credit card industries, to venally offering your name to the highest (or any) bidder. Consider the case of Richard Guthrie, ninety-two-year-old army veteran living in Iowa. He entered a sweepstakes which caused his name to appear in a database being peddled by infoUSA, one of the largest compilers of consumer information. (Running a sweepstakes that is primarily intended to collect names, addresses, ages, and habits is an ongoing practice in the info collection industry.) What kind of databases does infoUSA sell? According to the *New York Times* you can buy lists such as "Elderly Opportunity Seekers"—3.3 million older people "looking for ways to make money"; "Suffering Seniors"—4.7 million people with cancer or Alzheimer's; and "Oldies but Goodies"—500,000 gamblers over fifty-five years old. All of this for only 8.5 cents apiece. One list promises that "these people are gullible. They want to believe that their luck can change." Well, Mr. Guthrie's luck changed. After entering the sweepstakes, someone called his home, tricked him into revealing his bank account information, then emptied out his life savings. It's hard to believe that there's no connection between Guthrie entering the sweepstakes, having his name appear on an infoUSA list like the ones above, and the subsequent disappearance of his cash.

News of the occasional cheated old person may upset us, but it's only a tiny part of a much bigger story: the story of how the trade in personal information has been used to push people further and further into the kind of ill-advised debt that, at least in part, precipitated the financial meltdown and real estate crash of 2008. An article in the *New York Times* tells of Brenda Jerez of Jersey City, who fell ill with cancer, was forced to leave her accounting job, and ran up fifty thousand dollars on her credit cards before filing for bankruptcy protection. Not four months after she emerged from insolvency, "six to ten new credit and auto loan offers arrived every week that specifically mentioned her bankruptcy." There were even letters, like one from First Premier Bank, that "promoted a platinum MasterCard for people with 'less-than-perfect credit.'" This kind of minute targeting, which encourages people to get credit they can't afford and sign up for mortgages they don't understand and ultimately won't be able to pay was, as *Times* reporter Brad Stone writes, "one of the overlooked causes of the debt boom and the resulting crisis, which threatens to choke the global economy." Stone lays out the whole scheme, one which is both perfectly legal and perpetually enticing for all those who one day seek to own a castle of their own: "Using techniques that grew more sophisticated over the last decade, businesses comb through an array of sources, including bank and court records, to create detailed profiles of the financial lives of more than 100 million Americans. They then sell that information as marketing leads to banks, credit card issuers and mortgage brokers, who fiercely compete to find untapped customers—even those who would normally have trouble qualifying for the credit they were being pitched."

◻ ◻ ◻

Before Peep culture took over from pop culture, corporations generally acquired private information for what at least they purported were the essentials: calculating insurance risk, providing loans, assessing security. Bunkered down as we were in our castles, we were more circumspect about our private lives and less willing to spew forth our preferences for puffed rice breakfast foods and variable mortgages. But since pop became Peep, and we started discovering how much value there is in sharing (and oversharing), a whole new class of corporations have come to the fore. They help us watch ourselves and our neighbors, and in the process they help themselves to just about everything we care to entrust to their "free" services.

What's the saying? Nothing in life is free. In order to provide advertisements that are smarter, more effective, and more "contextual," Google, MySpace, and other Peep companies and Web sites are storing your searches and amalgamating them into useful kernels of data which don't necessarily identify you individually, but certainly create a very detailed picture of a person they think is like you. Yahoo! offers advertisers a customized advertising system that is constantly analyzing and responding to what its 500 million separate users are doing on the site, with the goal of connecting those users to ads immediately relevant to their real lives. Similarly, in 2007, MySpace pioneered something called "interest targeting," which involves gleaning likes and dislikes from its users' pages to sell ads in ten categories, including finance, cars, fashion, and music. Peter Levinsohn, head of Fox Interactive Media, proudly told an investor conference that this scheme would harness the power of the information that users were already putting on their pages for all to see. It's not so much privacy invasion as it is extending the reach of what we're already making public (though not for those purposes). We display ourselves for friendship, for attention, for convenience, and the corporate entity that makes it possible grabs up that information and uses it to generate profit. At the MySpace investor conference, Mr. Levinsohn talked about a hypothetical MySpace user named "Jill" who identifies herself as a "fashionista" and writes a blog about fashion. "She even goes so far as telling us she needs new boots for the fall," Levinsohn said. "How would you like to be an advertiser selling boots to her?" Remember, MySpace continues to be the number one social networking site in the world. "This is really just the beginning for us," Levinsohn promised. "No one else in the marketplace can offer this kind of concentrated reach."

It's just the beginning: advertisers are now starting to use the GPS feature incorporated into all new cell phones, including the iPhone and the BlackBerry, to track users, fix them in place and time, and send them location-specific ads via text message. This trend sends info-tech execs into high-salivation mode. As Google chief executive Eric Schmidt (whose company sends map information to iPhone users over AT&T's wireless network) told CNBC: "If you think about it, a mobile phone is much more personal and therefore the advertising can be much more targeted. And we win when we have more targeted ads." Online and cell phone advertising is booming: Greg Sterling of Opus Research in San Francisco forecasts that mobile advertising revenue for North America and Western Europe will hit $5 billion by 2012.

A good example of how this kind of thing works and how easily it can go awry came about when I ordered a book from Amazon called *Naked on the Internet: Hookups, Downloads and Cashing in on Internet Sexploration* (a somewhat misleading title for what turned out to be a pretty staid academic study of how sex and the Internet intersect). A few weeks later, Amazon sent me a list of books that I might also like, including *Working Sex: Sex Workers Write About a Changing Industry, Start Your Own Adult Web Site Business,* and *The Internet Escort's Handbook.* Amazon thinks that I'm starting my own adult Web site. (Probably a good idea, certainly more lucrative than writing.) Who else now thinks I'm planning to get into the sex business? My employer? My spouse? My parents? My insurance provider? My bank? My local police station? What might a private detective extrapolate from this little exchange?

It's all about the reach. How deep can the corporation get into the life of the consumer? Have you noticed how eager so many Web sites are to have you write reviews of books, movies, music, video games, vacations, and really anything at all? This too can be a kind of privacy invasion, a kind of monitoring. When you say what you like and why you like it, companies takes notice. There's an explosion of so-called interactive customer feedback happening on sites like Amazon, Netflix, TigerDirect, Yahoo!'s Web site–bookmarking and -sharing site Delicious, and so many more. Even staid department store Sears invited me to write a review when I availed myself of their online catalogue. Rate the product. Suggest a related product. Create a wish list. Make your favorites available to family, friends, anyone! This is Peep inasmuch as others derive entertainment from perusing your ordinary, nonexpert opinions about the Braun coffee maker, the latest Michael Ondaatje novel, or your favorite home-renovation Web site. It's also an easy way to gather information about customer preferences, information which can be repackaged, resold, and possibly attached to your name for the rest of your life.

Mark Andrejevic bitingly calls this "the model of willing submission to comprehensive monitoring as a form of participation." He also calls this "the work of being watched." What he means, basically, is that the smart companies are figuring out how to let you come to them. You generate valuable marketing and demographic information about your likes and dislikes and preferences on their site for free, even as you produce reams and reams of highly entertaining, utterly grassroots content. You design your own sneakers or jeans online, and in the process you tell them exactly what you (or someone like you or someone in your age group, in your zip code) might like. Your design might be open to other people voting, critiquing, discussing, all of which generates content and entertainment, and encourages more people to make more designs. Meanwhile the corporation lauds its transparency, flexibility, and interactivity. Company execs present the plan to the shareholders and await the applause they deserve for coming up with such a "great way to insert the consumer into the process of product development," as one retail consultant put it. Video-game makers, clothing sites, sneaker sites—even Lego lets you design and order your own customized set of interlocking Swedish fun. Reuben Steiger, head of a company that brokers commercial opportunities in the virtual world, Second Life (a very Peep environment where the main thrill comes from everybody watching what everybody else is doing) notes that the value of virtual environments for companies is that the buyer can endlessly customize. They can buy the virtual Toyota Scion for $1.50 (yes, Second Life money has a real value) and then customize it as much as they want. "You're interacting with the brand in a fairly intimate way, you can customize it to your heart's content, change the color, the rims, in ways that fit your fancy; that's very interesting to companies."

Let's not delude ourselves into believing that only vapid losers sucked too deep into commercial culture end up writing thousands of reviews for Amazon, custom-designing virtual cars in virtual worlds, and insisting on their own made-to-order Levis. This kind of Peep marketing is everywhere, and it's not necessarily limited to those who actively participate online. *Wired* magazine blogger Daniel Akst notes that even medical implant companies like Medtronics are getting in on the action, selling you not just a pacemaker but a cardiac implant that sends information about your health to you and your doctor, keeping you connected to the company and its products for as long as you live, via interactive, two-way communication that also generates valuable data about how fast the heart of an overweight sixty-year-old Caucasian male beats when he climbs two flights of stairs, and so on. You and your pacemaker are doing the work of Peep. Meanwhile Andrejevic cites TiVo as another example of a product of the Peep age. "TiVo?" you might be thinking. That liberating service that lets you record whatever TV you want, whenever you want, and fast forward through the commercials? The product that *Adbusters*, darling magazine of lefty ad designers, Hollywood liberals, and college vegans, lauded as "something revolutionary. Something almost purely democratic" that "sticks it to every broadcast advertiser"? Well, guess what? TiVo's goal, as Andrejevic writes, "is not to overthrow the corporate media, but to provide it with the most detailed information possible about viewers. . . . Far from fomenting revolution, TiVo promised to become the twenty-first-century realization of the Orwellian telescreens that watches viewers while they watch TV." While you're watching whatever you like, how you like, TiVo is watching exactly what you're watching, including when you rewind, when you fast forward, when you pause, what commercials you might actually watch, and everything else they can think of.

We keep slaving away for someone else's benefit. How many

of YouTube's top video posters, who draw millions of eyeballs to the site, are Google shareholders? But we don't think of it like that. We don't think of it as work. As Jason Pridmore said to me about loyalty programs, we're eager to participate: "It's great, they tailor things to my needs." As with the Peep phenomenon overall, we rarely, if ever, see what we're doing as giving away our private information. And even if we did, would we necessarily care? Corporations that facilitate Peep via various schemes ranging from pseudo-interactivity to custom design get value out of something that heretofore nobody really wanted—our regular lives. As with other Peep phenomenon, like blogging, social networking, and even appearances on reality TV, the perception is that we're utilizing a resource that didn't have any value before, so we really have nothing to lose. We can only go up in the world. We're so used to passively being fed our choices back to us, so used to being relegated to the tower in the castle, that we eagerly take up any option to communicate, no matter how conceivably compromised. In the age of Peep, Mark Andrejevic writes,

> the offer of participation has become its own reward which helps explain, at least in part, why people might be willing to pay more for customized products, why they might be willing to pay to share in some of the "duties" of production, and perhaps even why some of them might be willing to appear on reality TV shows that chronicle the details of their daily lives in exchange for payment that often amounts to less than minimum wage.

We're trading our personal lives for rewards, discounts, and opportunities to be noticed and notice others in turn. The social and personal consequences are subtle to the point of being largely invisible. A free flight, a company that promises to give you money if something bad happens to you, a forum to write book reviews that other people will actually read and respond to, an authorized service that lets you watch what you want when you want and skip the commercials—those are tangible, understandable gains.

Where all this information about you goes after you've agreed to the trade isn't nearly as interesting. As a result, we often don't realize what we've wrought until it's too late. "In the U.S.," explains Mike Neuenschwander, research director of Identity and Privacy Strategies at the Burton Group, a technology advisory service, "certain kinds of personal information aren't treated like property at all. It's very difficult to sue someone for misuse of personal information. And even if you do, they can never give you back your mailing address, your Social Security number, or your DNA, for that matter."

❐ ❐ ❐

"I think privacy is dead," Dave Sifry, the CEO and founder of live Web search engine Technorati bluntly tells me. "It's like it's had its knees already cut out from it and it's just a matter of when the body falls."

I dropped in on Sifry's Technorati office in San Francisco to find out how the founder of a popular tool for peering on the Internet now feels about what he's had a hand in creating. Technorati is a search engine that specializes in what Sifry calls the "live Web." From blogs to Tweets to YouTube, it purports to collect shifting material faster than Google and be better at penetrating the endlessly flowing online minutiae that most of us figure pretty much just disappears. Sifry, dressed office casual, looks more suburban dad than techno innovator and veteran of the dotcom booms and busts. As he talks it becomes clear that he's pulled between his role as a family man who doesn't want his kids revealing the details of their lives on the Internet, and what initially attracted him to online life—the anarchic joys provided by the possibilities of ubiquitous connection. Sifry describes this rupture as what happens when "we see misunderstanding get into conflict with the efficiency of the tool." What he means is that few understand the rules governing the way pictures, comments, and videos posted online can be found and disseminated. Who bothers to read the user agreements and privacy policies of the Web sites they use? And anyway, a 2008 study found that if every American actually stopped to read the privacy policy of every Web site they visited for a year, it would take them each an annual average of 200 hours, or almost eight and a half entire days of fine-print peering. Given that, who would then pause to further inquire into how material, once posted, can be permanently erased from corporate-owned hosting Web sites, from search engines, from caches, from back-up files, from the desktops of eager downloaders? And so the rotting corpse of privacy. Dave Sifry's update of the catchphrase first uttered by then Sun Microsystems CEO Scott McNealy in 1999: "You already have zero privacy—get over it."

But, I asked Sifry, does Technorati—or do Google, Twitter, Facebook, YouTube and Live Journal, for that matter—have any kind of responsibility to their users? Or do the architects and owners of systems that can instantly and efficiently spread the kinds of secrets and lies that ruin lives get a free pass? "Frankly, to me it comes down to how you use the technology," Sifry answered. "But where it starts to get really really tricky is when it has to do with third parties. What happens when you're at a party and you see someone else throwing up over the porcelain god and you take a picture and you post it?"

Sifry and his cohorts don't want to be put in the position of arbitrating what should or shouldn't be posted online. It's up to you how you "use the technology." If you do stupid stuff like put up information about your cocaine habit, that's your fault. Still Sifry believes that engineers and techies have *some* responsibility for how people use what they create. "I'm only human," he says, "and as a creator you have to recognize that even the best intentions sometimes go awry. Having said that, I think it's my responsibility to think carefully about how we design systems in order to have an effect that's positive." Part of that positive effect is creating and enforcing privacy policies. After all, Sifry notes, you aren't going to have many repeat customers if you constantly violate their trust. That's an argument that gets used quite often when it comes to online services and privacy. If you don't respect the user, the user will move on. It's in the best interests of Yahoo!, Technorati, and Facebook to make sure that a user's privacy isn't violated any more than he or she wants it to be. At the same time, there's also profit to be derived from keeping records of what we search for, what we reveal about our preferences, and so on. Furthermore, the very nature of these services depend on encouraging us to watch and be watched. We will guard your privacy even as we record everything you do and facilitate your ability to look at the minutiae of everything other people do, and encourage those people to do the same to you. What kind of "positive effect" will such a system ultimately render?

I don't think Sifry is trying to be disingenuous. Sifry runs a small company and he really does believe that if his users thought he was selling their search info to the highest bidder, he'd be finished. This argument might not work as well with a bigger company, though. The bigger the company, the less vulnerable it is to grassroots insurrection. Google and Microsoft don't have to worry about their customer the way Sifry does. That's why Sifry himself tells me that he advises extreme caution when putting your information online. You just never know how it is going to be used or, given the reach of these global companies, where it might turn up. By way of a warning, he tells me about the time his sister, a psychologist living in another city, called him. Sifry's sister said, "Dave, one of my patients came into my office and she said 'Oh, Dr. Sifry, your children, they're so beautiful.'" Apparently the patient had found Dave Sifry's Web site and thought she was looking at pictures of her therapist's kids. That was a wake-up call for Sifry: "From that day on I password-protected everything and I never again put up non-password-protected pictures of my kids." Sifry is also increasingly cautious about how he blogs. He takes pains not to reveal what conferences he's going to and when he'll be there, so that nobody can track his whereabouts and the whereabouts of his family.

Even as Sifry becomes more guarded, his livelihood becomes more and more dependant on people continuing to publicly post, blog, and reveal. This is where we are in a Peep culture age that literally cannot function without making use of our private information. Sifry can't run his business without sifting through the digital detritus of our lives, any more than Dad's insurance company can assess the risk of guaranteeing to pick up the tab of his (or Mom's) next accident without finding out what they're getting into. Caught between his family role as father-figure/protector and his corporate role as information liberator, Sifry preaches the impossible, asking us to relish the instantaneous possibilities of online revelation, while perpetually assessing a possibly risky future. "Ultimately," he tells me, "we have to recognize the role of unintended consequences."

❏ ❏ ❏

Unintended consequences are everywhere in a Peepville that at once preaches privacy *and* encourages methodical self-revelation.

Jeff White was a high school senior living thirteen miles out of Mitchell, South Dakota, when I first encountered him. I met Jeff when he added me on Facebook. He'd read one of my books and noticed I was signed up, so figured it would be cool to be my Facebook pal. I messaged Jeff and asked him if I could call and talk with him about how he and his friends use Facebook. Jeff said sure. When I called him, Jeff told me that although the majority of the kids in his school use Facebook, no one he knows has ever read the Facebook privacy code or adjusted their profile page to limit access. Jeff explained that putting up pictures of yourself at the right party, waving a bright-red cup in front of your bright-red face had quickly become something of a necessary ritual. "We've created a Facebook rite of passage where you can look cool on Facebook by posting that kind of stuff [pictures from drinking parties]," he told me. "I would say half of the college pictures show ones with cups in them. You can look cool, just like you would brag about it." But looking cool online comes with a price. Jeff recounted an incident at his high school in which kids who posted pictures of a beer party on their Facebook pages ended up getting called into the principal's office and threatened with expulsion.

Jeff's Facebook experiences are hardly unique to Mitchell, South Dakota. Principals are watching, teachers are watching, parents are watching, college admissions officers are watching, future employers are watching, even prosecutors and the police are watching. These are the "unintended consequences" of a new corporate Peep culture that commodifies our every utterance. In Tilsonburg, Ontario, two hours southwest of Toronto, police reportedly were tipped off to a Facebook group called "Wabash Party," which featured a picture of two people passed out on a pile of empty beer cans, and a guest list of 716 people who had confirmed attendance at the upcoming event. "This party is gonna be a real mess," one person posted enthusiastically. Or not. The Ontario Provincial Police issued a statement to the public, warning that anyone who attended the party would be monitored for underage drinking, illegal drug use, and trespassing. Why even bother then? The party was canceled. In Britain a Facebook invitation to a beach party led police to impose a twenty-four-hour ban on liquor consumption in the coastal area of Torbay. The press reported that 7,000 people had RSVP'd to the party, and the police got nervous. They banned liquor and the organizer put up the following message on the invitation site: "People attending beaches in Torbay on the weekend will be asked to leave or be arrested. Do not travel to Torbay. There will still be a high police presence around the coast. No event whatsoever will be taking place in Torbay, and we urge you to inform all others you know that are planning to attend that it is no longer going ahead."

If you do go ahead and do something stupid like drink a bunch of beers and then plow your car into a bunch of other cars, you can now expect that your online demeanor, both before and after, will be taken into account. Two weeks after college student Joshua Lipton was charged in Rhode Island with drunk driving leading to a three-car smash-up that seriously injured a twenty-year-old woman in another car, Lipton hit the party circuit. He headed to a Halloween party wearing a striped prison shirt and an orange jumpsuit labeled "Jail Bird." He thought it was funny, partying while his crash victim was still in the hospital, but the judge didn't. After the prosecutor showed a PowerPoint slide show of recently posted Facebook pics (innocently tagged and posted by Lipton's pals, no doubt), Lipton got the maximum two-year sentence. Similarly a California college student by the name of Jessica Binkerd, charged with a fatal drunk-driving crash, failed to heed calls from her Santa Barbara lawyer to take down her MySpace page. She left it up, and prosecutors made hay out of the pictures they grabbed off the site. In one, Binkerd is wearing a shirt advertising tequila. In another, she's sporting a belt lined with plastic shot glasses. Binkerd ended up with a sentence of more than five years in jail. "When you take those pictures like that," said Binkerd's rueful lawyer, "it's a hell of an impact."

"Many young people and students probably think of the MySpace community that they're participating in as somewhat of a closed community," Deirdre Mulligan, clinical professor of law and director of the Samuelson Law, Technology & Public Policy Clinic at Berkeley tells me. "It turns out that it's not. There are voyeurs in that community and those voyeurs might not share their values. When you let loose on spring break, you didn't leave a permanent record, it was a transient activity, there [were] a few other witnesses. People have the ability to forget, so who knows what really happened? But now the whole point of letting loose is to document."

In the age of Peep, that's what we do: We document. We take

pictures. And then we share those pictures. We don't care about our privacy because we figure what we're doing is pretty much only of interest to us and our pals. Of course we're totally wrong. In the age of Peep, our every location, purchase, and thought has value, which is why companies are archiving like crazy and previously excluded authority figures and agents of law and order now have access to a closed network that used to be composed of whispers and rumors. As a result people are being accused of breaking the law before they even do anything. Or they're being hauled into the principal's office after the fact, simply for being in a snapshot. Or they're being denied admission to a college, rejected for a scholarship or a job, or sentenced to a prison term, all because of what they, themselves, put up online.

We've already met a number of people in this book who were fired, sued, or dumped for various acts of oversharing. Most of those people were not, ultimately, surprised by what happened to them, and many even relished the drama their oversharing created, watching with glee as their product-person-persona was enhanced by scandal. The cases we're looking at now are different. In these cases, people are, for the most part, accidentally providing information to "the system." They're doing something that they are encouraged to do or cannot avoid doing as they go about their lives, and then they discover that their everyday actions are being used against them in some way that they could never have intended or imagined. (Ways that, indeed, were impossible before the Peep age.) These people and their confusion demonstrate just how badly we need a New Deal on privacy, one that enables people to understand how, when, and why their private information is being gathered. I don't expect that people will stop putting their private lives out there; the rewards are too great. We need a new conception of privacy so that people can limit unintended consequences and derive maximum benefit from what, in the age of Peep, is becoming an increasingly valuable commodity—the gestures, acts, and choices we make every day, that constitute our private lives.

The need for education regarding the nature of privacy in the age of Peep is obvious when you consider a developing trend in law enforcement: teenagers being arrested and charged with child pornography for taking pictures or videos *of themselves.* The poster child for this was a fifteen-year-old girl in Ohio who was arrested for sending nude photos of herself to her buddies. She was originally charged with felony criminal offenses for illegally using a minor (herself) in the process of making nudity-oriented material. The teen could have been forced to register as a sexual offender annually for ten years. After public outcry, charges were dropped, due to an undisclosed agreement with her family. In another incident in Michigan, police did a drug-bust-like raid and confiscated dozens of cell phones that all contained pictures of a fourteen-year-old girl's face and genitals. (She, of course, had willingly sent the pictures to a friend, who passed them on to a friend who—et cetera.) Then, in Florida, a sixteen-year-old and a seventeen-year-old were arrested after taking pictures of them-selves having sex with each other, and sending the pictures only to each other via e-mail. In these cases, teenagers never sought (however misguidedly) to gain attention, notoriety, approbation, and even community by trading on their own intimate moments. They didn't publish the photos, didn't post them online, didn't seek to deliberately challenge society. Even so, they found out that there are limits and unintended consequences to what they thought was nothing more than fun and games.

❑ ❑ ❑

Congratulations, you've graduated high school without being ar-rested in a cell-phone sex scandal. But that alone isn't going to get you into university. A University of Massachusetts-Dartmouth study in the fall of 2007 questioned 453 college admissions de-partments and found that 26 percent were actively researching students through search engines and 21 percent are checking out social networking profiles on the likes of MySpace and Facebook. Commentators have suggested that by now that number is probably much higher.

Once you're in, you have to stay in. Swimmers at Louisiana State University criticized coaches on Facebook and were kicked off the team. Police busted an underage drinking party at George Washington University after they found invitations online. It's happened enough times, from Jeff's high school to Jane's university, that there is now a new phenomenon amongst the college set—Sunday morning "de-tagging" sessions. "The event happens, pictures are up within twelve hours, and within another twelve hours people are de-tagging," Chris Pund, a senior at Radford University in Virginia, tells a newspaper. "If I'm holding something I shouldn't be holding, I'll untag," reports Robyn Backer, a junior at Wesleyan College. "And if I'm making a particularly ugly face," she continues, "I'll untag myself. Anything really embarrassing, I'll untag." Untag, untag, untag. The latest trend is for parties to simply ban camera phones, in what one tech commentator describes as a "last-ditch attempt to preserve privacy."

Okay, so you manage to untag and earn a diploma. Now it's time to get a job. As early as 2003 (around the same time Heather Armstrong was getting famous for being "dooced"), the *Boston Globe Magazine* was reporting on Michael, a thirty-four-year-old working in a professional job at a Boston medical school. When Michael was seventeen he had a drug problem and did some time. He later wrote a few articles about his past as a teenage criminal, and those articles got online, attached to his name. Now he's having trouble advancing in his career and getting dates. Three years later the *New York Times* ran a similar story that included, among other things, the testimony of a corporate recruiter who rejected an applicant after doing a Google search and finding the quote "I like to blow things up" attributed to the student, a chemical engineering major. Another college student, Tien Nguyen, a senior at the University of California, Los Angeles, "signed up for interviews on campus with corporate recruiters" but rarely got any invites. Then a friend suggested that he look himself up on Google. He found a link to a joking essay he'd published on a Web site for college students. The essay was called "Lying Your Way to the Top," and soon after he had it removed, he found himself invited to interviews and offered positions. "I never really considered that employers would do something like that," he told a reporter. "I thought they would just look at your résumé and grades." By the way, these searches aren't just aimed at new grads: A study done by a recruiting consultant firm found that 77 percent of executive recruiters use search engines to help screen candidates. A survey of 3,169 hiring managers by online job site Career-Builder.com found that 22 percent of them screened potential staff via social networking profiles, up from 11 percent in 2006.

Not long ago, a fellow named Dylan e-mailed the magazine I publish, *Broken Pencil*, a guide to zines and independent creativity, asking if we would remove a review of his zine from our online archives. He wrote: "I am a struggling filmmaker looking for work. I recently found out that a potential employer googled my name and came up with the following: 'A zine chock-full of repugnant humour. Yes Dylan thinks jokes about kiddie porn are funny—and guess what! So do I. He also posits that KFC causes AIDS (as decent a theory as any) and suggests [*sic*] that killing rock stars is not only easy, but fun! Dylan you sick fuck, send the next issue over my way but otherwise, keep your distance.' The employer was unimpressed." In asking us to remove the review from our Web site, Dylan says, "I wrote that zine when I was 15 years old and I had no idea that it would cause so many problems for me when I was 29." When Dylan was fifteen he was probably thrilled with the review we gave him. Now it's an embarrassing remnant from a juvenile past he needs to distance himself from if he hopes to be able to make a living. In any other era, Dylan could expect his zine to have long since disappeared along with a juvenile hilarity over AIDS and kiddie porn jokes. But today, in the era of Peep, you never know what past silliness is going to stick to your name forever.

Teenagers and college kids aren't the only ones who get caught up in the nexus where privacy meets technology, and reputation meets Peep. More than one hundred men responded to a fake ad that a malevolent blogger posted to Craigslist. The ad purported to be from a woman looking for a "str8 brutal dom muscular male." After stringing along all the respondents, the hoaxer posted their names, pictures, e-mail addresses, and phone numbers to his blog. In the aftermath, several of the men lost their jobs. More and more, things we had no idea could or would ever be made public and used against us are coming to the fore. At a murder trial in which a man claimed self-defense in the shooting of one of a group of teenagers yelling threats and racial epithets, the prosecutor wanted to know why the man didn't simply call 911. He then went on to note that since 1989 the accused had called the emergency number nine times, including a call made "at 1:21 p.m. on January 13, 2001, to complain about his sister-in-law; the two calls to report paint balls on his lawn; the one to report his missing garbage can; the one on Christmas Eve of 1993 to report a barking dog." The prosecutor also presented the 911 call record of the accused's wife, who apparently had made eleven calls since 1993, "including complaints of a loud party, a dog biting her dog, and again, the sister-in-law." Meanwhile, various states are keeping records of your travels through the toll booths. If you've signed up for E-Z Pass, the system that speeds your collection by automatically billing you for tolls, where you have paid tolls and when is on the public record. And eleven states now supply that information in criminal cases. Seven of those states provide information in civil cases such as divorce, "proving, for instance, that a husband who claimed he was at a meeting in Pennsylvania was actually heading to his lover's house in New Jersey." (New York divorce lawyer Jacalyn Barnett has called E-ZPass the "easy way to show you took the offramp to adultery.")

So untag, if you can, but often you can't because your data is sucked into an interface you have no control over and don't even know exists. Google's Street View service offers street level views in a select but growing number of cities across the United States and UK. One Brooklyn resident complained when she checked her address and found that you could clearly see her cat sitting on a perch in the living room window of her second-floor apartment. "If the government was doing this, people would be outraged," she told the *New York Times*. Her husband added: "It's like peeping." One person's outrage is a million people's enjoyment: a new way to see how people you meet and know live. As Google headquarters explained, responding to the cat story: "Street View only features imagery taken on public property. This imagery is no different from what any person can readily capture or see walking down the street." Street View is pretty much pure Peep. If you want to see how someone lives and you have their address, type it into Street View and see what comes up. The service is otherwise pretty much useless. It's not useful as a map, and doesn't really help you to familiarize yourself with a new area you'll soon be visiting—the disconnected shots it provides as you move down a street are too difficult to process. I checked out the address of my publisher, City Lights Books in San Francisco. A bus partially obscured the building. But there a man and a woman were walking. Maybe one of them was my editor? I zoomed in. Too blurry to quite tell. Unfortunate. Other stuff you could at one time see on Google Street View: a clearly identifiable man standing in front of a lap dance establishment in San Francisco; a man entering a porno bookstore in Oakland, face not visible; license plates of cars entering the Brooklyn Battery tunnel. A Pittsburgh suburban couple sued Google after they found their home on the Street View, claiming that Google could only have gotten the shot by going up a private drive and violating their privacy. "A major component of their purchase decision was a desire for privacy," the lawsuit says. Google says all the couple had to do was go to the site and ask to have the pictures taken down. Furthermore, in statements in court, Google made the following defense: "Complete privacy does not exist in this world except in a desert, and anyone who is not a hermit must expect and endure the ordinary incidents of the community life of which he [or she] is a part."

Here Google, which won the case, seemed to be generally missing the point (as were the plaintiffs, for that matter). It's not so much that there might be a picture of you on the street in front of City Lights Books or a picture of the front of your house that's worrisome. I mean, you're walking down a street in a public place and anyone can see you anyway, right? But how could that information be used after the fact when it's stored for all time in a massive archive? Maybe you were supposed to be at work when that shot was taken? Maybe claimed that you were at a conference in good old Pittsburgh? And who's that with you there? Oh, just a good friend? Excuse me Google, but we'd like to know what time and day that photo was taken, please. We don't expect privacy when we're walking down the street, but that doesn't mean we expect the moment to be chronicled by a for-profit company and permanently stored in a database designed expressly for the purposes of instant retrieval.

◻ ◻ ◻

Unintended consequences. I'm thinking of my dad again here: living the American dream as an immigrant made good in the shadow of such monuments to liberty as the White House and the Lincoln Memorial, and yet he feels betrayed. Who let him down? Who stole his trust? Exactly who violated his expectation of personal privacy?

In many ways, it was nobody and everybody. Peep is so interwoven with other social and cultural forces that it's possible to argue that even the smartest of us don't really know what we're doing and why. There was no single moment when privacy moved from human need to human right, and from human right to commodity. In fact, as I've suggested, privacy remains all three of those things at the same time, in communities around the globe. And so there's no way to explore every conceivable scenario that might emerge, and it's doubtful that the next time you order a product on a Web site, update your blog, or check your Facebook page you'll be running every hypothetical calculation through your head.

What's the moral of this confusing story? It's not that Big Brother is watching. That was fifty years ago. And it's not that privacy is dead, either. In fact, the idea of privacy—as a right, as a moral imperative, and as a source of cash—is more potent than ever. In cases where privacy is seen by us (quite rightly) as an impediment to connection and success, we are more than willing to jettison it. Meanwhile, when we think we're due privacy because we paid into the system that promised us a padlock for every castle, we have no problem invoking our rights as citizens or consumers. This confusing relationship to privacy is mirrored by how it's manipulated in the new era of Peep business. Every single day we're encouraged to share everything and anything by various corporations and information-collecting entities who, at the same time, promise to safeguard our privacy. How does that work? It works because governments and corporations have a vested interest in making sure that we believe in the possibility of privacy.

Privacy, after all, underlies an entire ethos of acquisition-as-success. The better we do, the more property and stuff we have, the more privacy we deserve—checking our surveillance cameras, tracking our kids, activating our alarms, and generally having a great time acting as celebrity-kings in our own castles. Ultimately there's a lot of money to be made off of privacy, both as a symbol of status and attainment, and as a commodity we're willing to exchange due to our inherent desire to connect and be connected.

Government and business leaders preach privacy even as the citizenry experiments with the possibilities of instantaneous connection and total transparency. As a result, over and over again, our eagerness to exchange privacy for connection is abused—by law enforcement, by teachers and admissions officers and coaches, by employers, and by faceless corporations. What's the moral of this story? There isn't a clear one. As private detective Stephen Rambam happily tells us, we're in the gray zone.

chapter seven

Future Peep: Why No One Came to My Party and Other Semi-Transparent Conclusions

Certainly if you had all the world's information directly attached to your brain, or an artificial brain that was smarter than your brain, you'd be better off.
—Sergey Brin, cofounder of Google

One day, a day like any other, I woke up and went through what has now become the obligatory process of clicking on the links sent to my e-mail inbox from Facebook headquarters. Facebook HQ e-mails me hourly, telling me that I have been invited to such and such an event and that so-and-so has requested the honor of my friendship. After dealing with the various requests, I scanned the handsome visage looking out at me (otherwise known as my "profile picture"), considered a "status update," and, gaze dropping down the page, noticed that I was very near to breaking the 700 mark in friends. Not bad, I thought to myself. But the number also made me uneasy. I had just pretty much ended a friendship I'd devoted a lot of energy to over the years. I'd lost a few other friends to the usual demands: jobs in other cities, the pressures of family life, et cetera. In my non-cyber existence I probably had fewer friends then at any other time in my life. A two-year-old kid taking up a lot of my time, a workaholic irritability, a love of being left alone to read and think, and a lack of any kind of office environment or mysterious association with the Masons from which to derive an instant network of cronies, all were all putting a serious crimp in my social life. And yet, here was evidence to the contrary. Seven hundred friends.

A few of the 700 were actual friends, some were contacts and acquaintances, but the majority were basically just people who had requested to be my Facebook friend in a city, Toronto, that sports one of the largest number of Facebook users in the world. I was in the middle of doing research for this book and so, I thought, here's a great way to learn more about Peep culture and revive my faltering social life in the process. I decided to have a Facebook party. I used the Facebook event feature to invite all the people on my friends list I had never met before to join me for a drink at a neighborhood bar. Some of them, of course, didn't live in Toronto, but I figured it's summer and people travel so you never know who might be around. If they lived in Buffalo or Vancouver, they could just click "not attending" and that would be that. I also posted the invitation on my blog, which was garnering a stunning thirty to fifty readers a day. I wrote: "If you haven't met me, if you're in the city, come by and hang out. No obligations, no stress, I'm buying the drinks." I sent a similar invitation to the thirty or so people following me on Twitter.

On Facebook, which automatically gives people the option to respond by choosing one of three categories (attending, maybe attending and not attending), fifteen people said they were attending and sixty said maybe. A few hundred said no and a few hundred just ignored the invitation altogether. Based on that result, I thought it would be safe to assume that at least twenty people would show up to my impromptu shindig. After all, if, say, eight of the people who said they were definitely attending showed up, and a quarter of the maybes dropped by, that would be a respectable twenty-three people. Throw in two or three surprise walk-ins from the blog, and away we go. I planned for twenty-five attendees.

As a fun icebreaker and out of curiosity too, I put together a questionnaire: "What Do You Know About Hal?" Ten questions about my personal life: "Has Hal ever had a one-night stand?" "Can you list two of Hal's hobbies?" Regular readers of my blog and careful scrutinizers of my Facebook page would be able to get a perfect score. Giggling at my cleverness, I took a shower. I shaved. I splashed on my tingly, men's perfume. I put on new pants and a favorite shirt. Brimming with optimism I headed over to the neighborhood watering hole and waited.

And waited.

And waited.

Seven hundred Facebook friends, thirty Twitter followers, and who knows how many readers of my blog, the bulk of them living in Toronto. But only one person showed up.

One.

How could that be?

I would probably have met more prospective real-life friends by simply sitting at the bar and offering to buy drinks for whomever happened to be on the stools next to me.

Let me tell you about the woman who showed up. Her name is Paula. She works in corporate communications. She plays on a soccer team. She has a boyfriend. She's read a few of my books. She became my Facebook friend after noticing my profile on a friend's page. She thought it would be interesting to drop by and meet me. She got a six out of ten on the quiz, which, much to my relief, disqualified her for stalker status. She was a delight to hang out with but, alas, she had to work in the morning and only stayed for an hour. I picked up the tab on her Tom Collins and she strode out into the night, both of us not entirely sure, as these things go, if or how our friendship might grow. But time will tell in that regard.

In the meantime, I renewed my friends vigil. It was getting

on ten o'clock now and all my rationales—people needing time to get home from work, eat dinner, relax a bit—were starting to wear out. I ordered another beer and glumly flipped through my stack of unanswered questionnaires. Inevitably, the combination of alcohol and solitude turned my thoughts to self-pity. Was I really that big of a loser? Was it possible that, out of all those people, only one actually wanted to be my real-life friend? Paula had expressed shock and bemusement when she discovered that, so far, she was the one and only potential friend to turn up. She said, very kindly, that she almost didn't come, figuring that a guy like me would be swamped with all kinds of well wishers, networkers, and new potential pals. Well, I mused, maybe that was the problem. Maybe everyone just figured that everyone else was going to come, that the event would be so packed that they would hardly get to know me anyway, so why bother. Or maybe people thought I was being disingenuous, not really trying to meet new friends at all, but just conducting an obnoxious social experiment. (Which, of course, I was, but at the core of my disingenuous experiment was a true desire to make a new friend, something I'd never been particularly good at.) Whatever the reason for the evening's utter failure and total rebuke of my social standing, by now it was past eleven and pretty clear that no one else was coming. I ordered one more beer, a British import: Young's Double Chocolate Stout. It was deliciously bittersweet.

The next day, head somewhat less clouded by booze, I returned to the problem of why only one person showed up to meet me. As a method of making new friends my evening had been an abject failure, but as a social experiment it was a clearcut success. While one night could hardly be called "proof," the utter lack of attendance obviously suggested something about the kind of relationships we're building on the many networks that promise to better connect us via Peep. People don't want to make the leap. As despairing a thought as it may be, the bulk of us have no desire to use the mass-mediated environments of social networking, blogging, instant update, and "tell me your secret" to connect in the real world. We'd rather be at home peering at each other online than putting ourselves out there for friendship, messy emotional connection, and all the responsibilities and frustrations that come with forming attachments to others. We're tired, we're stressed, and we're conditioned now to get home from our daily labors and lose ourselves in virtual environments, whether they be TV, video games, other people's profiles and blogs, or our own.

This puts the success of something like PostSecret in a whole new light. It's not just that we use PostSecret to anonymously get things off our chest and get insight into what other people are struggling with. It's that we actually prefer it that way—why get into the whole messy quid pro quo of friendship, the whole I'll-listen-to-you-if-you-listen-to-me burden of the thing, when we can do it online, no mess, no fuss, no one calling you up next week and saying, "Listen, I need help, can I borrow a hundred bucks?"

Virtual friendship, like exploring someone else's virtual secret, is without consequence. You can say you're coming, and not feel any actual obligation to attend. "Definitely attending" on Facebook seems to mean "maybe" and "maybe attending" seems to mean probably not—that is, "I like the idea of attending, just not the actual process of having to go through the tiresome ordeal of showing up somewhere." One of the maybes explained all of this to me after the fact: "Hi Hal, It's funny because I often say 'maybe' I'll come to things when I can't come. I'd have liked to come to meet you but I live in British Columbia. Saying I'm not coming always seems so final . . . So I usually say Maybe." Another person who said she was definitely coming explained that she was going to come but that she lives an hour's drive away: "gas . . . you know." Now if you can't afford the gas, I understand completely, but it's not as if the price of gasoline changed so dramatically in the week between when that person said she was coming and the day of the actual event.

Most of the events we get invited to on Facebook are relatively anonymous. They aren't dinner invitations or parties. They're
book launches, gallery openings, notices that a band is playing.
As a result, people treat the event invitation as the equivalent
to being handed a flier from an acquaintance—"Yeah, cool, I'm
gonna try and make it." We want to go to things. We want, at the
very least, to be seen as the kind of people who go to things. But
more and more, we don't actually go to things because, let's face
it, there's plenty of social interaction and entertainment to be had
without ever leaving the house.

Another "maybe" told me that instead of coming out she
played Wii and smoked a joint at her boyfriend's friend's place.
She made it sound way more exciting than anything I could
have ever come up with: "We smoked some killer weed . . . then
the games began. i virtually bowled, boxed my man (and won)
played a lego version of Indiana Jones, walked a tightrope. it was
pretty nifty." A "definitely" told me that in lieu of attending she
"had a (first) date that night with an experimental theatre artist. we ended up making out by the train tracks at spadina and
dupont!" An apologetic fellow had a job interview the next day.
Another "maybe" was going to come but decided against it because she had to work in the morning. Another "maybe" ended
up having an Ultimate Frisbee night and a confirmed attendee
bailed out to go to, of all things, a George Michael concert. (Can't
compete with that, I guess.) A "maybe" spent his evening returning tiles he bought for his basement after his wife nixed them
as too expensive: "So, I had to haul back 25 boxes of heavy tiles,
bring them down to the basement, one box at a time, and carry
back the other boxes of tiles which were already in the basement,
load them up in the car, drive to Home Depot and get my money
back." We're so busy working, scheduling, and renovating (both
our virtual and actual properties) that it's actually far more efficient to stay home and digitally delve into other people's lives
than it is to make new friends. Far from assisting us in alleviating

the loneliness and even desperation that underlies our constant motion, our perpetual drive to redecorate, upgrade, change jobs and cities, social and connective media put even more pressure on us and leave us even less time to meaningfully encounter each other: In addition to everything else, I've also got to update my status, vet new online friends, and spend an hour just, well, watching.

People are, in fact, more likely to attend a relatively anonymous public event they are invited to via Facebook than accept an invitation to a personal encounter from a Facebook friend they've never met. Writes a "maybe": "I wanted to go, and had plans to attend with my friend Jennifer. When Jen bailed, I didn't have enough confidence to go on my own. Sad but true. I can and do travel alone, go to movies and restaurants alone, attend literary and gallery events, and do a myriad of other things alone. But going to a bar alone to meet a stranger who obviously already has a terribly fascinating cabal of friends I just didn't feel I had the social stamina for." The more disengaged we are, the more comfortable we feel. This is, surely, one of the ironic consequences of Peep culture. Or you could flip it around and put it this way: The more we learn to "engage" with each other through mediated environments, the less comfortable we are just meeting up. "Meeting you would make you 'real'," noted a perceptive commentator on my blog, "[the people meeting you] would have an emotional connection which brings in all that emotional baggage like guilt (for not following Twitter, skipping your blog a few times, etc.)." These days, it's easier to take part in community from in front of a screen. It's much harder to make an emotional connection and then have to live up to another person's expectations, hopes, and desires. Social media create distance, even as they fill in gaps. The result is something like my New Friends Night: online enthusiasm to meet that becomes a kind of generalized real-world reluctance to get involved.

In the end, we're still human. After I posted the story of my

failed party on my blog and Facebook page, people were genuinely, endearingly mortified for me. Several expressed true re-
pentance, at least two people sent me their phone numbers and
told me I should call them if I still wanted to hang out, and many
people promised (albeit vaguely) to buy me a beer when and if
our paths crossed in the future. Also, weirdly enough considering
the circumstances, hundreds added me as a Facebook friend out
of pity. Everyone felt, if not sorry for me, then sorry for how the
night turned out and for being one of those people just a little too
busy, too distant, or too (dis)connected to attend. People are kind
and caring. It's just that life, the way our lives are structured and
organized, gets in the way. People want to hear other people's secret. But do they want to discover something that might obligate
them to take action? Either way, my secret's out: 700 friends and
I ended up drinking alone.

□ □ □

When I set out to write this book, I wanted to explore the social and cultural forces pushing us to watch and be watched. After two years of research, after putting myself through various
Peep experiments, after traveling all over the place to meet a cast
of Peep characters who revealed far more to me than I actually
wanted to know, two big-picture ideas emerged. These two big
ideas became my frame for understanding why Peep is suddenly
such a powerful force in the world.

First, I believe that Peep emerges from and is made possible
by the primacy of pop culture. For the last hundred or so years,
pop culture has relentlessly peddled hyper-individualism as the
path to fulfilment and success. The celebrity, the ultimate hyper-
individual, a mythical yet real creature who is everywhere and
nowhere, everything and nothing, is presented to us as the para-
mount being. We aspire to be celebrities, and our Peep culture
gives us an entrée into that world. Meanwhile our desire to mimic

the celebrity lifestyle by generating our own personal mythologies for consumption, complete with press releases, videos, moment-by-moment updates and more, has been noted, and indeed encouraged, by the for-profit culture makers. Increasingly, they are realizing that the survival of their kind of gatekeeping, blockbuster entertainment is bound up in perpetuating the evolving myth of the star next door. Keep watching because you might be next. Pop merges with Peep. Talk and reality TV merge with the rise of celebrity gossip. This strange amalgamation of chitchat and caught-on-tape becomes the main entertainment commodity of the twenty-first century—a surefire strategy to sell tickets, boost ratings, get hits, peddle books and magazines, and otherwise generate dollars.

The process of turning the minutiae of celebrity life into big business entertainment has sped up the means by which we've come to see the details of our lives, our divorces, addictions, and daily routines, as valuable and interesting to others. And so we delve deeper into Peep, following our favorite celebrities into the cellar of self-revelation and debasement—the inevitable result of creating commodity out of our every gesture, habit, struggle, interest, and antic.

Pop culture morphs into Peep culture, but there's something else underlying this transition. In many ways, pop culture was just an early phase in what is and will continue to be a massive transformation of human life as lived in postindustrial capitalism. As the traditional ties of kinship, locality, ethnicity, and religion are cut, we are increasingly free to do what we will, but in many ways we're stunned and confused by our relatively sudden newfound freedom. This rapid and wholly unnatural cleaving of individuals from their cultures and communities is exacerbated and buttressed by the promise that the more you own the happier you'll be, enjoying your possessions in the privacy of your own home. This is not a pretty picture. Behind the locked doors of our castles we sit alone, desperately trying stave off the inevitable discouragement, depression, and anxiety that are the by-products of our antihuman society.

But as Peep constantly suggests, human beings are endlessly adaptable. Since we're hardwired to be in near constant social contact with each other, we instinctively seek connection, despite the fact that our culture encourages us to stay safely alone in our mansions, suburban bungalows, or subsidized apartments. We Peep because we still long for that lost, preindustrial world of constant contact, the way we once knew each other through lengthy, instinctual sessions of grooming that let us connect to each other without a business card, a sales pitch, or a come-on.

There's a dangerous desire to see Peep as our savior, a way out of this pained and painful alienation from ourselves and each other. We'd like to imagine that Peep culture, despite its problems, is nevertheless going to usurp capitalism and usher in the new world order of meaningful connectivity that we've been searching for since the ruptures of the Enlightenment and the Industrial Revolution. But the consequences of a new culture of instantaneous oversharing, so far mostly unnoticed, make it clear just how difficult it will be for Peep in current and even future incarnations to return us to the global village and bring about a revolution of small-town utopias.

Peep is a hybrid phenomenon. It's a combination of hyper-individualist excess, cutthroat capitalist self-preservation, longing for lost community, and our inherited hardwired need to make sense of life through narrative. These contradictory interests mostly end up canceling each other out. When we seek to connect to others through electronic networks, others join up and lie in wait, eager to undermine the foundations of our shaky, fledgling cyber communities by using our revelations for unannounced and unexpected purposes. By and large, as we've seen over and over again, when we put our craving for connection ahead of pragmatic self-preservation, we pay a price. Peep is not some benevolent shtetl of like-minded, kindly villagers always willing to bend an ear, offer advice, and pitch in. As the various college students who have seen themselves denied jobs and even jailed based on their public profiles can attest, Peep is inextricably connected to the forces of bureaucracy, capitalism, and law and order that keep our society focused almost exclusively on the production and consumption of wealth. Because Peep offers only the illusion of the village, only a facsimile of community, the vast amount of material we generate about ourselves and those around us serves not only as a way to connect to others but as a way to evaluate us as potential participants in the main event—earning and spending, buying and selling. This comes as a continual surprise to us. Wait a minute, we say. There are people out there who are actually judging us on our profile pages, status updates, and blogs? Don't they know it's just for fun? Can't they see that it's just a show—not who I really am?

But if people *could* know and trust each other in an intrinsic, communal way, could see us for who we really are, we would never have seen the rise of Peep culture in the first place. The whole reason we do Peep is because we *aren't* living in the small town and *don't* know who anyone is anymore. All we have to go on is what we can dig up via Google searches, NetDetective, and anything else that has been inadvertently or purposely entered into the official digital record. Since it's impossible to know who is just pretending versus who really is a party animal with a penchant for blackouts and drunk driving, so far the age of Peep culture has also been an age of literal interpretation. Nothing goes away, everything is assumed to be fact. And yet nobody quite wants to admit that reality; it just seems more civilized for all concerned to pretend that we are somehow using technology to return to the idealized, proverbial global village.

It's time to stop pretending. Unlike life in the sixteenth-century hamlet, there's no nuance to tilt the gossip, there's no collective sense of who you are, who your family is, where you come from. If you say you like to blow things up, we take that at face value; if you were arrested once for doing drugs, even if that was twenty years ago when you were seventeen, well, sorry, as far as we know you're a junkie; if you made a joke about child molesters in your adolescent zine, well, buddy, you're a sicko for life.

Moreover, the demands of moneymaking almost always take precedence over the needs of individuals and communities. We're sharing everything from our innermost secrets to our daily shopping patterns, and a vast array of for-profit entities are feasting on our every detail. Time and time again, we pay the price for our oversharing. We pay the price when our personal information is used in ways we don't know about or understand—ways that enrich massive corporations and shareholders, offer us little or nothing in return, and eventually enable other massive corporations to better cajole, convince, or just plain swindle us into buying things we don't want and don't need. We pay the price when what we chose to make public for one reason is scooped up by admissions officers, law enforcers, principals, neighbors, lawyers, and so many others for entirely different reasons. Enter the dominion of Peep culture and pay the price.

I'm not saying that individuals who chose to overshare or otherwise make poor decisions about their sending of personal information into the public realm don't share the blame and the responsibility. Nor am I saying that the urge to share, connect, and create community is necessarily bad. There's amazing potential in the rise of Peep culture and, as I've said, Peep isn't about how we're all turning into voyeurs or pathetic snoops. Peep is, in fact, a bold attempt to decentralize power, a grassroots campaign to return to individuals the capacity to tell their own stories about who they are and how they live. That's why Peep is situated so firmly in the landscape of pop culture. It was popular culture's centralization that hijacked our right and ability to tell our own stories to each other in the first place. Now we want that back.

The problem, of course, is that almost as soon as some grassroots Peep phenomenon takes off, it becomes infiltrated by the agents of social control and profit. Peep is many different things to many different people and the more confused we are about ideas like privacy, celebrity, and community, the more likely we are to find out too late that what we're doing is infected by alien agendas and fraught with all of those good old "unintended consequences."

□ □ □

One of those unintended consequences is the rise of the notion of the "transparent" society. Many are now arguing that the future of Peep, the future of our burgeoning culture of oversharing, perpetual GPS tracking, ubiquitous surveillance, blogging, loyalty cards, and all the rest of it is an egalitarian society in which nobody can lie, cheat, or steal because everybody is always watching everybody else. "Transparency" is today's buzzword, but I first encountered the concept almost ten year ago when I was collaborating with Steve Mann, cyborg extraordinare, on his book about the future of humanity in the age of the wearable computer. Perched on a stool in his University of Toronto laboratory, I listened as Mann, surrounded by transducers, wires, and circuit boards, and looking every bit the mad scientist, argued that if everyone was monitoring everyone else and instantly uploading the footage (so that their cameras couldn't simply be confiscated and destroyed), it would be impossible for anyone to abuse their authority or take advantage. He called his plan *sousveillance* and to this day dreams of equipping us with wearable computers that can instantly record and broadcast everything we see and say.

Today just about everyone's talking about transparency. Why not? It seems like such a great idea. No more lying. No more hiding. A concept that applies equally to cheating boyfriends, scheming politicians, and thieving muggers. No wonder Mann's argument is such a powerful one. Not only does it suggest the ways in which Peep technologies and practices can be forces for good, it's also something we can actually see in action. In the past, singular, unexpected pop-culture phenomena have served to challenge orthodoxies, change minds, and fundamentally alter perspectives. Now we have the Peep culture equivalent: sudden, unexpected, digital disruptions of transparency.

And there have been such moments, moments that make us look at Peep with a renewed sense of its possibilities and promises. Consider a story reported in the summer of 2008. The first line says it all: "A New York City police officer was stripped of his gun and badge on Monday after an amateur video surfaced on the Internet showing him pushing a bicyclist to the ground in Times Square during a group ride on Friday evening." This mundane, comparatively minor incident, is just one of many examples of something that happens consistently all over the world in the age of Peep culture: abuse of power is accidentally recorded by an amateur (in this case a watching tourist), made public on one of the mechanisms of Peep, reported on by the news media, and used as evidence to contradict official explanations. A few more examples: In October 2007, an elite unit of the Chicago Police Department was disbanded after video emerged of its members shaking down barroom customers. A policeman in Puerto Rico fell under FBI investigation when video shot by a bystander and sent to the local news media (and eventually uploaded to YouTube) showed him executing an unarmed man. When Dennis Kyne was arrested during a protest held outside the New York Public Library coinciding with the 2004 Republican National Convention, video of his arrest directly contradicted police officer statements: "A police officer testified that he and three other officers had to carry one protester, Dennis Kyne, by his hands and feet down the library steps. Videotape showed that Mr. Kyne walked down the steps under his own power, and that the officer who testified against him had no role in his arrest. The charges were dismissed."

The more repressive the society, the more likely it is that a video clip can have a dramatic effect. In Kuala Lumpur, Malaysia, in 2005, a video surfaced showing twenty-two-year-old babysitter Hemy Hamisa Abu Hassan Saari being repeatedly forced to do naked squats. This video spread from e-mail to e-mail before ending up on YouTube. Saari had been arrested because one of the members of a group of people she was with had been in possession of drugs. The tape of her "interrogation" was originally created by a male police officer secretly filming the incident for his own enjoyment. The recording ended up forcing the Malaysian prime minster to announce the formation of an official inquiry into police practices. This in a country where one party has ruled with impunity since 1957. Meanwhile in Iran a video of a married cleric having adulterous sex topped the charts of Balatarin.com (an Iranian version of Digg.com). The video's omnipresence led to a rare public discussion of the hypocrisy of a society that permits the arrest of a medical student for sitting with her fiancé in a public park (forty-eight hours later her family was told to come collect her inexplicably dead body from prison) but looks the other way when the clerics who impose these laws have illict affairs.

All of the above are inspiring examples of the way Peep culture mixes "entertainment" with truth telling and social change to create new possibilities, particularly for those who find themselves accused, repressed, and silenced. Why, then, does the thought of this kind of transparency strike me as so devastatingly sad?

I don't want us to have to live in Steve Mann's world. I don't want us to be afraid to leave our castles because our wearable cam armor is on the blink.

Over and over we've seen the way that Peep justice gets meted out. Peep, inextricably intertwined with entertainment, encourages us to rush to snap judgments and instant expressions of high-pitched emotion—the more extreme the better. That's why turning us all into walking, talking, recording and transmitting computers might not be such a hot idea after all. For every righteous moment of transparency, there are hundreds of thousands of moments of prurient invasion—videos and photos nobody wants to be in, making money for people and companies profiting off the misery, unhappiness, and delusions of others. When everyone is recording everyone else, things seem to move very quickly from citizen activism to mob justice. Rumor and gossip, unfiltered by collective community standards and shared purpose, rendered permanently digital, can do damage with just a click of a mouse. Do you really want self-appointed citizen deputies filming you every time you leave the house, drive too fast, spit on the sidewalk, light up a joint, or do a funny jig? (Case in point: Since the 2005 incident involving the babysitter, the Malaysian police have been trying to turn Peep technology to their own advantage. They are asking citizens to send digital images of traffic violators, double-parkers, and people who otherwise add to the capital city's apparently epic traffic jams.)

In the ahead-of-its-time book *The Transparent Society* (1998), futurist David Brin argued that "no other populace has ever had so much known about them, both in groups and as individuals—and no populace has ever been so cantankerously individualistic or free." Brin is basically making a connection between the free flow of information and the free flow of freedom. But ten years later we're not nearly as free as we think we are. Corporate mergers (particularly in the IT industries), the politics of fear that became de rigeur after 9/11, and widening income gaps that have shrunk the middle class and made a small fraction of the population ridiculously wealthy are just some of the factors that have led to us having less and less control over the not-so-free-flowing information that determines many aspects of our lives. What will it be like in another ten years? Will we have solved these problems? The more we are encouraged to reveal everything, and discouraged or even actively prevented from knowing exactly how and why our various revelations might be used, the less we can be said to be truly free.

Now more than ever we live in an era of illusion: the illusion
that we're in control, the illusion that we have (or should want to
have) privacy, the illusion that we're smart enough to avoid the
pitfalls of Peep.

So many smoke-and-mirrors mazes. When I first conceived
of this book I thought I would be able to end with a rallying cry. I
wasn't sure which way I'd go, pro- or anti-Peep, but I felt sure that
I would be able to reach a strident, gratifying conclusion. But I'm
at the end of the book and I'm as undecided as ever. I still don't
know where I stand. I still waver between getting personal on my
blog and keeping it strictly business. I still can't decide if I should
close down my Facebook page or keep generating free content for
a corporation partially owned by Microsoft. Do I avoid Google?
Do I install every possible privacy protection on my computer?
Do I track my friends and let them track me?

I have come to at least one concrete conclusion: My three-
year-old daughter should be given the opportunity to make her
own decisions. I won't put her picture up on my blog, Web site,
or social network. I won't even mention her name online. I think
that's the only thing I'm absolutely sure about when it comes to
Peep. This isn't a decision made out of fear, a sense that I need
to protect her from all the creeps lurking online. It's a decision
based on the idea that she should have the right to control her
own destiny. I don't want her to spend the first years of her adult
life detagging. Instead it'll be up to her if she wants the video of
her first bath to become public property.

Mind you, that doesn't mean I've figured out the parameters
of Peep culture as related to my kid. By the time she's old enough
to read this book and understand it, I'll probably be tempted to
watch her every move for her own good. She's on chapter one
and I'm struggling with the compulsion to track her school attendance, spy on her keystrokes, and monitor her nights out. Will
I give in? It's pathetic, but again I have to confess indecision.

That's not much of a conclusion is it? My daughter deserves

better (not to mention everyone else reading this book). So let me try again.

A lot will have happened by the time my daughter hits her teen years. Possibly the warnings and worries I've written about will just be history—amusing nuggets of reportage based on an earlier, more primitive era. More likely this is just the beginning of a long struggle to understand a Peep culture that, in the same day, can instantly evoke transparency, transgression, and totalitarianism. Peep is all about contradictions, which is why it's so hard to come to firm conclusions about it as a phenomenon. Peep culture enhances our potential for empathy, even as it—like all incarnations of mass media—makes it more difficult for us to truly feel for others. The temptation is to advise my daughter to just stay away. But to lock yourself in your castle is to miss playing a part in the most fundamental transformation of Western society since the Industrial Revolution. If you lock yourself away, you'll be safe but, oh, so lonely. You'll be safe, but shut out from possibly the most exciting, democratic, and empowering way to make meaning and tell stories that human beings have ever experienced. Peep is a risk. But sticking your head in the sand and refusing to participate is, in many ways, an even greater risk. More and more, Peep will be at the core of how we talk with each other. For my daughter's generation, Peep may well be the way that young people learn how to make others laugh, cry, and feel. In the future, not partaking in Peep culture may mean your disappearance; you'll be a living ghost; you'll move amongst the rest of us, but if we can't access your profile, we won't notice or care about you.

Then again, that might be better than the equally ghostly alternative. Do you remember Brian Hill? He blogged for five solid years, from December 2003 to January 2008, about his slow, inevitable death from the rare and incurable disease ALS (amyotrophic lateral sclerosis). Brian died a month after posting his final goodbyes on his blog. Now Brian, like all those people who have passed on but continue to exhibit their likes, dislikes, dating status, and hopes for the future, exists solely online. He, too, is a kind of ghost, a digital fragment, just another pit stop as we cruise the Internet, just another flick of the channel as we surf the tide of other people's lives. Is there some way that Brian can be more to us than a fleeting moment of entertainment? We need to figure out a way to allow people to be memorialized and remembered through the contrivances of Peep culture without being consumed, reduced, and debased.

Thinking about Brian, I'm reminded of the story of Russel Ogden, a Canadian sociologist who wanted to witness assisted suicides—though not himself assist in any way—as part of a study he hoped to conduct. (Welcome to the age of Peep science.) At the last minute, after his study had been approved by his peers and passed through his university's ethics committee, it was quashed. Why did the university suddenly quash the study? Because there are some things we don't want to know. There are some things we believe should be left to transpire in the murky twilight between decision and indecision, between afternoon and night, between life and death. To do otherwise is to risk too much. To do otherwise is to risk what's always at stake in Peep culture—turning people's lives into nothing more than commodities to be bought and sold like lima beans. Brian Hill made his choice, decided how much to reveal and why, but so many others aren't getting to decide, are finding themselves suddenly nothing more than fodder for the latest entertainment craze: other people's real-life misery.

So I think I have finally come to the one thing I know for sure, the one thing writing this book has made me absolutely convinced of. Here goes: If there's one thing I now know, it's the value of not knowing. Our pragmatic, bureaucratic society sees it differently, of course. But so much of the mystery of life, so much of its inherent unquantifiable worth, comes from that which remains a mystery. It's *not* knowing that makes us fall in love, that allows us to appreciate beauty, that permits us to revel in the moment despite the indisputable fact that one day we will be sick, and that one day we will be dead.

Why didn't people come to my Facebook party? Because they felt they didn't have to. They felt they already *knew* me. So why waste an evening getting to know someone you already know?

Many times during the course of researching this book I heard a familiar refrain: "They think they know me, but they don't really know me." It's as if, having revealed everything, having laid bare every potential mystery, we want to pull back and reclaim that insoluble, essential something we've given away. They don't know me. I'm still a singular human being—an enigma, an unknowable. Do we want to be known or don't we? I keep coming back to the RedClouds posers taking pictures under the table, passing the camera around. In many ways we're all in danger of becoming RedClouds posers, accidentally draining the beauty and mystery of human existence by transforming it into its still-life doppelganger.

Not knowing is an option, too. It's a choice I hope my daughter's generation will be able to occasionally make.

As for us right now, well, we're busy frantically trying to know everything and anything, no matter how garish, invasive, or better left alone it may be. We're frantic about filling the void. But a void is a vacuum—it sucks everything into it, it's never full, and it's never satisfied. Peep is bad when it exists to feed the all-knowing void. And, at the risk of getting all chicken-soup-for-the-grown-up-daughter here, Peep is good when it feeds that which is uniquely human: our capacity to care without needing to know why.

Notes

Chapter 1

Burns, John F. "Trial about Privacy in Which None Remains." *New York Times*, July 9, 2008.

Stelter, Brian. "A.P. Says It Wants to Know Everything about Britney Spears." *New York Times*, January 14, 2008.

Levin, Thomas Y., et al. *Ctrl [space]: Rhetorics of Surveillance from Bentham to Big Brother*. Boston: MIT Press, 2002.

Lee, Felicia R. "Survey of the Blogosphere Finds 12 Million Voices." *New York Times*, July 20, 2006.

Leung, Wendy. "Blogging to a Better You." *Globe and Mail*, April 17, 2008.

Hartley, Matt. "Money and Relationships: It's Love 3.0." *Globe and Mail*, February 14, 2008.

Hartley, Matt. "Toronto Tops the Twittersphere." *Globe and Mail*, December 23, 2008.

Catone, Josh. "35 Ways to Stream Your Life." *ReadWriteWeb.com*, February 29, 2008.

Rosen, Jeffrey. "Google's Gatekeepers." *New York Times Magazine*, November 30, 2008.

Associated Press. "Search Engines Gaining in Use, a Study Says." *New York Times*, November 21, 2005.

Andrejevic, Mark. *iSpy: Surveillance and Power in the Interactive Era*. Lawrence: University Press of Kansas, 2007.

Holden, Stephen. "That Beautiful but Deadly San Francisco Span." *New York Times*, October 27, 2006.

Boyes, Roger. "Dying to See Gregor Schneider's Latest Work? Don't Worry—You Could Be In It." *Times* [London], April 23, 2008.

Holson, Laura M. "Privacy Lost: These Phones Can Find You." *New York Times*, October 23, 2007.

Chapter 2

Kredo, Adam. "Web of Caring." *Washington Jewish Week*, January 1, 2009.

Keizer, Garret. "Requiem for the Private World." *Harper's*, August 2008.

Ryan, Claudine. "Blogging Boosts your Social Life: Research." *Abc.net. au*, March 3, 2008.

Thompson, Clive. "Brave New World of Digital Intimacy." *New York Times Magazine*, September 7, 2008.

Twenge, Jean. *Generation Me : Why Today's Young Americans Are More Confident, Assertive, Entitled—and More Miserable Than Ever Before*. New York: Free Press, 2006.

Halpern, Jake. *Fame Junkies: The Hidden Truths Behind America's Favorite Addiction*. Boston: Houghton Mifflin, 2007.

Levin, Thomas Y., et al. *Ctrl [space]: Rhetorics of Surveillance from Bentham to Big Brother*. Boston: MIT Press, 2002.

Andrejevic, Mark. *iSpy: Surveillance and Power in the Interactive Era*. Lawrence: University Press of Kansas, 2007.

Tanz, Jason. "Internet Famous: Julia Allison and the Secrets of Self-Promotion." *Wired*, July 2008.

Rhode, Eric. *A History of the Cinema from its Origins to 1970*. New York: Hill and Wang, 1976.

Chapman, James. *Cinemas of the World: Film and Society from 1895 to the Present*. London: Reaktion Books, 2003.

Gledhill, Christine, ed. *Stardom: Industry of Desire*. London: Routledge, 1991.

Trebay, Guy. "Shes Famous (and So Can You)." *New York Times*, October 28, 2007.

Armstrong, Heather. "I Have Something to Say," *Dooce.com*. February 12, 2002.

Rosen, Jeffrey. "Your Blog or Mine?" *New York Times Magazine*, December 19, 2004.

Apuzzo, Matt. "Sex Blogger Files for Bankruptcy." Associated Press, June 1, 2007.

Kaufmann, Leslie. "When the Ex Blogs, the Dirtiest Laundry Is Aired." *New York Times*, April 18, 2008.

Steenhuysen, Julie. "Most Teens Too Risky on MySpace, Study Finds." Reuters News Agency, January 6, 2009.

Gould, Emily. "Exposed." *New York Times Magazine*, May 25, 2008.

Haber, Matt. "New York Times Magazine Blog Article Tears Media Blogosphere Asunder." *Observer.com,* May 23, 2008.

Chapter 3

Calvert, Clay. *Voyeur Nation : Media, Privacy, and Peering in Modern Culture*. Boulder: Westview Press, 2000.

Barnouw, Erik. *Documentary: A History of the Nonfiction Film*. New York: Oxford University Press, 1974.

Rhode, Eric. *A History of the Cinema from its Origins to 1970*. New York: Hill and Wang, 1976.

Horkheimer, Max, and Theodor W. Adrono. *Dialectic of Enlightenment*. New York: Continuum, 1988.

Carlson, Peter. "For 20 Years, a Pleasure So Guilty It's Criminal." *Washington Post*, February 19, 2008.

Wiltz, James, Steven Reiss. "Why America Loves Reality TV." *Psychology Today*, September/October 2001.

Peters, Jeremy W. "When Reality TV Gets Too Real." *New York Times*, October 8, 2007.

McNett, Gavin. "The Wacky World of Television." *Salon.com*, March 13, 2000.

Appleyard, Diana. "We Were Ruined by Reality TV: The Humiliated Families Who Dreamed They Would Be Stars." *Daily Mail*, January 3, 2008.

West, Latoya. "Brat Camp Kids in Trouble with the Law," *About.com*, August 8, 2005.

Hinckley, David. "Pity the Kids on 'I Know My Kid's a Star.'" *Daily News*, March 20, 2008.

Mechanic, Michael. "Torture Hits Home." *Mother Jones*, March/April 2008.

Chapter 4

Solove, Daniel. *The Future of Reputation: Gossip, Rumor, and Privacy on the Internet*. New Haven: Yale University Press, 2007.

Saranow, Jennifer. "The Snoop Next Door." *Wall Street Journal*, January 12, 2007.

Ben-Ze'ev, Aaron, and Robert F. Goodman, eds. *Good Gossip*. Lawrence: University Press of Kansas, 1994.

Dunbar, R. *Grooming, Gossip, and the Evolution of Language*. Cambridge, MA: Harvard University Press, 1996.

Schwartz, Mattathias. "Malwebolence." *New York Times Magazine*, August 3, 2008.

Chapter 5

Schwartz, Mattathias. "Malwebolence." *New York Times Magazine,* August 3, 2008.

Whitaker, Reginald. *The End of Privacy: How Total Surveillance Is Becoming a Reality.* New York: New Press, 1999.

Regan, Tom. "Poll: Most Americans Support Surveillance Camera Use." *NPR News Blog,* July 30, 2007.

Hohmann, James. "Washington, D.C. Puts Itself under Surveillance." *Los Angeles Times,* June 16, 2008.

Zetter, Kim. "NYPD Helicopter Views Faces from Miles Away." *Wired. com,* June 5, 2008.

Brown, Paul. "Demand for Closed Circuit TV Triggers Fear of Crime." *Guardian,* January 9, 1998.

Angus Reid, "Canadians Back Use of Surveillance Cameras."*Angus Reid Global Monitor,* March 16, 2008.

Nagourney, Adam, and Janet Elder. "New Poll Finds Mixed Support for Wiretaps," *New York Times,* January 27, 2006.

Lichtblau, Eric. "Senate Approves Bill to Broaden Wiretap Powers." *New York Times,* July 10, 2008.

Nevius, C. W. "Front-window Spy Cam Puts Tenderloin on the Web." *San Francisco Chronicle,* December 6, 2008.

Honan, Matthew. "I Am Here: One Man's Experiment With the Location-Aware Lifestyle." *Wired.com,* January 19, 2009.

Nakashima, Ellen. "When the Phone Goes With You, Everyone Else Can Tag Along." *Washington Post,* July 12, 2008.

Vanderburg, Willem H. *Living in the Labyrinth of Technology.* Toronto: University of Toronto Press, 2005.

Vlahos, James. "Surveillance Society: New High-Tech Cameras Are Watching You." *Popular Mechanics,* January 2008.

Seifman, David. "'Track' Man Is Sacked." *New York Post,* August 31, 2007.

Leach, David. "Freelance Slackers, Beware: Big Brother Is Watching." *Globe and Mail,* August 11, 2008.

Caruso, David. "NY Taxi Drivers Sue to Stop GPS Units," *Globe and Mail,* September 19, 2007.

Parenti, Christian. *The Soft Cage: Surveillance in America from Slavery to the War on Terror.* New York: Basic Books, 2003.

Derene, Glenn. "Is Your Boss Spying on You? Inside New Workplace Surveillance." *Popular Mechanics*, January 2008.

Brin, David. *The Transparent Society: Will Technology Force Us to Choose Between Privacy and Freedom?* Reading, MA: Addison-Wesley, 1998.

"FBI Ditches Carnivore Surveillance System." Associated Press, January 18, 2005.

Campbell, Duncan. "The Spy in Your Server." *Guardian*, August 10, 2000.

Levin, Thomas Y., et al. *Ctrl [space]: Rhetorics of Surveillance from Bentham to Big Brother.* Boston: MIT Press, 2002.

Calvert, Clay. *Voyeur Nation: Media, Privacy, and Peering in Modern Culture.* Boulder: Westview Press, 2000.

Solove, Daniel. *The Future of Reputation: Gossip, Rumor, and Privacy on the Internet.* New Haven: Yale University Press, 2007.

Roman, James W. *From Daytime to Primetime: The History of American Television Programs.* Westport, CT: Greenwood Press, 2005.

Carlson, Peter. "For 20 Years, a Pleasure So Guilty It's Criminal." *Washington Post*, February 19, 2008.

Morrison, Blake. *As If: A Crime, a Trial, a Question of Childhood.* New York: Picador, 1997.

Andrejevic, Mark. *iSpy: Surveillance and Power in the Interactive Era.* Lawrence: University Press of Kansas, 2007.

Simmel, Georg. *The Sociology of Georg Simmel.* New York: Free Press, 1967.

Holton, Kate. "Modern Killers Turn to Video to Get Message Out." Reuters, November 7, 2007.

Mydans, Seth. "The Police Verdict: Los Angeles Policemen Acquitted in Taped Beating." *New York Times*, April 30, 1992.

Chapter 6

Solove, Daniel. *The Future of Reputation: Gossip, Rumor, and Privacy on the Internet.* New Haven: Yale University Press, 2007.

Stone, Brad. "Our Paradoxical Attitudes toward Privacy." *New York Times*, July 2, 2008.

Cheng, Jacqui. "Users Talk the Talk, but Don't Walk the Walk on Privacy." *ArsTechnica.com*, August 11, 2008.

Andrejevic, Mark. *iSpy: Surveillance and Power in the Interactive Era.* Lawrence, Kansas: University Press of Kansas, 2007.

Etzioni, Amitai. *The Limits of Privacy*. New York: Basic Books, 1999.

Albanesius, Chloe. "Can Internet Activity Ever Be Truly Anonymous?" *PC Magazine*, July 10, 2008.

Duhigg, Charles. "Bilking the Elderly, With a Corporate Assist." *New York Times*, May 20, 2007.

Stone, Brad. "Banks Mine Data and Woo Troubled Borrowers." *New York Times*, October 21, 2008.

Gentile, Gary. "MySpace Data Mined for Advertisers." *Globe and Mail*, September 18, 2007.

Nakashima, Ellen. "When the Phone Goes With You, Everyone Else Can Tag Along." *Washington Post*, July 12, 2008.

Akst, Daniel. "2-Way Talk." *Wired*, March 2007.

Caruso, Denise. "Securing Very Important Data: Your Own." *New York Times*, October 7, 2007.

Anderson, Nate. "Study: Reading Online Privacy Policies Could Cost $365 Billion a Year." *ArsTechnica.com*, October 8, 2008.

Tucker, Eric. "Facebook Pics Come Back to Haunt Defendants." Associated Press, July 21, 2008.

Guernsey, Lisa. "Picture Your Name Here." *New York Times*, July 27, 2008.

Thompson, Clive. "Brave New World of Digital Intimacy." *New York Times Magazine*, September 7, 2008.

Swidey, Neil. "A Nation of Voyeurs: How the Internet Search Engine Google is Changing What We Can Find Out About One Another." *Boston Globe Magazine*, February 2, 2003.

Finder, Allan. "For Some, Online Persona Undermines a Résumé." *New York Times*, June 11, 2006.

Sapieha, Chad. "Your Google Reputation Could Cost You a Job." *Globe and Mail*, January 25, 2008.

Reuters. "Bosses Screening Applicants' Web Lives." *Globe and Mail*, September 11, 2008.

Schwartz, Mattathias. "Malwebolence." *New York Times Magazine*, August 3, 2008.

Kilgannon, Corey. "911 Has a Long Memory." *New York Times*, January 6, 2008.

Vlahos, James. "Surveillance Society: New High-Tech Cameras Are Watching You." *Popular Mechanics*, January 2008.

Chapter 7

Parsa, Telmah. "Iran's Hottest Porn Video." *TheDailyBeast.com*, January 9, 2009.

Barron, James. "Officer Investigated in Toppling of Cyclist." *New York Times*, July 29, 2008.

Babwin, Don. "Chicago Police to Disband Elite Unit." Associated Press, October 9, 2007.

Soto, Tom. "Puerto Rico Community, Public Demand Justice after Police Execution of Worker." *Worker's World*, August 23, 2007.

Dwyer, Jim. "When Official Truth Collides with Cheap Digital Technology." *New York Times*, July 30, 2008.

Padania, Sameer. "Cell Phones Expose Malaysian Police." *PostGlobal*, November 20, 2006.

Brin, David. *The Transparent Society Will Technology Force Us to Choose Between Privacy and Freedom?* Reading, MA Addison-Wesley, 1998.

"Brian Hill Dies—He Blogged about His Illness." *San Francisco Chronicle*, Monday, February 25, 2008.

Jaschik, Scott. "When a University Kills Suicide Research." *InsideHigherEd.com*, July 7, 2008.

Index

"Passim" (literally "scattered") indicates intermittent discussion of a topic over a cluster of pages.

3